EXCAVATIONS AT
THE NEW ROYAL BATHS (THE SP/
BELLOTT'S HOSPITAL 1998–19yy

By Peter Davenport, Cynthia Poole and David Jordan

with contributions from

Ian M Betts, Ian Brooks, Lisa Brown, John Clarke, Mark Corney, Lorrain Higbee, Alice Humphrey, Andrew K G Jones, David Jordan, Lynne Keyes, Marek Lewcun, Ruth Pelling, Alan Vince, Felicity Wild

Illustrations by

Sophie Lamb and Lucy Martin

Oxford Archaeology monograph 3
Archaeology in Bath

Published for Oxford Archaeology as part of the Oxford Archaeology Monograph series

Designed by Oxford Archaeology Graphics Office

Edited by Ian Scott

This book is part of a series of monographs from Oxford Archaeology which can be bought from all good bookshops and Internet Bookshops. For more information visit thehumanjourney.net

ISBN 978-0-904220-45-2

Typeset and Printed in Europe by The Alden Group, Oxford, UK

Contents

List of Figures

List of Tables

Summary

Excavations took place in the south-west quadrant of the Roman and medieval town of Bath in advance of the redevelopment on the site of the former Beau Street Baths and Nos.7–7a Bath Street. The deep and extensive foundations of the new Royal Spa building required total excavation in advance of the destruction. Associated hydrological investigations also provided the opportunity to study artefacts derived from the Hot Bath spring. Possible early Mesolithic ritual activity was associated with the Hot Spring, whilst exploitation of the river gravels for flint occurred in the late Mesolithic. Evidence for activity after the late Mesolithic period was absent until the Iron Age. An Iron Age coin had been deposited in the Hot Bath Spring, and represents the first evidence of a pattern of votive offering otherwise confined to the Roman period. In addition a few sherds of Iron Age pottery occurred residually in the Roman contexts, the first such find in central Bath.

During the 1st and early 2nd centuries AD the area of the site appears to have been derelict and overgrown waste ground, cut through by a drainage ditch. In the Antonine period, a substantial and architecturally impressive building, which must have stood somewhere close by, was demolished to make way for a major redevelopment of the area. Materials from the building were incorporated in the new construction, which seems to have been a large public building with at least two wings arranged around a central courtyard. It was bounded by roads to the south and west and may have been associated with a baths complex known to the south. The development may have been built to create a major religious-leisure complex centred on the Hot Bath spring. Evidence for votive offerings at the Hot Spring was recovered in the form of numbers of Roman coins, which ranged in date from the 1st to 4th centuries.

Nineteenth century truncation had destroyed the upper levels of the large building, together with much of the stratigraphy of later periods, resulting in an absence of evidence for buildings until the Georgian period. There is evidence for robbing of the Roman building in the late or sub-Roman periods, followed by its decay and the accumulation of a thick dark earth, possibly indicative of cultivation. Renewed occupation occurred in the 11th century with evidence for the digging of pits, an activity which gradually decreasing in successive centuries. Little trace of earlier post-medieval activity survived, the deposits having been almost entirely destroyed by the late Georgian spa facilities built in 1829–30, which were subjected to various alterations and rebuilds during the 20th century.

At Bellott's Hospital, observation of engineers' test pits had shown that well-preserved stratified deposits of Roman date and a probable post-Roman dark earth were present over the entire site. In 1998 all post-Roman deposits, including the dark earth, were removed by machine with only minimal recording possible. The new construction level largely coincided with the top of the Roman structural layers, in which were also visible the remains of medieval pits following the lines of earlier walls and interpreted as robbing pits. The upper surface of the Roman deposits was planned and limited investigations were undertaken.

Nearly a metre of Roman structural deposits representing three phases of Roman masonry buildings fronting a street were revealed together with the underlying buried soil. Hints of timber buildings preceding the masonry phase were also recorded. The latest building contained extremely well-preserved evidence of a Romano-British blacksmith's workshop, with slag deposits and an anvil base.

Acknowledgements

The Project was commissioned by Bath and North East Somerset Council as a mitigation excavation in advance of the construction of the new Spa complex, now named the New Royal Baths. The project was part-funded by the Heritage Millennium Fund. The authors are grateful to Bob Sydes, both as curatorial archaeologist and as representative for the client, for his constant help and advice throughout the project. We would also like to express our appreciation to Keith Gibson, Clerk of Works for B&NES, who visited the site regularly and was a constant source of useful advice, information and good cheer. He also was responsible for alerting us to the presence of artefacts in the borehole material from the Hot Bath Spring, thereby preserving a vital data set. The council's project manager for the relevant stages of the whole project was Mike Gray to whom we are likewise grateful. The Archaeological Project Manager until well past the post-excavation assessment phase was Michael Heaton, who sweated blood putting together the project design, and kept a tight hold on its financial side. Much of the success of the project is due to him. The project was directed day-to-day by Cynthia Poole, who would like to thank all the staff who worked on the excavation, and especially Margaret Heslop and Leslie Cross, who worked on all three phases of the excavations and were invariably cheerful and helpful. Dom Barker and Bill Moffat were the area supervisors. John Wilson was the Education officer who dealt with the web site, and in particular school children's visits to the site and the setting up of a small visitor centre. Thanks are also due to all the specialists who have contributed to the report and especially to those involved at a late stage and who managed to produce reports within very tight deadlines. Vanessa Straker, the area English Heritage Environmental Advisor was of enormous help in clarifying and prioritising the post-excavation environmental analysis.

The draft manuscript was read by Dr Nick Barton, Prof Barry Cunliffe, Dr Martin Henig, Dr Warwick Rodwell and Dr Vanessa Straker, who all made extremely useful comments on the contents and structure of the report. The authors are grateful for having been made to think harder about what we had written. Nonetheless all errors and omissions are on the authors' heads alone. The volume was edited for publication by Ian Scott and illustrations were prepared by Sophie Lamb and Lucy Martin.

List of contributors

A number of people, listed below, contributed specialist reports on the material from the excavations reported in this volume. A number of the reports have not been included in the publication, although information they contain has informed the published results, and acknowledgement is made in the text. Other reports only appear in summary form. The full specialist reports will be found in the site archive.

Richard Bailey   OSL dating
Ian Betts   Ceramic building materials
Ian Brookes   Flint
Lisa Brown   Roman pottery
John Clarke   Small finds
Mark Corney   Roman coins
Rowena Gale   Wood analysis
Lorrain Higbee   Animal bone
Alice Humphrey   Fish bone
Julie Jones   Archaeobotanist
Andrew Jones   Fish bone
Lynne Keys   Iron slag assessment
Marek Lewcun   Clay tobacco pipes
Ruth Pelling   Planr remains
Heather Tinsley   Pollen assessment
Roger Tomlin   Graffito
Alan Vince   Medieval and post-Medieval pottery
Felicity Wild   Samian ware
Lesley Zienkiewicz   Painted wall plaster

Chapter 1:   Introduction

Figure 1.1   General View of Bath Spa Excavation & Bath cityscape.

GENERAL INTRODUCTION

This publication presents reports on the excavations undertaken in 1998–9 by Bath Archaeological Trust on the Spa Redevelopment site (now known as the New Royal Baths) together with associated work on the Hot Bath Spring and separate excavations on the nearby Bellott's Hospital site. The opportunity to excavate on the site of the Beau Street Baths arose from proposals in the late 1990s to create a new spa facility. This was needed to replace those that had

been closed in 1978 following the discovery of the pathogenic *Naegleria* amoeba in the spring water feeding the former facilities. The excavations were required as mitigation, as the massive piled footings and basements of the new development removed all archaeological deposits within their footprint. The sites all lie within the south-western quarter of the old walled City of Bath. The Spa Redevelopment excavations interlock with work carried out at Beau Street in 1989 (Davenport 1999, 22–37) and

1

the records made by James Irvine in 1864–7 (reproduced in Cunliffe 1969, 151–4). Recording of the standing buildings was carried out by Archaeological Investigations of Hereford, and will be reported upon separately.

ARCHAEOLOGICAL AND HISTORICAL SETTING

The City of Bath, in south-west England (Fig. 1.2), lies in the valley of the River Avon 3.4 km upstream of its tidal reach, on the oolitic limestones and clays of the Jurassic series. The City is a World Heritage Site reflecting its importance in World and European culture. Before the Georgian expansion, the city was contained within its medieval walls set on gently rising ground above the flood plain within a southward meander of the River Avon. The walls were demolished in the mid 18th century. The city then grew rapidly and growth has continued since, albeit sporadically. The historic core is now surrounded on all sides by industrial and residential suburbs.

The sites reported here lie within the City of Bath Conservation Area, a local statutory designation to control development. The Hot Bath, a Grade II* listed building, is next to one of three hot springs within the City, deposits in and around which have produced evidence for human exploitation dating back to post-glacial times. The springs were known to, and seemingly venerated by, the local populations before the Romans arrived in the area in or soon after AD 43. The existence of the tutelary

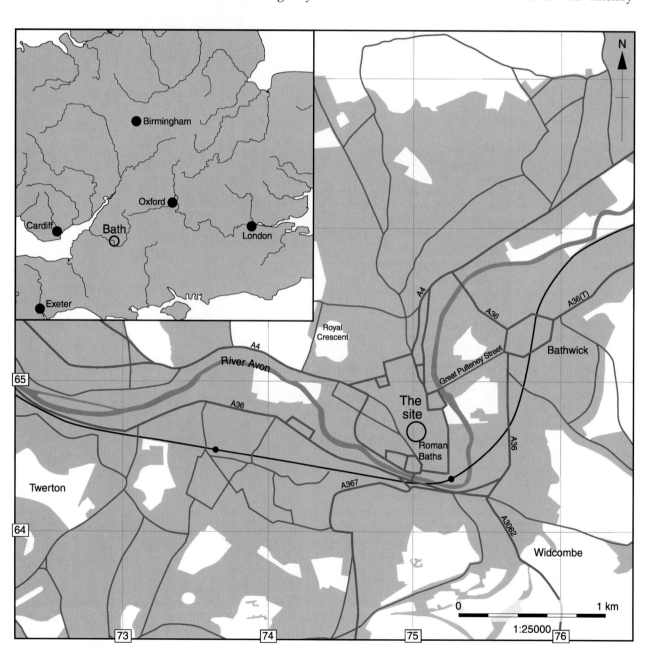

Figure 1.2   Site location map.

2

goddess, *Sulis*, and the deposition of coins in at least two of the hot springs prior to the conquest indicate religious and ritual practices which continued into the Roman period (Cunliffe 1988 and Corney, Chapter 9). Within the first few decades of Roman occupation the area occupied by the present city centre was encompassed within a temenos wall and the first masonry spa structures were erected (Cunliffe and Davenport 1985).

The enclosed area around the springs seems to have been fortified in the late Roman period and became the core of the medieval city, but is now thought to have been a civic or sacred centre in Roman times, the residential and commercial area being along the road leading to London and the Fosse Way, modern Walcot Street (Davenport 2000, 7–26). This belief is based on substantial discoveries of typical urban occupation along Walcot Street in the last 15 years and the recognition of a noticeable lack of domestic material from excavations in the central area. The pattern of finds recovery was repeated in the Spa excavation. Thus the site is in the centre of a Roman religious and ceremonial site, transformed at some point in the early middle ages to a more normal (but still unusual) urban centre.

The Hot Bath and adjacent Cross Bath springs, even combined, have a flow smaller than the principal source, which formed the nucleus of the Roman temple of *Sulis Minerva* and the medieval and Georgian 'Kings Bath' complex.

The buildings on site prior to excavation were the latest in an architectural palimpsest spanning nearly two centuries of bathing establishments. The kernel of the complex is John Wood the Younger's Hot Bath of 1776, itself a re-siting of an earlier structure originally situated in the middle of what is now Hot Bath Street, actually over the spring. This was redesigned and augmented by a 'tepid' bath (swimming pool) in the early 19th century, traditionally attributed to Decimus Burton, but now known to be by a local architect, G P Manners. The building continued to be altered throughout the later 19th century. In 1925 the Tepid Bath was completely rebuilt by A J Taylor, and Wood's Hot Bath was re-ordered once again. Finally the baths were given another refit in 1956, leaving them in the state they were in when they finally closed in 1978. Elements of each major phase were evident in the standing structure, interspersed with the less easily-interpreted features of numerous intermediary episodes.

Bellott's Hospital was founded in 1608 by Thomas Bellott, Steward to Lord Burleigh and an important benefactor of the restoration of Bath Abbey. Bellott intended it for "poor strangers", visitors to Bath, prohibiting any inmate for staying longer than 28 days. A doctor was also provided to attend the inmates – a startling innovation. His foundation was a single storey building around a courtyard entered through a pillared gateway, off which opened fourteen apartments. The building was torn down to be replaced by the present building in 1859. Unlike its predecessor, this was cellared, the digging of the cellars removing all deposits down to those of the early post-Roman period.

Archaeological investigation of the immediate environs of the development area has been intermittent since 1776. In that year foundation digging for John Wood the Younger's new Hot Bath Building produced Roman finds from the Hot Bath Spring (Cunliffe 1969, 152). The only subsequent opportunity for archaeological investigation occurred in 1986, when a possible stone block floor of a former Hot Bath building around the well head was revealed (unpublished archive, Roman Baths Museum, Bath). The earliest archaeological records were made by J T Irvine in 1864 during an extension of the Royal United Hospital, where he identified the remains of a large bathing establishment (Cunliffe 1969, 151–4). In 1908 during building work on the north-west side of Hot Bath Street, massive walls of Roman type were observed, which appear to form a continuation of the same bathing establishment (Cunliffe and Davenport 1985, fig. 107).

Investigatory and remedial work on the Cross Bath has led to archaeological discoveries on a number of occasions, the earliest in 1809 when a Roman altar was discovered. This was followed by the recovery of a relief sculpture in 1885, at the same time as part of the Roman stone-built tank was discovered (Irvine papers, and Davenport 1999, 37–40). Between 1983 and 1988 repair work allowed limited excavation and survey to be carried out, which clarified the Roman and later structural history (Davenport 1999, 37–40).

To the north-west of the Cross Bath at St John's Hospital excavations in 1954 exposed Roman gravel surfaces and a ditch, reused medieval architectural fragments and burials (Wedlake 1979). The latter must have been from the burial ground of the hospital itself (Manco 1998, 40). Further north-west, excavations at Citizen House (Greene 1979) revealed several phases of Roman building followed by post-Roman soil accumulation, pit digging and a 13th century building.

To the east of the development site limited excavation took place at 30–31 Stall Street in 1965 (Cunliffe 1969, 179–181), where pre-Roman ground surfaces and Roman floor and yard surfaces possibly associated with timber buildings were revealed along with a subsequent phase of Roman masonry building. To the north-east the complex of the Roman Baths, Kings Bath Spring and the Temple Precinct form the central focus of the city, even today (Cunliffe and Davenport 1985).

Most recently extensive excavation was undertaken on the north side of Bath Street during 1986 (Davenport 1999). The pre-Roman ground surface was excavated producing Mesolithic flints. During the Flavian period a road associated with gravel spreads cut across the site. It was later diverted around the Temple Precinct colonnade, when this was built *c* 150 AD, and was put out of use in the later 2nd century, when masonry buildings aligned with the baths were constructed. A new road was

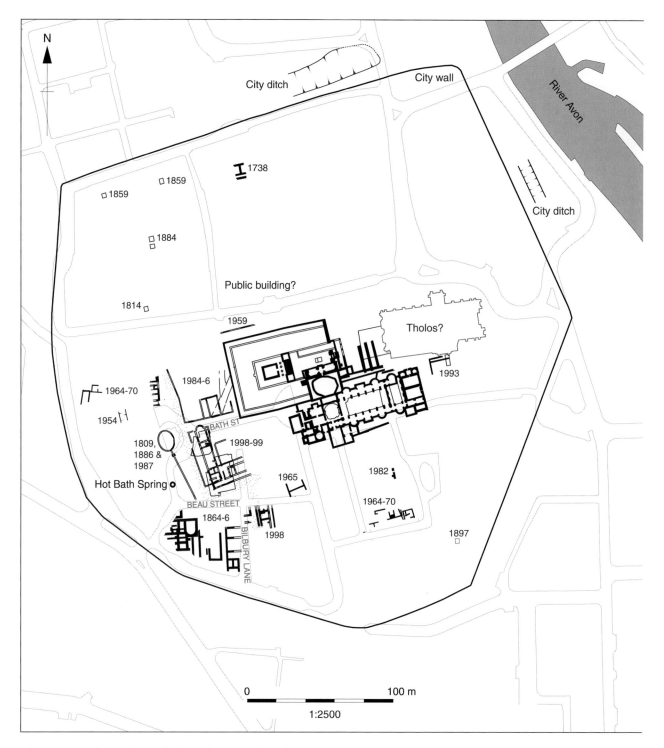

Figure 1.3 The position of the Bath Spa and Bath Street excavations in relation to the south-western quarter of the walled area of Bath, together with previous archaeological investigations.

laid out along the west side of these buildings, although possibly not until the 4th century. A building with an apsidal north end (Building D) was identified during these excavations and assigned a 4th century date. In one area stratified deposits from the Roman period to the 13th century survived with evidence of accumulation of dark earths, a street and bank of Late Saxon date, a thick layer of organic clay (possibly midden material) and a series of late 11th century hearths. The lane, referred to as ''The Way to the Cross Bath'' in medieval deeds, was laid out in about AD 1100, sealing earlier deposits. It was cobbled and resurfaced several times during the 12th century. Medieval pits of 11th-12th century date were common throughout the area.

Within the area of the present project several trial trenches and excavations were carried out by Bath Archaeological Trust in 1988 and 1989 (Fig. 1.3 and Davenport 1999). These included trenches in some of the cellars of 7–7a Bath Street, a small trench within the John Wood Hot Bath and a large excavation within the base of the Beau Street swimming pool. This revealed complex stratified deposits to a maximum depth of one metre between the base of the swimming pool and the upper surface of underlying fluvial gravels. A broad range of archaeological deposits were revealed, from which a considerable variety of artefactual material as well as animal bone was recovered for analysis. The evidence from these interventions is referred to and reconsidered with the more recent excavation results.

GEOLOGICAL SETTING
By David Jordan

The complex geological history of the city and its region has been studied since the early days of scientific geology when the pioneering geologist William Smith first developed the techniques of stratigraphic correlation and mapping while working on mining and canal projects nearby. (A fuller study of the geological background and issues arising from its study is available in the site archive.)

The geology of the valley side has had an important influence on the formation of the Bath Spa archaeological site. A succession of rock strata of varied lithologies is exposed in the sides of the Avon valley at Bath. From the valley floor to the plateau these are Lower Lias clay, Midford Sands, Inferior Oolite limestone, Fuller's Earth and Great Oolite limestone. There are important variations within the strata – in particular within the Oolitic limestones, which contain hard, shelly beds of quite different physical properties to those of the softer oolith-dominated limestone.

Subsequent weathering of the soft Fuller's Earth has caused blocks of the limestone plateau capping to tip gently towards the valley. The rocks have been very prone to slippage, bringing eroded upper strata down over the valley sides in the debris of large landslides. Creep and colluviation have also brought disaggregated soil downhill.

The valley floor is partly filled with well-rounded Pleistocene fluvioglacial sand and gravel derived from a large area to the north, north-east and north-west. This material is of much broader lithology than is found locally because it includes rocks transported into the catchment by the Anglian ice sheet and reworked from the alluvia of earlier river systems. The gravel and sand are found in the valley bottom and as terrace remnants on the valley sides. The valley floor is covered in fine-grained Holocene sediments, which extend as far as the Spa site.

The hot springs rise through funnel-shaped gravel and sand-filled 'pipes' which the water has eroded through the Lower Lias clay. Some of this clay may have been redeposited in depressions around the springs, although the spring water carries almost no sediment under normal circumstances.

The site lies on a gently sloping terrace at about 20 m above OD – about 5 m above the valley floor and 280 m from the present course of the river. The terrace occupies part of a promontory within which lies the medieval city, extending south-eastwards into a large meander of the Avon. Kellaway's reconstruction of the Holocene valley geomorphology (Cunliffe and Davenport 1985, fig. 1) shows the Roman river Avon flowing 100 m to the north-west of its present course. More recent work (Jordan 1999) broadly supports Kellaway's findings and suggests that the medieval course of the river also lay closer to the site than it does today. Excavations in the same Southgate area have, however, shown that the distribution of archaeological and natural deposits is very complex and that Kellaway's model of the channel needs to be greatly refined if it is to faithfully describe the Roman and post-Roman geomorphic history of the area. The information required to produce such a refinement is not yet available but may become so through site investigations in advance of further development in this part of the city.

The terrace on which the Spa site lies consists of Lias clay overlain by about one metre of gently dipping gravel and sand lenses which were probably deposited by the river Avon during the Devensian glaciation. These are overlain by about 0.5 m of silty clay in which are found slightly more organic units, root hollows, pores and peaty depressions which represent a complex of horizons and strata which formed the natural soil before the Roman occupation of the site. This is argued to be alluvial rather than colluvial, possibly deriving in part from the hot springs themselves.

BACKGROUND TO THE INDIVIDUAL EXCAVATIONS

The 1998–9 Excavations for the Spa Redevelopment Project at the New Royal Baths

The New Royal Baths occupy the site of the old Hot Bath/Beau Street Baths complex in the south-west part of the walled city (Fig. 1.3). The development area was of approximately 1430m^2. The present day ground level is at approximately 22 m OD, with a slight rise towards the north and east.

There were three main areas of excavation: on the site of the old mineral water swimming baths, the Beau Street Baths; in the cellars to the north beneath Nos. 7 and 7a Bath Street, a Grade I listed Georgian building which was to be converted to offices and an entrance foyer for the new development; and in a cellar under Bilbury Lane, part of the Tepid Bath of 1830 (although this latter area was subsequently withdrawn from the development, following only limited excavation). In 1989 part of the site of the Beau Street Baths and 7 and 7a Bath Street had been excavated as part of the mitigation for a spa scheme which was subsequently abandoned (Davenport

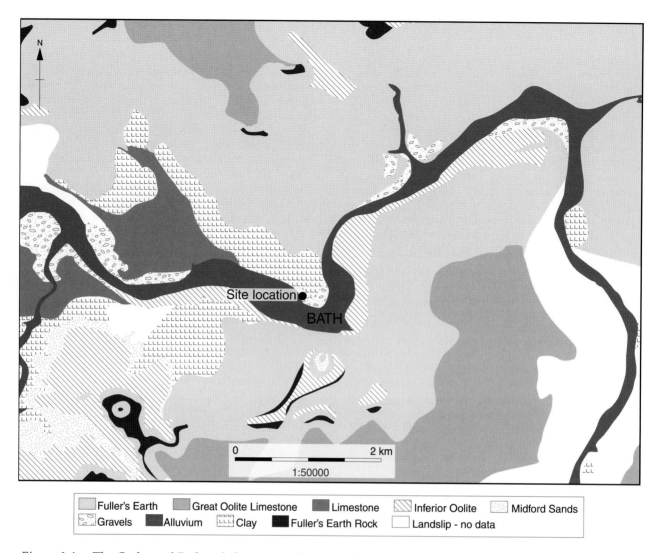

| Fuller's Earth | Great Oolite Limestone | Limestone | Inferior Oolite | Midford Sands |
| Gravels | Alluvium | Clay | Fuller's Earth Rock | Landslip - no data |

Figure 1.4 The Geology of Bath and the surrounding area. (Based upon Geological Map sheet 265 reproduced by permission of the British Geological Survey. ©NERC. All rights reserved. IPR/59–18C).

1999). This area was re-excavated in the current work. The total area of archaeological excavation was 571.5 m². Depths of excavation varied from 0.5 m to 4.0 m; giving a total volume of investigations of approximately 593.5 m³. The extent of the excavations is shown in Figure 1.3.

The 1989 work showed that significant but truncated archaeological deposits, including pre-Roman soils, survived under what was believed to be the most heavily damaged part of the site, the northern end of the 1925 swimming pool. Two small evaluation trenches were dug in 1997 to ascertain the degree of survival west of the pool, where it was thought that deposits might have survived as much as two metres higher. No evidence of cellars was known in these areas, for example. The results from these trenches, though limited, did seem to indicate that *in situ* archaeological deposits survived immediately beneath existing slab level. If representative, they would indicate the presence of post-medieval, early and late medieval, Roman and prehistoric deposits to a depth of 2.5 m–3.0 m. However, neither

the extent nor severity of existing disturbances to these deposits was known outside of the limited area of evaluation and further investigation of the exposed deposits was not allowed.

As a result of the 1989 and 1997 work, it was determined that environmental sampling would form a key element of the on-site methodology, with the main emphasis on soil studies, pollen analysis and bulk sampling for recovery of animal bone, molluscs and plant macrofossils. It was thought this would be most appropriate for studying post-Roman dark earths and the pre-Roman stratigraphy.

During the course of excavation it soon became apparent that most areas were heavily truncated, and that no post-Roman dark earths remained. However, the environmental programme was continued although constrained by the limitations of survival of appropriate deposits. Following the assessment stage of the project it was clear that preservation of certain categories of material was poor, and that for others the character and quality of deposits from which these materials derived would

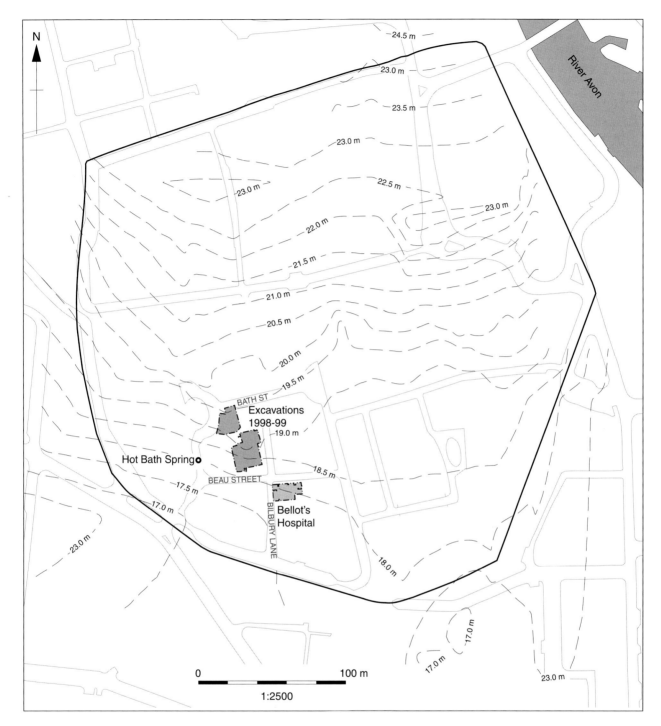

Figure 1.5 Contour survey of the pre-Roman ground surface and the Spa excavation in the centre of Bath (based on survey data from excavations by Bath Archaeological Trust).

limit their research potential and did not justify the scope of work originally envisaged. As a result of these conclusions at the assessment stage, it was decided that full analysis should only proceed for soil micromorphological analysis and further funding was only sought for this aspect. During the course of full analysis of the stratigraphy, it became evident that a more flexible approach would be more rewarding and that more reliable information and results could after all be obtained from a more

detailed analysis of certain contexts and materials. The client released more funds to allow further work on certain aspects of the record, but it has only been possible to undertake a limited amount of this work.

It was clear that preservation of pollen, molluscs and diatoms was poor and no further work has been undertaken on these materials following the assessments. All large mammal bone was recovered during hand excavation, but a small number of contexts, which contained large quantities of bone, were wet sieved. Plant macrofossils, small mammal, fish and bird bone were recovered from 169 bulk samples. The animal bone has been fully analysed. An assessment of all plant macrofossil samples was completed, but further analysis has been undertaken on the waterlogged material, including wood, and on carbonised wood from the Roman culvert trench.

Research Design

Prior to commencement of the project the research potential of the Spa site was fully explored in the Design Brief and Project Specification. Many of the research topics identified were entirely dependent on good preservation of well-preserved and well-stratified deposits providing data of sufficient quantity and quality for the topics to be addressed. In the event the quality and extent of the archaeological deposits was such that many of the identified research topics had to be abandoned; they are not listed here.

The principal research themes that it was thought might still be pursued were:

The early prehistoric landscape and environment of Bath
The Roman to medieval transition
The post-medieval to Georgian transition
Residuality within urban deposits
Soil micromorphology of urban deposits

Further work made it clear that, although the site produced data that could be relevant to these topics,

analysis of the chronological issues required adequate stratigraphic/artefactual and environmental data on either side of each chronological divide, which was not forthcoming. Analysis of residuality would require not only assemblage populations sufficiently numerous and varied to be statistically valid, but also comparable for all periods. As a result of the limitations of the site, the post-excavation analysis has been directed towards a reduced number of themes: namely to characterise urban deposits through the soil micromorphology, to elucidate the prehistoric landscape and the transition to Roman occupation, to understand the major developments in this quarter of Roman Bath during the 2nd century AD and to analyse the primary and secondary uses of the medieval pits. It has been possible to examine the Roman to medieval transition to a limited extent.

Description of Site

The remains of the Tepid Bath and its associated structures of 1829 dictated to some extent the approach taken to the earlier deposits (Fig. 1.6). The deep foundation trenches for these walls effectively subdivided the site into discrete areas (designated Eastern, Central, and Western for ease of reference); Northern refers to the area below the 1989 excavations and NE to the area investigated immediately to the east of this. In only one small area did the earlier archaeological deposits physically link across these subdivisions. In addition, the 1829 construction work had truncated all deposits to a lesser or greater extent.

Figure 1.6   General view of Bath Spa excavation.

In the eastern area the natural gravels were truncated to a depth of *c* 18.7 m OD leaving only the basal remnants of the deepest Roman foundations below. A two metre wide strip to the east of the pool and the area to the north (the latter sampled in 1989) survived to 19.2 m OD. Some Roman stratigraphy survived here, especially towards the south end where Roman road surfaces remained. The buried pre-Roman soils \ sediments also survived. The excavation of 1989 had removed all Roman deposits in the northern half of the 1925 pool but had only sampled the pre-Roman contexts. In the western area the 1829 foundation trench had cut down to a depth of *c* 19.75 m OD to hard Roman deposits, removing almost all post-Roman stratigraphy apart from the truncated bases of negative features.

The central strip had a mixture of deep truncation at the south end into the natural gravel, but with shallower truncation in the middle comparable to the western area. To the north were two small baulks of pre-1829 deposits (separated by a deep 19th century cellar), which had survived to just below the 19th and 20th century floor levels (*c* 21.1 m OD). The southern of these had originally been exposed in Trial Trench D (Heaton 1997), which encouraged the original supposition that deeply stratified deposits survived to the west of the swimming pool. A similar level of preservation occurred in the north-east corner, east of the pool (surviving to *c* 20.8 m OD), but could only be observed in section during demolitions in 1999. These latter deposits may have been continuous with those in the cellar under Bilbury Lane, although here the floor of the cellar was 0.4 m lower.

This meant that the pre-Roman buried soil was well-preserved outside the footprint of the 1829 structures and where not removed by deep Roman footings or drains. The Roman deposits were truncated vertically and horizontally by the 19th century works and by medieval robbing and rubbish pits. The rubbish pits were truncated by a range of activities, but predominantly by the 19th century works. Below the floor level of the 20th century Beau Street Baths, the 1829 baths survived very well.

The sequence of activity and phasing is summarised in a simple site matrix (Fig. 1.7). The full site matrix in which all contexts are shown in their stratigraphical relationship can be found in the site archive together with full details of all contexts.

Hot Bath Spring (Fig. 1.3)

The Hot Bath Spring (sometimes erroneously referred to as the Hetling or Hetlin Spring) lies outside and immediately to the west of the John Wood Hot Bath building, situated below the present day road surface of Hot Bath Street. During the preparations for the Spa redevelopment, it became necessary to drill a borehole approximately 230 mm in diameter (9 inches) into the spring. This had not originally been included within the archaeological programme,

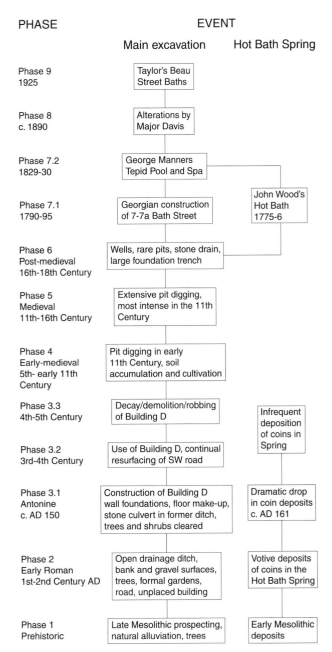

Figure 1.7 Summary matrix block diagram of the main phases of the Bath Spa excavation.

but the work coincided with the excavations in the cellars of 7–7a Bath Street, and the excavation team was informed by the Clerk of Works of the appearance of coins in the spoil skip. The spoil, essentially loose sands and gravels, came from a depth of 5–12 m below the present road surface. No archaeological excavation was involved but all the spoil pumped up from the borehole was wet-sieved. An entire skip full of material was processed in this way and a very high percentage of artefactual material was recovered. Despite this, it is unlikely that everything was recovered as not all the slurry from the borehole went into the skip.

Bellott's Hospital (Fig. 1.3)

Bellott's Hospital lies opposite the Spa site on the south side of Beau Street. Work there was undertaken in late 1998 during refurbishment and extension of the building, which dated from 1859, but originated in a foundation of 1608. This site had gained development approval without benefit of PPG16 procedures and, in the absence of an archaeological programme of mitigation, Bath Archaeological Trust undertook a watching brief. Limited excavation and recording were possible and were carried out with the full co-operation of the builders but without funding from the developers, St John's Hospital, Bath.

The cellars were deepened to gain headroom for new rooms to be fitted out in them. This involved the removal of the cellar floors and the machine excavation of an area of 187 sq m of archaeologically stratified deposits to a depth of 0.4 m. Service trenches were subsequently excavated into the underlying archaeological deposits.

The account of the excavation presented here is of an interim nature only since as a consequence of the financial background to the project no funding has been available to undertake full analysis of the stratigraphic sequence, or of the artefact and ecofact assemblages.

REPORT STRUCTURE AND ARCHIVE

The majority of the report is taken up with the account of the Spa Redevelopment excavations, based on the successive archaeologically recognised periods of the site. The stratigraphic and structural narrative seeks to describe and interpret the sequence using the geoarchaeological study to enlarge and clarify aspects of it. The geoarchaeological comments on each period are therefore given prominence at the beginning of each section where they are relevant. Finds and environmental evidence is incorporated into the period-based narrative, either as summaries of or as extracts from the relevant specialist reports, in order to present an integrated account of the discoveries relating to each period. In particular the geoarchaeological discussions have been recast to make their character more comparable to that of the rest of the text. A general discussion is given for each period where appropriate, drawing on all the evidence presented.

The report is linked to site archive, which contains supporting site and specialist data in digital form. The specialist reports, either full analysis or an assessment where this was the limit of study, can all be found in full in the archive.

The accounts of the work at the Hot Bath Spring and at Bellott's Hospital are self contained, incorporating discussion of finds and environmental evidence where possible, although in the case of Bellott's Hospital this is confined to a summary assessment of the important metalworking debris. The specialist reports for the Hot Bath Spring can also be found in full in the site archive. The project archive is held by Bath and North East Somerset Heritage Services, Roman Baths Museum, Stall Street.

Chapter 2: Spa Period 1: Prehistoric

OVERVIEW

This period can be summarised as a long process of natural alluviation with evidence of tree growth and of two main phases of deposition. Optically stimulated luminescence (OSL) and carbon 14 dating suggest it is a finely stratified series of deposits of early postglacial origin that continued to be deposited until at least the neolithic. The alluvial clays contained a scatter of artefacts in the form of worked flint and occasional ceramic material. Though originally regarded as a prehistoric or pre-Roman soil, it has become clear during the analysis that the upper phase continued to form the ground surface during the early Roman period until it was completely covered over at the beginning of Period 3. As anticipated, the old ground surface survived over much of the site. The main areas where it was present are shown in Figure 2.1. These were, broadly, the western area, the eastern strip and much of the northern area. The largest area of absence was below the tepid pool, which had cut into the underlying gravels for almost its full extent.

SUMMARY OF THE GEOARCHAEOLOGY OF THE PRE-ROMAN DEPOSITS
by David Jordan

The site sits on a thin layer of terrace gravel and sand – 0.5 m to 1.5 m thick – overlying Lias clay. The gravel and sand lenses show well-developed current bedding representing deposition from fast flowing water in the braided river Avon, probably during the latter half of the Devensian glaciation. Earlier excavations in central Bath had consistently encountered a clayey deposit underlying the Roman strata (*inter alia* Cunliffe 1969, figs 67 and 70; Davenport 1999, fig. I.59). A large area of this pre-Roman deposit was revealed here, providing the opportunity to analyse it and the natural strata immediately beneath it.

The deposit was found to be a clayey silt or silty clay, which contained small but varying amounts of coarser matter derived from the gravel and sand below. The deposit was stratified into bands of slightly different texture, some of which were darkened by a small proportion of almost completely humified organic matter. Artefacts, other than Mesolithic stone tools, and charcoal fragments are rare. The strata were discontinuous across the site and varied considerably in depth and thickness, suggesting that whatever soil profile development had taken place had been punctuated by repeated episodes of renewed surface deposition. A number of hollows through the silty clay and down into the

gravel beneath were filled with a dark and internally consistent humified organic clay with abundant root channels in the underlying gravels. The hypothesis was that the larger organic clayey masses might represent the remains of tree boles still embedded in the soil: radiocarbon dating showed some of them to be Late Mesolithic or Neolithic.

The palaeosol was of variable thickness, around 0.5 m, with a clear upper contact with the lowest early Roman deposits and a gradual lower contact with the sands and gravels of the Devensian fluvioglacial terrace on which the site lies. The profile was divided in two with a lower sequence of horizons developed within the sands and gravels of the upper Devensian terrace deposits and an upper sequence developed in silty clays above. Both showed well-developed mottling and micromorphological evidence of persistent wetness. The upper surface of the lower sequence was a well-developed organic-mineral horizon resembling a much-degraded gley Ah (organic surface) horizon, although not as excessively organic as such wet soil surfaces can become. The upper sequence, however, showed no such organic surface although there were clear signs of some horizonation (the formation of horizontal zones) within it. This is most likely to be due to the mixing of the upper part of the soil profile with the Roman strata above, as shown by the presence of Roman artefacts in the upper sequence.

The silty clay deposit extends, with variations, over the whole area of the site and represents a process of formation which was continuous over the same area and, by inference from the earlier excavations, a much larger area beyond. The same broad themes of stratigraphy and post-depositional change are found within it almost everywhere. A gradual fall in the surface from the north-west towards the south-east corresponded with a slight deepening and darkening of the clay.

The profile through the strata shows horizonation caused by gradual processes of soil formation, water movement and biological activity, which have worked down from the surface above to leave approximately horizontal zones.

Analyses showed low magnetic susceptibility, which suggests that the soil was persistently wet since these conditions make susceptibility enhancement less likely. It also suggests the absence of significant mixing of Roman occupation and the rarity of such debris within the clay also indicates that mixing – and thus biological activity – largely ceased when Roman construction began: Roman construction debris is, with few exceptions, absent from the clay beneath. Thus it can be concluded that the beginning of the first significant

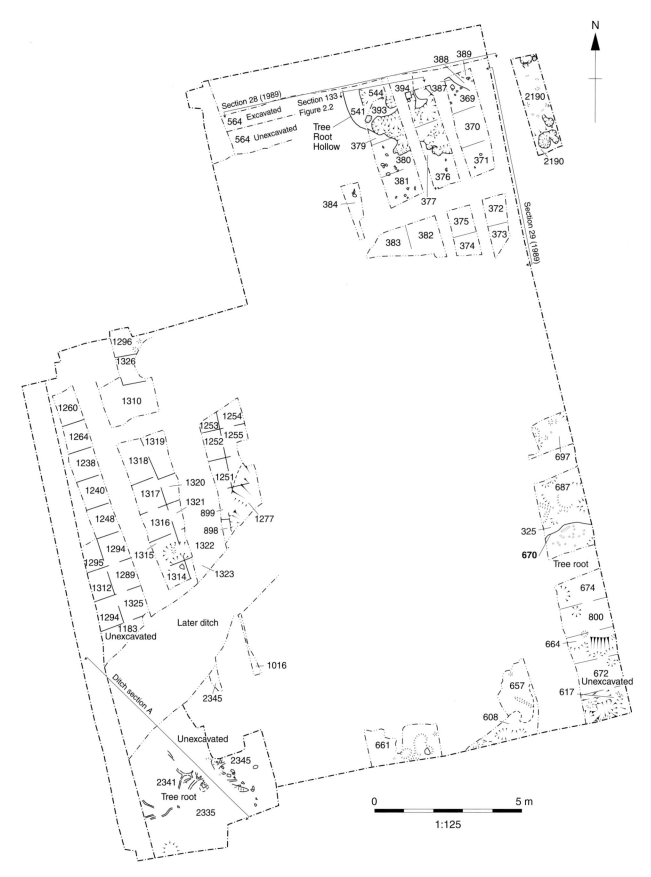

Figure 2.1   Bath Spa Excavations: Plan of Period 1: the prehistoric level, showing subdivisions of the palaeosol as excavated.

Roman construction phase brought soil activity below to a close, implying that the soil was rapidly buried by biologically sterile deposits such as solid floors, compact gravel surfaces and building debris.

The pre-Roman buried soil was non-calcareous. This lack of calcium carbonate through most of the buried soil suggests either that it was never calcareous or that it has become decalcified. If it was decalcified, then this probably took place before the strata above were deposited.

The soil structure was massive or weakly developed large-blocky, in contrast to finer structures, whose absence suggests that regular wetting-drying cycles and biological activity had not been taking place within the soil since it was buried. Evidence of organic activity taking place *before* it was buried is largely due to plant growth and the biological mixing going on is evidence that the soil was sometimes dry enough for an active soil biota to have developed. The organic component was found to be largely amorphous confirming that the organic matter was almost completely humified.

The origins of the soil material help understanding of the site conditions faced by the earliest occupants. Deposition of the silty clay immediately after the underlying sand and gravel during the last glaciation seems unlikely in view of the presence of organic matter and Mesolithic flints in it. A colluvial origin seems equally unlikely since the deposits contained very little sand, a significant component of all the soils uphill caused by admixing of the Midford sands. This leaves deposition by water flowing out of the hot springs or by high floods of the river Avon. The surface of the buried soil was slightly ridged, perhaps by rill erosion, and mineralised deposits, perhaps deriving from warm spring water, were observed during excavation. However, it seems unlikely that such a spring clay deposit would be as uniform as that found, instead it is likely to have been made up of a more complex sequence of overlapping splays of clay. Moreover some root and tree-bole organic masses had been buried by later clay deposits, and this is more easily explained in terms of alluvium deposition from high floods rather than by laterally restricted deposition from spring water flow. However, the silty clay may have been deposited both by spring water and by floods, so to resolve this XRD analyses were carried out on the Lias clay, river alluvium and the buried soil. The XRD evidence suggests that the soil is derived more from river alluvium than from the Lias clay and thus is most likely to have been laid down by the river Avon in flood.

The organic clay found filling depressions within the buried soil, and interpreted initially as decayed peat, was analysed in more detail and two radio-carbon dates obtained. Large root pores extended from these hollows, suggesting that they were more likely to represent tree-boles, which had been preserved *in situ*, although it was suggested on site that they might have been associated with tree-throw hollows. Organic clay masses were sometimes separated from the mineral soil and gravel to each side by a steep boundary, which is unlikely to have survived exposure without slumping or eroding. This suggests that the mineral soil was supported by the organic masses as might be expected with a decaying tree stump.

The OSL dates indicate that the buried soil strata span 'dates' in the Mesolithic (ref OxL-1035, 5,780 ± 330BP and ref OxL-1036, 9,210 ± 520BP), whilst the radiocarbon determinations on the organic masses gave dates of late Mesolithic to Neolithic. The radiocarbon determinations were 6475 + 75 BP (GU-10859: cal 5610 BC – 5590 BC (1.5%) and 5570 BC – 5300 BC (93.9%) at 95.4% probability), and 7745 + 65 BP (GU-10860: cal 6690 BC–6450 BC at 95.4% probability). Dates on both the mineral and organic matter significantly pre-date the Roman strata. Their stratigraphic and date order is consistent with the strong evidence for sedimentary stratigraphy within the deposit itself.

The XRD analyses suggest that the buried soil minerals are similar to those of the alluvium of the river Avon, as sampled at the bottom of a deep trench close to the modern river course. The dating, artefact and micromorphology data agree with observations on site that, although the deposits have been strongly mixed, the buried soil retains a great deal of relatively fine stratigraphy as well as volumes with a fairly high proportion of organic matter, albeit highly humified.

Taken together this evidence suggests that there is a sequence of strata in the buried soil, which survived the natural processes of mixing from the Neolithic to the Roman occupation of the site. The analyses of the strata suggest that Devensian fluvioglacial deposition of a sandy-gravelly terrace, later dissected, gave way to soil formation during the Mesolithic which resulted in a shallow profile with a greater proportion of organic matter and clay at the surface. Further high floods, in the later Mesolithic or Neolithic, buried this soil surface and left a new stratum of alluvial silty clay overlying or incorporating organic masses which may, given the strong evidence for tree-roots within the lower soil, have been the remains of trees. Human activity occurred here during the Mesolithic and artefacts representing this extensive use of the landscape became buried within the accumulating alluvial strata. The micromorphological evidence shows that the buried soil became mixed by the normal soil-forming processes, but there is no evidence that the artefact stratigraphy is due to downward movement. The location of the artefacts seems more likely to reflect where they were originally deposited.

The survival of so much organic matter, and the micromorphological evidence for mixing taking place under very wet conditions, indicates that normal soil activity was strongly suppressed because the soil was very wet for much of the time. The survival of Neolithic organic matter, however, suggests that the lower soil horizons never dried out fully and thus some persistent source of water must have been keeping the soil wet. It is possible that this source will have been the spring itself, although, as the XRD evidence suggests, the buried soil minerals were not derived from the Lias clay and there is no evidence that the soil, before it was buried, was enriched in the soluble minerals abundant in the spring water.

STRATIGRAPHIC EVIDENCE

The surface of the palaeosol had a distinct slope from the north and west towards the south and east. On the west side of the excavation it lay at 19.25 m OD sloping down to 19.1 m OD on the east and as low as 18.8 m OD in the south-east corner. At the north end of the main site it lay at *c* 19.2 m OD, and further north in the cellars of 7–7a Bath Street at a maximum of 19.5 m. This follows the natural trend of the hillside north of the Avon meander.

The excavation provided an opportunity for a detailed study of these deposits to elucidate the development of the prehistoric environment and the natural setting encountered when the Romans began to develop the area. The study of the soil micromorphology (David Jordan above) has shown the palaeosol to be an alluvial deposit possibly laid down in two main phases of flooding with subsequent evidence of tree growth. At the low south-east corner of the excavation it may have supported an alder carr-type vegetation and have been (semi-) permanently waterlogged. Jordan indicates the soils were subject to persistent wetness, but dry enough at times for bioturbation to take place. The lower horizon is described as a degraded gley type with a well-developed organic surface horizon. In the upper horizon no clear organic surface was identified, and this may have been destroyed post-deposition.

Two samples for Optically Stimulated Luminescence assay were taken from the upper and lower horizons of the palaeosol in the north-east area utilising the section originally cut in 1989 (Davenport 1999, fig.I.29 section 19). The results give dates of 5,780±330 years BP (3,780±330 years BC) and 9,210±520 years BP (7,210±520 years BC) for the upper and lower formation respectively (Bailey 'The soils' report in archive). This long time span may be interpreted as reflecting evidence for alluviation and soil formation over a considerable length of time. Alternatively, in view of Jordan's results from the soil micromorphology, they may reflect the two discrete flooding episodes, when the main sediments were laid down.

The alluvial deposits are described in detail by Jordan in a report in the archive. Broadly they took the form of a firm, mid-dark greyish brown silty clay with little sand (contexts 353, 1183, 1285, 1347, 2335). They contained a light scatter of small flint gravel and pebbles and variable quantities of charcoal flecks. In some areas mottles from iron staining were present. The deposits graded into yellowish or reddish brown silty clay, again with little sand, in the lower horizon (367, 396, 1286, 1348, 1349, 2340). In some areas a darker grey, more organic lens occurred towards the base of the upper horizon

(1240, 1299, 1312). A similar lens was noted in the Bath Street cellars in the lower horizon (1790) and in the western area as a middle horizon (1258). A sparse scatter of chert and flint pebbles sometimes provided a marker band between the upper and lower horizons of the alluvial deposits. The lower horizon exhibited greater variation in colour with fine flecks of iron staining or more diffuse and extensive brown mottles. The density of flint and limestone gravel and cobbles and sand also varied, in some areas becoming very sandy towards the base.

A small number of contemporary features, probable tree root hollows and one possible tree throw (385–387) (Fig. 2.2), were identified within these deposits. They took the form of bowl shaped or irregular shallow hollows of various sizes often pock-marked with small depressions, which had the appearance of root holes. These were concentrated in the north-east area and the largest was an irregular, basin-shaped hollow (385) *c* 2.2 m wide by 0.6 m deep, which contained a variety of layers of humic silty clay, sandy clay and gravel layers asymmetrically tipping into the hollow (Fig. 2.2). The excavator Poole feels this is consistent with a tree throw, though Jordan disputes this interpretation (full report in the archive). Nonetheless, this is the only tree depression that can be argued to be an actual throw. The only artefacts recovered from this root hollow were struck flints. Brooks ('Flint Assemblage', below) has suggested that the concentrations of flint may have resulted from a tree throw pulling up suitable raw material or providing easier access to it (there is no archaeological evidence of excavations into these deposits to obtain flints from the gravels).

Jordan ('Geoarchaeology', above) identified the more amorphous humic material (388, 394) within these areas as tree boles, rotted *in situ*. The radiocarbon assay of these tree roots (above) has given a determination compatible with a late Mesolithic-Neolithic date and he suggests that clearance may have been taking place sometime during the Neolithic. This date ties in with the association of the late Mesolithic flints with these contexts.

However, the situation is not so straightforward that all tree root hollows found can be regarded as being of the same date. The evidence suggests that certainly one and possibly two are the remains of trees growing in the Roman period (2341, 670). In the case of 2341 it is clear that the tree was not uprooted but that the base of the trunk and roots radiating from it were left to rot *in situ*, the root channels being preserved as voids coated in calcium carbonate. This tree certainly appears to have continued growing into the early Roman period, not being cut down until as late as the redevelopment of the site at the beginning of Period 3. The rotting stump appears to have been the cause of subsidence of Roman surfaces to the south of Building D. In the case of 670 it is possible that the tree was cut down as part of this same activity, but in this case the stump was burnt out, resulting in layer 648.

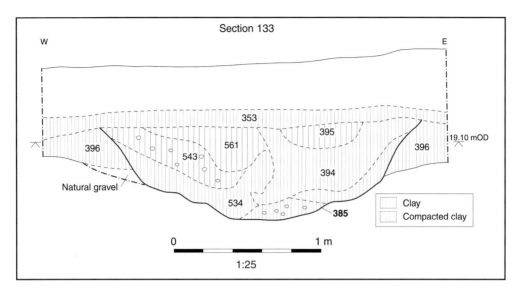

Figure 2.2   Bath Spa Excavations: Section through possible tree root hollow 385.

Cultural activity is represented primarily by worked flint and chert, nearly all of late Mesolithic date. Other flint artefacts indicating activity in other periods comprise a heavily rolled flake, probably of Palaeolithic date and assumed to originate from the underlying river gravels, and a Bronze Age style scraper found in a Roman gravel layer and probably imported into the site (late Bronze Age activity is now known near the Royal Crescent, an area used for gravel extraction in the 18th century (Davenport 2004, passim). The palaeosol was excavated in small units, wherever possible as metre squares, and in selected areas bulk samples were taken for environmental analysis and artefact recovery. In addition large unworked flint pebbles and cobbles were retained for comparison as the source of artefactual material. The report by Brooks (below) shows that a large number of the flints consisted of broken flakes, worked lumps and spalls (65%). This taken with the high cortical index (52.7%) and the low number of tools (2%) suggests that preliminary testing and preparation of flint derived from the underlying gravels was the major activity taking place on the site during the late Mesolithic. There is no evidence of extraction pits on site, but the people may have been taking advantage of fallen tree boles, other natural exposures of the gravel in the vicinity or material brought to the surface of the soil by animal activity. The flint assemblage is similar to other groups found in excavations in this area of Bath, but is in stark contrast to the early Mesolithic assemblage recovered from the Hot Bath spring (Chapter 9).

Apart from the Mesolithic material, evidence of human activity appears to be absent for the following prehistoric period. A small number of Iron Age sherds were found residually within layers in the Period 3 culvert ditch [1280], mixed with the re-used demolition material, and had probably been brought onto the site from elsewhere. However, the presence

of early, middle and late Iron Age sherds derived from close by suggests that the centre of Bath was not entirely devoid of activity during the Iron Age. Prior to this Iron Age material had been identified no closer than at Sion Hill (Cunliffe 1979, 127–8), Lower Common (unpublished BAT excavation, Roman Baths Museum archives) and Bathampton Meadows (unpublished BAT excavation Roman Baths Museum archives) and more distantly at Stanton Field (Bath & North East Somerset Heritage Services), Bathampton Down (Wainwright 1967) and Solsbury Hill (Dowden 1957).

ENVIRONMENTAL EVIDENCE

It has not been possible to characterise the plant cover in any detail, as pollen and mollusc analyses showed these indicators to be poorly preserved, whilst plant macrofossils were sparse.

Very little is known of the environment of the Avon valley during the prehistoric period and how this changed when the Romans founded *Aquae Sulis*. It is of course possible to make educated guesses. The steep slopes of the valley were probably heavily wooded throughout much of the prehistoric period. The valley floor was perhaps a mosaic of woodland and more open marshy ground criss-crossed by braided streams, providing excellent areas for hunting. Brooks (1999) has suggested that late Mesolithic flint assemblages found at various sites in Bath probably represent a series of hunting camps, whilst the occasional presence of projectile points of Neolithic-Bronze Age date found in the King's Bath spring (Care 1985) probably represent casual loss during episodes of hunting.

The soil characteristics and presence of tree root hollows in the excavation indicates the presence of trees, some dating to the late Mesolithic or early Neolithic, but others still present at the start of the Roman period. There was probably a gradual change through prehistory to permanent pasture along the floodplain, though this could have been interspersed with standard trees or small spinneys. Areas of the alluvial floodplain near to the site were certainly accreting after the Mesolithic suggesting clearance and soil erosion upstream. The Ham and Kingsmead were water meadows and pasture throughout the Middle Ages (as their names indicate) and the pollen evidence (Tinsley, report in site archive) suggests that this was probably the case during Roman times as well.

Prehistoric settlement from the Neolithic onwards is well represented on the higher ground around Bath such as at Lansdown and Charmy Down (Cunliffe 1986, 6; Grimes 1965, 223–232). Extensive field systems providing evidence of pre-medieval arable agriculture occur in Bathwick Wood and on Bathampton and Claverton Downs, with the field lynchets continuing down the valley side to within a few hundred metres of the recently excavated Iron Age site at Bathampton Meadows (Davenport in prep). Here field banks and ditches were identified, though these are not necessarily lynchets indicative of arable agriculture being practised on the valley floor, but could equally be field boundaries in pasture for grazing.

It was hoped that pollen analysis might provide a more detailed picture of the environment during this period. The prehistoric palaeosol was sampled (layers 672, 673 and 674 below the road in the SE area, layers 365 and 366 and sediment from a tree root hollow in the north-east area) but the assessment showed that pollen was sparse and poorly preserved. The identifications that could be made and their quantities are shown in Table 2.1. Clearly the poor preservation and low concentrations of pollen prevent any meaningful conclusions being drawn about the prehistoric to early Roman plant communities. All that can be said is that the plants identified were growing somewhere in the pollen catchment area between the Mesolithic and early Roman period. The presence of heather (*Calluna*) is interesting as it is unlikely to have been growing in the immediate vicinity of the site and may indicate that anthropogenic activity introduced it

into the spectrum. It may have been brought in as roofing or flooring material. The presence of fine charcoal (mostly too small to be identified) may indicate that the area was burnt off from time to time to encourage new growth for pasture or to encourage game if the area was used for hunting.

The assessments of macroscopic plant remains (Jones and Pelling, full report in site archive) show these to be equally sparse. Twenty-nine samples were taken from the prehistoric levels, predominantly from the palaeosol, together with two from a tree root hollow. All the flots were small, many producing no charred material. Cereal grains were noted, singly or in small numbers in ten samples and included *Triticum* sp. (wheat) and *Avena* sp. (oat). Another sample produced a single possible *Bromus* sp. (brome grass) seed. Non-charred seeds of *Sambucus nigra* (elder) were present in some flots and may represent contamination. The limited range of material provides no indication of date.

The cereal grains may have been incorporated in the soil at any time from the Neolithic onwards. There is no evidence to indicate that crops were being grown or processed in the immediate vicinity and Jordan's analysis of the soil would suggest it was not ideal for arable cultivation. It is most likely that the few carbonized seeds found were incorporated in the soil during the earliest Roman activity, which also resulted in artefactual material being introduced into the soil.

A small number of what appeared to be spade marks (1743–1747) were observed in cellar 4 of 7–7a Bath Street cutting into the surface of the palaeosol. Although they could be interpreted as representing prehistoric spade cultivation, there is no evidence to support this and they are more likely to relate to garden activity during Period 2.

MATERIAL EVIDENCE

Flint Assemblage
by Ian Brooks

A total of 994 artefacts were found, of which 742 are from the palaeosol and associated deposits. The remaining 252 artefacts are assumed to have been

Table 2.1   Period 1: Pollen and spore types and numbers from the prehistoric palaeosol.

Contexts	Quercus	Alnus	Corylus	Poaceae	Lactuceae	Calluna	Pteridium	Filicales	Unid
199 [5900]						1			2
365 [5900]	2			2			+	+	
366 [5900]							+	+	
672		2	1	4	3		35	+	
673								+	+
674								+	+
368 [5901]						3			+
2332			1	1	2				
2340									

derived from the underlying deposits or to have been accidentally brought onto the site as part of some other activity. The 18 flint artefacts recovered from the excavations in the cellars of Bath Street have been included within the appropriate section as these are an extension of the open area excavations.

Residual assemblage

241 flint artefacts, assumed to be residual, were recovered from the Roman and later deposits from the Spa and Bath Street excavations. The majority of the artefacts recovered from the post-prehistoric contexts were flakes of various forms. One hundred and thirty flakes or broken flakes were recovered (64.4% of the assemblage from the post-prehistoric contexts), of which 66 (32.7%) were broken. The complete flakes consisted of only 10 primary flakes (5.0%), 29 secondary flakes (14.4%) and 25 tertiary flakes (12.4%).

Only five tools (2.5%) were found, as follows (for full descriptions see report in site archive):

Side scraper on a rolled secondary flake. (Fig. 2.4, 4) Context 361, SF 6110.
Side scraper on a secondary flake. The style of the tool might suggest an Early Bronze Age date. (Fig. 2.4, 12) Context 1215, SF 6122.
Hollow side scraper on slightly rolled, broken fragment of a tertiary flake. (Fig. 2.5, 4) Context 1215, SF 6123.
Dihedral Burin on tertiary flake. (Fig 2.5, 6) Context 1231, SF 6121.
End scraper formed reusing an already patinated flake. (Fig. 2.4, 7) Context 2332, SF 6126.

Whilst only two (1.0%) fragments from formal cores were recovered a further 57 (28.2%) worked lumps were also found. The core fragments were both core face rejuvenation flakes from small blade cores. A further eight spalls and worked fragments were also found in the post-prehistoric contexts.

Period 1 assemblage

Some 742 artefacts were recovered from the prehistoric soil at the base of the sequence. Of these, 234 (31.5% of the assemblage from Period 1) were complete flakes and a further 217 (29.2%) broken flakes. The complete flakes consisted of 43 (5.8%) primary flakes, 95 (12.8%) secondary flakes and 96 (12.9%) tertiary flakes. The relatively high number of cortical flakes would suggest that initial knapping, or possibly the testing of nodules, was taking place on or near to the site. This was also reflected in the broken flakes, 115 (53% of the broken flakes) of which had cortical surfaces. The size and shape of the flakes from the Spa excavation is summarised in Figure 2.3.

Only a limited number of formal cores or core debris was recovered (8 or 1.1%). Three cores

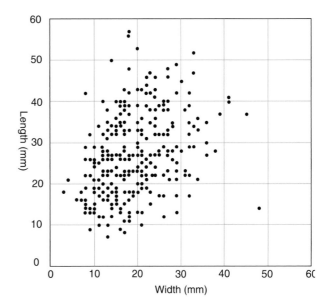

Figure 2.3 Bath Spa excavations: Scattergram showing distribution of flint flakes by size.

(Fig. 2.5, 8–10) or broken cores were found, all of which were from the production of small blades. Further evidence of on-site production of blades consisted of four core rejuvenation flakes, two core face rejuvenation flakes and two core platform rejuvenation flakes. A crested flake was also found.

A further 152 (20.5%) worked lumps were also collected together with 115 (15.5%) spalls and flint fragments which are assumed to be the result of knapping events. The high number of irregular worked lumps is partly a reflection of the quality of the flint being exploited and, probably, a reflection of the testing of the local gravel resources. The small size of the elements of the resource being exploited can be seen from the average weight of the cores and worked lumps from the site, only 10.2 g.

Sixteen (2.2%) tools were recovered from pre-Roman contexts. Whilst the majority of these are assumed to be contemporary with the formation or disturbance of the prehistoric soil, one artefact would appear to have been derived from the underlying gravels. This was SF 6104 (from context 543), a heavily rolled and patinated secondary flake. It is assumed to have been derived from the underlying gravels and therefore is most probably Palaeolithic in date. At least four large removals along the left hand edge may suggest that this flake had been further modified, although the degree of rolling has removed any fine detail. (Fig. 2.5, 11)

The majority of the remaining tools were scrapers of various forms. Ten scrapers (1.3%) were collected being a mixture of side, side/end and end scrapers (Figs 2.4–2.5). One distinct group were two side/end scrapers with a rectilinear plan (Fig. 2.4, 1 & 2). The scrapers are summarised in Table 2.2.

Table 2.2   Quantification of flint scraper types.

Type	Number
End Scraper	3
Side Scraper	3
Side/End Scraper	2
Rectilinear Scraper	2
Total	10

The remaining tools consisted of two microliths, three burins, a notch and a possible crude fabricator. These are summarised here and fully described on the web site:

Distal end of a broken/snapped **microlith**. (Fig. 2.5, 13) Context 392, SF 6128.

Rod microlith on a narrow blade, 5 mm wide. (Fig. 2.5, 12) Context 1264, SF 6117.

Dihedral burin on a fragment from a tertiary flake. (Fig. 2.5, 7) Context 533, SF 6107.

Dihedral burin on a secondary flake. (Fig. 2.5, 5) Context 6124, SF 6124.

Notch on a rolled secondary flake. (Fig. 2.5, 3) Context 346, SF 6112.

Possible Fabricator with a triangular cross section. (Fig. 2.4, 6) Context 1240, SF 6119.

Illustrated flint tools:

Figure 2.4

1   **Side scraper**, Context 543, SF 6105
2   **Double sided scraper**, Context 533, SF 6106
3   **Side scraper**, Context 699, SF 6114
4   **Side scraper** on a worked lump, Context 361, SF 6110
5   **Side/end scraper**, Context 357, SF 6108
6   **Possible fabricator**, Context 1240, SF 6119
7   **End scraper**, Context 2332, SF 6126
8   **Side/end scraper**, Context 833, SF 6113
9   **End scraper**, Context 1320, SF 6118
10 **End scraper**, Context 1318, SF 6125
11 **End scraper**, Context 1248, SF 6115
12 **Side scraper**, Context 1215, SF 6122

Figure 2.5

1   **Side scraper**, Context 1255, SF 6120
2   **Side scraper**, Context 395, SF 6111
3   **Notch on a secondary flake**, Context 346, SF 6112
4   **Hollow side scraper**, Context 1215, SF 6123
5   **Burin**, Context 1335, SF 6124
6   **Burin**, Context 1231, SF 6121
7   **Burin**, Context 533, SF 6107
8   **Blade core fragment**, Context 2335, SF 6127
9   **Single platform blade core**, Context 1251, SF 6116
10 **Single platform blade core**, Context 356, SF 6109
11 **Rolled secondary flake**, Context 543, SF 6104
12 **Microlith**, Context 1264, SF 6117
13 **Microlith**, Context 392, SF 6128

The limited range of tools and the high quantity of cortical material, particularly worked lumps, would suggest that the main activities taking place on the site were related to the extraction of flint from the gravels of the Avon Terrace and possibly the limited maintenance of existing tools. The relatively low numbers of tools, particularly scrapers and burins, may suggest that domestic occupation was not a primary activity on the site.

The excavation of the prehistoric soil in a series of sub-units allows for the distribution of the lithic assemblage across the site to be investigated. Only remnants of soil survived, cut by later features, and the size of the collection units varied, but the majority were approximately 1 m square by *c* 0.15 m thick. The density of flint artefacts varied from below 5 artefacts/m^2 to above 40 artefacts/m^2. The variation within these densities was uneven, however, and there was a concentration of both tools and general artefacts in the north-east corner of the site (Figs 2.6–2.7). Minor concentrations were also noted in the mid eastern side and the mid western side of the site. This uneven distribution is assumed to be related to the area in which the testing of extracted flint nodules was taking place. The correspondence of the concentration in the north-east corner of the site with the possible tree root holes [385, 386, 387] suggests that a fallen tree may have given access to the underlying gravels. Unfortunately no similar correspondence can be seen for the other possible concentrations.

Raw material types

A wide range of flint and chert types was recognised within the assemblage. In order to study the selection of flint types a type sequence of macroscopic raw materials was built from the assemblage. Twenty-nine flint types and a further six chert types were recognised. (These are summarised in Appendix 1 to the full report in the site archive.)

The site is on the Avon gravels and in order to characterise the flint resources immediately available a random selection of 200 pieces of the non-worked material collected as part of the excavation was compared to the raw material type sequence. The selection of raw materials is discussed in more detail below.

Sourcing studies

Initial impressions suggested that the flintwork from the Spa excavations was possibly related to the extraction of flint from the underlying gravels. It was decided to test this assumption. A two-phased examination of the raw materials used in the assemblage was carried out. Initially a set of raw material groups was defined. These were based on the macroscopic characteristics of the flint. Non-worked flint samples collected as part of the excavation were used as a sample of the raw materials available on the site. It was then possible to compare the relative

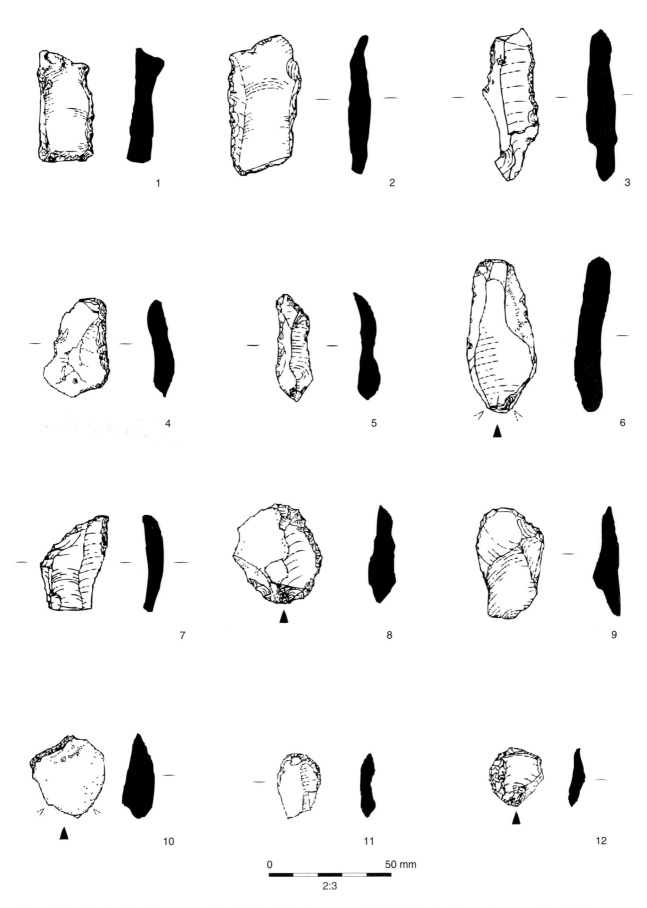

Figure 2.4   Flint tools: side scrapers (1–4, 12), side/end scrapers (5, 8), fabricator (6), end scrapers (7, 9–11).

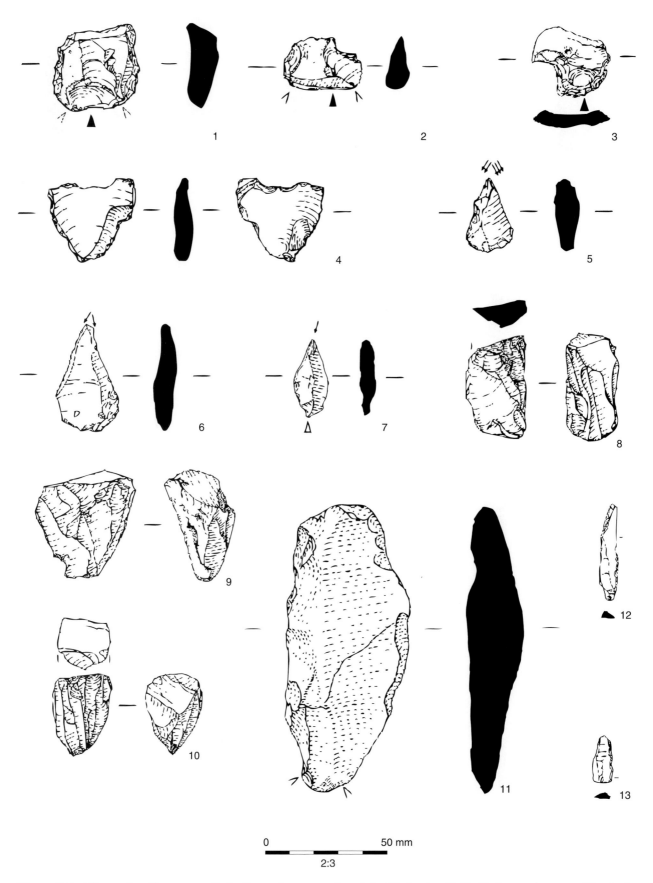

Figure 2.5   Flint tools: side scrapers (1–2, 4), notch on secondary flake (3), burins (5–7), blade core fragment (8), single platform blade cores (9–10), rolled secondary flake (11), microliths (12–13).

Figure 2.6 *Bath Spa Excavations: Plan showing distribution density of all flint artefacts within the palaeosol.*

Figure 2.7 *Bath Spa Excavations: Plan showing distribution density of flint tools within the palaeosol.*

quantities of each of the raw material groups within the archaeological and geological groups. This is illustrated in Figure 2.8.

This macroscopic analysis may suggest that the raw materials used for the artefacts probably came from the underlying gravels. Generally the range of raw materials used for the artefact group follows the range of those within the gravels, suggesting that little selection of raw materials more widely available was taking place. The slightly increased values of Raw Material Types 16 and 23 suggest that these flint types were slightly preferred although not actively selected.

The second phase of examination was based on the microscopic analysis of a limited number of samples. This method is based on an initial examination of the macroscopic characteristics, followed by a microfacies analysis (general appearance of the thin-section) and detailed microfossil analysis. The methodology is described in full on the linked web site. Two groups of material were examined. A group of ten samples were selected from the archaeological assemblage reflecting the major macroscopic flint types present within the assemblage. Ten further samples were selected from the flint within the natural gravel underlying the site to represent the material immediately available on the site.

Previous research (Brooks 1989) has shown that the microfacies of flint varies along a band of flint as well as between successive flint band and depositional zones, thus the technique can be extremely sensitive in investigating whether more than one nodule was used to create a knapping cluster

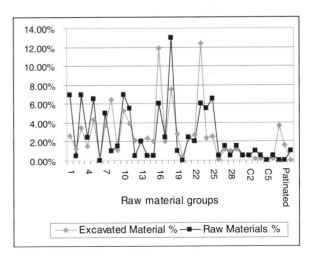

Figure 2.8 *Graph showing correspondence of flint raw materials occurring in the artefact assemblage compared to the river gravels.*

Table 2.3   Matches of flint raw material groups.

Sample	Macroscopic Group	Microscopic match
Sample A	23	8
Sample B	23	23A
Sample C	16	10B
Sample D	8	16A
Sample E	3	3
Sample F	10	10A
Sample G	18	18A
Sample H	18	18B
Sample I	16	16A
Sample J	10	10A

consisting of flint artefacts with similar macroscopic characteristics (Brooks forthcoming). The potential source being investigated is a gravel and as a result even macroscopically similar flint types within it may have been derived from similar, but different sources. It was therefore important to select the raw material comparators with extreme care so that they were as macroscopically similar to the archaeological samples as possible. Flint sources from other than the Avon Gravels on the site were not investigated.

The best fit between the archaeological samples from the Spa excavations and the geological samples is shown in Table 2.3. In seven of the samples the macroscopic analysis is confirmed showing the relationship between the underlying gravels and the material used for the archaeological assemblage. The remaining three had best fits with other samples. The macroscopic variability between these possible matches suggests that different nodules were being used. The source of those nodules is uncertain and it is possible that other material within the gravel on site would have produced a better match or that some material was brought on to the site.

Discussion

The assemblage from the excavations on the Spa sites can be conveniently divided into two sub-assemblages. The lower assemblage was found within the prehistoric soils at the base of the excavations and can therefore be largely regarded as in situ. The upper assemblage is from the Roman or later contexts and is regarded as largely residual, although the possibility of some ad hoc use of flint cannot be ruled out.

That the site is on gravel deposits is probably the key to some of the activity on the site. The limited number of diagnostic tools and cores within the assemblage would suggest a broadly late Mesolithic date for the assemblage. This would be consistent with the optically stimulated luminescence dates of 5,780±330 yrs BC (3,780±330 yrs BC, OxL-1035) obtained from the upper levels of the prehistoric soil.

Large numbers of broken flakes, spalls and worked lumps (65% of the total assemblage) were found on the site. This together with the low number

of tools and high cortical index (52.7%) suggests that the extraction of flint from the underlying gravel may have been a major activity on the site. The raw materials within the archaeological assemblage match those within the gravels underlying the site, although the possibility remains that some of the flint was brought on to the site from elsewhere.

The presence of a tree root hollow on the site may suggest a possible initial source for the flint. The root balls of trees, which had fallen or were blown down, could have served as an easily exploited source of flint. Whether this then developed into the digging of extraction pits is not evidenced within the excavation.

The residual assemblage would appear to be largely derived from the underlying assemblage, generally matching the style of knapping and the macroscopic raw material types being used. There are, however, a few artefacts, such as the Bronze Age style scraper (Context 1215, SF 6122), which arrived on to the site by other means.

Prehistoric Pottery
by Lisa Brown

Seven small body sherds (77 g) of prehistoric pottery were identified. All were probably Iron Age in date, and were derivative elements incorporated within the fill of Period 3.1 culvert trench 1280, in association with late 1st-early 2nd century Roman pottery. Although the prehistoric pottery is likely to represent activity on or close to the site, its provenance is insecure since even the Roman assemblage with which it was associated is likely to have originated from a site some metres to the south.

Four prehistoric fabrics were recognised (full fabric descriptions can be found in the site archive):

Fabric 1: A clay containing common inclusions of oolitic limestone. The fabric is of local or near local origin. Early or middle Iron Age.
Fabric 2: Wareham-Poole Harbour, Dorset ware, related to BB1 SED almost certainly an example of the Durotrigian precursor of Roman period BB1. Middle or late Iron Age.
Fabric 3: Very finely sanded, glauconitic and slightly micaceous ware containing sparse fragments of powdery dark red ferrous material. Early or middle Iron Age.
Fabric 4: Fine, slightly micaceous glauconitic clay with quartz particles. Probably middle or late Iron Age.

Calcareous fabrics similar to Fabric 1 are common in the Bath region and several varieties of calcareous tempered wares were identified amongst the Iron Age assemblage from Batheaston Bypass (Morris forthcoming). Black burnished ware from the Poole Harbour area of Dorset is very common within the Roman assemblages of Bath from the Flavian period onwards but the occurrence of a possible pre-conquest Durotrigian sherd from the same region (Fabric 2) is interesting, especially considering the find of a Durotrigian coin from the site. The four glauconitic burnished sherds (Fabric 4) probably belong to a single vessel. The fabric resembles that of middle to late Iron Age pottery thought to have a source in the Wiltshire area (Brown 1984, fiche 8:C1–7).

GENERAL DISCUSSION

Human impact on the landscape during the prehistoric period left little impression on the area studied, but our understanding of the character of this area has increased immensely as a result of the detailed analysis of the soils. In the 1999 report on the excavations in this area Davenport comments that it was surprising that the Mesolithic flints could not be interpreted as a domestic camp-site, which might have been expected on what was thought to have been the well-drained gravel terrace (Davenport 1999, 41). It is now clear that the soils were, on the contrary, persistently wet and would have been unattractive for domestic activity, which should perhaps be sought higher up the valley sides. Instead, the analysis of the flint has confirmed that this area was favoured as a source of raw material for stone tools in the late Mesolithic. Evidence of later prehistoric activity is all but absent (consisting literally of a handful of sherds of late Iron Age pottery in early Roman contexts), although the area was wooded and, if extensively so, could have provided a rich hunting ground throughout prehistory. Other evidence suggests that later prehistoric settlement occurs along and above the Avon Valley, if not immediately around the springs. There may even have been active management of the plant cover, either to encourage the presence of the wild animal population or to improve grazing to benefit domestic herds in the later prehistoric period. The evidence for a ritual component of the Mesolithic activity, however, here adds another, less directly utilitarian, element to the use of the valley floor (see The Hot Bath Spring, Chapter 9).

Chapter 3: Spa Period 2: Early Roman Development 1st-mid 2nd centuries AD

OVERVIEW

Roman activity during the 1st and early 2nd centuries AD was limited in scale. The defining features of Period 2 are an open drainage ditch cutting across the site with low banks of spoil to either side, some possible fences, a scatter of trees and shrubs in a damp, boggy environment, and a possible formal garden impinging on the north-west area (Fig. 3.1). It is equivalent to period 2 of the 1989 excavations and pottery indicates a date of late 1st century AD to early 2nd century AD. Stratified deposits that could be assigned to this period occurred as a narrow strip along the eastern edge of the excavations to the east of the Manners pool and partly below the Taylor pool, and in the south-west corner south of the ditch. Elsewhere only negative cut features survived.

The boundary between the prehistoric soil and the Roman stratified deposits was distinct, but it is clear from the soil analysis (below) that the ground surface remained exposed for some time after the Roman conquest allowing small quantities of Roman artefacts to be incorporated. Although the actual soil surface does not survive, this is not taken to represent any form of deliberate truncation of the soil in the Roman period, but probably represents severe trampling and churning of the surface occurring at the start of construction of Building D in Period 3.1, or the digging of the ditch 2355.

During the assessment and preliminary analysis contexts were assigned to this period on the basis of ceramic dating and correlation with the 1989 interpretation. It was concluded late in the analysis that very little stratigraphy and few features could be assigned to this phase. It was the soil analysis (below), which raised concerns that the early Roman levels represented even more ephemeral activities than at first thought. The report of the 1989 excavation (Davenport 1999, 22–9) suggested that three Roman phases preceded the construction of masonry buildings, but it was increasingly difficult to fit the later results with the earlier interpretation. The difficulty in defining Period 2 arises from the fact that the majority of the dated artefacts incorporated within contexts of Period 3.1 were of 1st and early 2nd century date, resulting in the lowest layers of Period 3.1 being initially designated as Period 2. There is no intention to rework the 1989 results in detail here, but a limited review of the contexts is required to allow some reinterpretation to form a coherent picture from the two excavations. In essence, the 1989 results have been reinterpreted as

a very short lived set of activities immediately predating or forming part of the early Period 3.1 activities. Context numbers used in the 1989 excavation ran from 1 to 263, those in 1998–9 started from 300, eliminating any need to differentiate between the excavations.

GEOARCHAEOLOGY OF THE EARLY ROMAN DEPOSITS
by David Jordan

There was a very restricted range of Roman deposits and little occupation debris – even in contexts where it might be expected to have accumulated. The scarcity of finely-divided artefact and charcoal fragments is particularly interesting because it implies that occupation debris was not being incorporated into the soil on or around this site in significant quantities, in turn suggesting that a restricted range of non-domestic processes was responsible for the formation of most of the strata.

The early Roman deposits are quite different from the buried soil below and represent a phase of extensive (rather than intensive) development, which have left a restricted range of strata. Most contain very little charcoal – even microscopic charcoal fragments – and, although there are pottery fragments, bone and evidence of hearths, there is only a small proportion of domestic or industrial debris when compared with later levels.

Magnetic susceptibility values are mostly low – between 6 and 15SI – values which arise only where domestic debris, typically of much higher susceptibility, is either absent or highly diluted. Even those deposits that contained some artefacts had only a slightly raised susceptibility, suggesting either that such debris had become greatly diluted by other mineral matter or that this debris did not include much finely divided matter derived from hearths, ovens or from the gradual decay of coarser susceptible material such as ceramics. This, in turn, suggests that the range of debris being incorporated into these deposits was restricted and does not represent the full range of domestic activity or material derived from the long, slow decay and mechanical degradation of coarse debris components. This contrasts greatly with the characteristics of the medieval pit fills discussed in Chapter 6, and suggests that there may have been relatively little domestic occupation around the site in the early Roman period and that the debris which it generated was too briefly exposed to decay very much before it

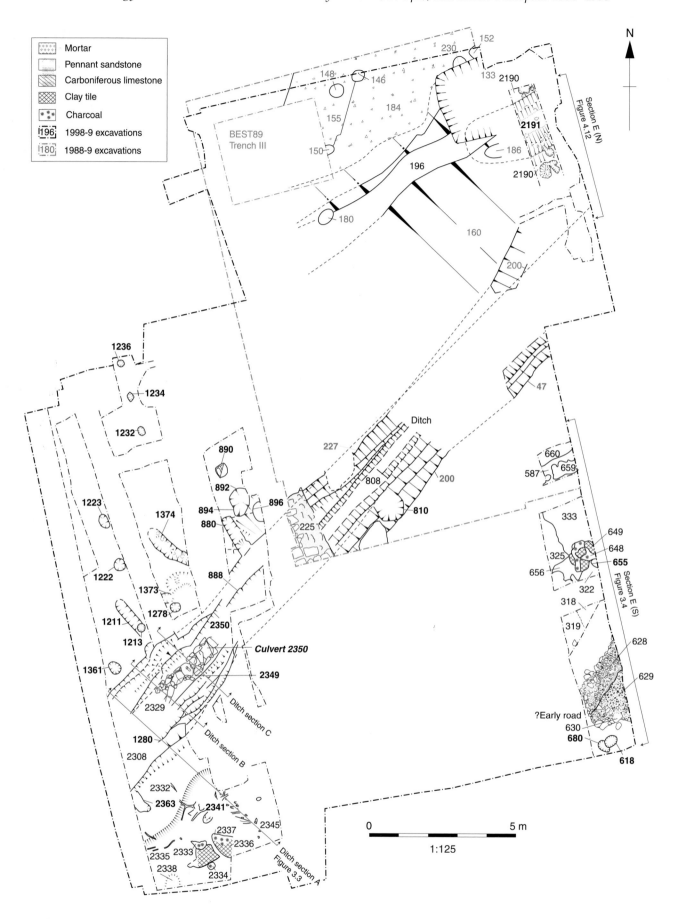

Figure 3.1 Bath Spa Excavations: Plan of Period 2: the early Roman features, including features found in 1989 excavations.

was incorporated into the excavated deposits. Further analysis showed that the ceramics had not been incorporated into these deposits for long enough to break down physically into small fragments, implying that the deposits were quite fresh and unweathered when laid down.

The deposits varied greatly in their physical make up, but analyses suggest that much of this variability is explained in terms of the relatively few parent materials from which they were formed rather than a wide range of processes or a complex sequence of redeposition. In the majority of the other strata studied, it appears that the deposits consist of components derived from a very few parent materials and that there had been very little mixing of these parent materials before the strata were deposited. This strengthens the impression that the early Roman strata were derived directly from the buried soil and fluvio-glacial deposits beneath with relatively little material derived from elsewhere, other than some building and domestic debris which was rapidly incorporated into the deposits.

The early Roman deposits are less finely structured and show less evidence of soil biological activity after burial than most of the more recent strata. Much of the structure appears to post-date burial, since it does not relate to the boundaries or surfaces of the Roman strata themselves and may be associated with later events affecting soil formation. It seems likely that most of the fine soil formation took place within the Roman deposits after the Roman occupation but before the Georgian reconstruction sealed the soil surface above.

Drainage was clearly a concern for the occupants of the site since the most prominent early Roman feature is a large drainage ditch. The ditch may have lowered the soil water level over a much wider area since it cuts through the fluvioglacial sand and gravel which will have tended to form an aquifer carrying water from upslope. Thus the ditch may have significantly improved the local drainage and been sufficiently large to divert both the regular flow through the aquifer and occasional high-floods of the Avon itself. The need to deal with both these sources at once may explain why the ditch was cut so deep.

STRATIGRAPHIC AND STRUCTURAL EVIDENCE

Ditch and banks (Figs 3.2–3.3)

The major feature in this period was a drainage ditch [2355] running diagonally north-east to south-west across the site. Almost all the evidence of this ditch had been removed by the trench [1280] cut for the later culvert [2350], which follows the same alignment. No evidence of this ditch was found in the 1989 excavations, when the culvert trench was taken to be the earliest feature. The digging of the ditch resulted in the creation of low banks on either side, with a pronounced soil bank on the south side (2332) (Figs 3.2–3.3). Gravel spreads (2099, 2331) dumped to the south of the earthen bank may also have derived from the digging of the ditch. In the 1989 area the same pattern was found to the north of the ditch, where a low gravel bank (199, 196) with more

Figure 3.2 Bath Spa Excavations: Roman culvert trench 1280, with stone-built culvert 2350, looking to the south west. The low banks to the north and south of the culvert trench are clearly visible.

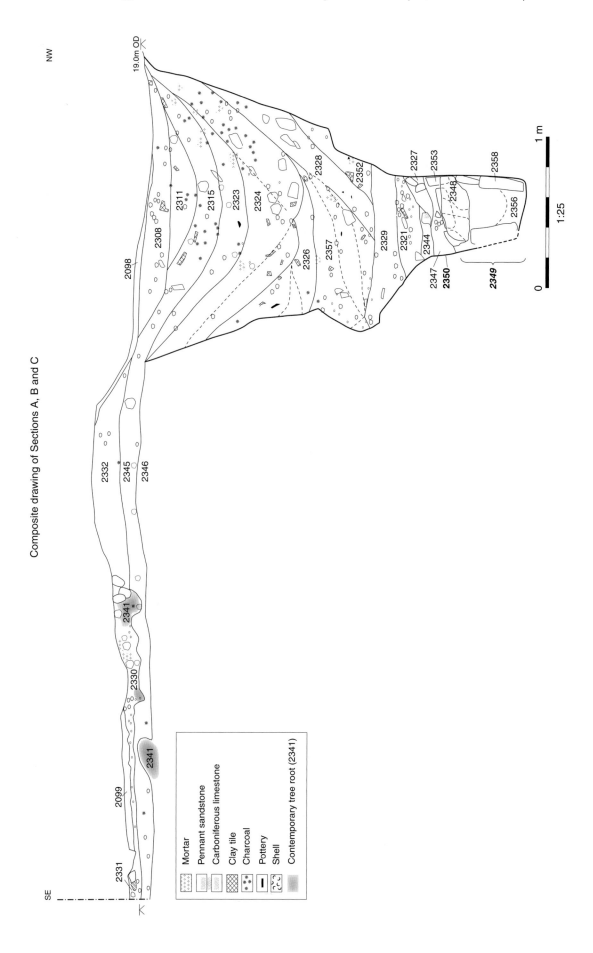

Composite drawing of Sections A, B and C

Figure 3.3 Bath Spa Excavations: Section across culvert trench 1280 and bank 2332.

level layers of clay, sand and gravel (197, 198, 232) spread behind it to the north. From the bank (2332) came a few fragments of pottery, including samian ware, dated 1st–2nd century AD, bone and flint. The ditch was in use for sufficient time for trees or shrubs to spring up along its side: remnants of a tree stump identified as elm (Gale, see site archive), were rooted into the north edge of F1280. This had been cut down immediately prior to the construction of the culvert and Building D. The presence of this substantial tree root is the reason for postulating an open ditch in Period 2, the direct evidence of which is admittedly very flimsy. The tree could not have grown up in the fairly short period that the later culvert trench was open.

Contemporary activity

To either side of the ditch was a scatter of small features (Fig. 3.1). In the 1989 area a few postholes and other features were found cut into the bank and this pattern continued in adjacent areas. In the narrow north-eastern strip adjacent to the 1989 excavation the boundary between deposits of Periods 2 and 3 is unclear, but the accumulation of several thin surfaces composed of river gravels (2184, 2193) and gravelly clay (2185, 2192, 2194) may belong to this early period (see Fig. 4.12). The clay tile and brick assemblage from the features and layers overlying these is similar to material used in the construction of Building D and implies that very few of the deposits in the north-east area predate that construction.

The gravel bank did not continue west of the 1989 area, which suggests it was a discrete area of upcast rather than a continuous bank. In the western area the earliest features cut into the old ground surface were a number of postholes, which included one line of three small postholes 2.4 m long aligned NNW-SSE, each *c* 0.3 m wide (1232, 1234, 1236) (Fig. 3.1). Another three (1213, 1222–3) may also have formed a post line on a similar alignment, but the sizes and fills of these formed a less convincingly coherent group. One of these postholes (1213, fill 1214) contained pottery dated to the late 1st century AD. Four more (894, 1278, 1361, 1373) occurred a short distance from the lip of the ditch (2355) and may have related to a boundary alongside the north edge of the ditch. Another group (890, 892, 896) occurred on the east edge of this area and included one square cut hole (890) filled with large limestone blocks, whilst the others were shallow circular hollows. No clear arrangement of structures could be discerned and although these features may hint at the presence of early timber buildings, the postholes are more likely to represent fences or more ephemeral structures. In view of the evidence for garden features further north, it would be possible to interpret them as representing more horticultural activity in this part of the site. The more confidently interpreted postholes may have provided supports for climbing plants, whilst some of the other features,

though interpreted during excavation as postholes, could in fact be small bedding pits for shrubs. Equally it is possible to interpret them as preliminary activity in preparation for the construction of Building D.

South of the ditch in the western area irregular areas of burning (2333, 2334, 2336, 2337) (Fig 3.1) up to 1.4 m long on the surface of the alluvial clay have the appearance of casual bonfire sites. These were overlain by the gravel spreads (2331, 2099), which may represent the earliest phase of a metalled track or lane in this area. Evidence of a second large tree [2341] was found in the form of extensive root voids through the low bank of alluvial clay (2332), along the south edge of the ditch. Only a few sherds of pottery dating to the late 1st-early 2nd centuries AD were recovered from these contexts.

In the narrow south-eastern strip were postholes, (618, 655, 680), indistinct layers of trampled soil and gravel surfaces (331, 333, 586, 646–7, 650, 659–60, 678) (Figs 3.1 & 3.4). A roughly circular area of *in situ* burning (648/649), 1.0 m wide, was initially interpreted as a hearth, but the presence of an underlying tree root hollow (656, 670) may indicate that a tree stump was burnt out here, representing vegetation clearance immediately prior to the construction of Building D.

Formal Garden ? (Figs 3.5–3.6)

Within cellar 1 of 7–7a Bath Street the excavation was at first thought to have produced evidence of internal features within Building D, within the rooms VII and VIII (see below) and this remains a possible interpretation. However, though the relationship to Building D structures was not clear, it was concluded on circumstantial evidence that the features pre-dated Building D and have been interpreted as gardening features. A series of shallow slots [1708, 1710, 1712, 1748, 1750] *c* 0.2 m wide by 1.2–1.6 m long ran east-west and between were two small pits (1702, 1716), which appeared to be bedding pits for shrubs (Fig. 3.5). The pits were clearly dug features but root holes radiated from them. In one case (1716) the root had been burnt out, possibly indicating that one plant had replaced another, as they were very closely spaced for both to be growing at the same time. These features may represent part of a formal garden, as twigs of box found in the culvert trench suggest that this shrub had been growing somewhere close by shortly before the construction of Building D. The linear slots could have been dug as bedding trenches for small box hedges (Fig. 3.6). On the other hand, it must be admitted that the evidence could just as well represent a vegetable patch, neatly laid out in rows.

The features produced minimal quantities of Roman pottery (none of which can be dated more closely), bone, glass, wall plaster and residual flint, but one of the underlying layers (1752) produced pottery of 2nd century date. This pottery included forms that peter out towards the latter half of the 2nd

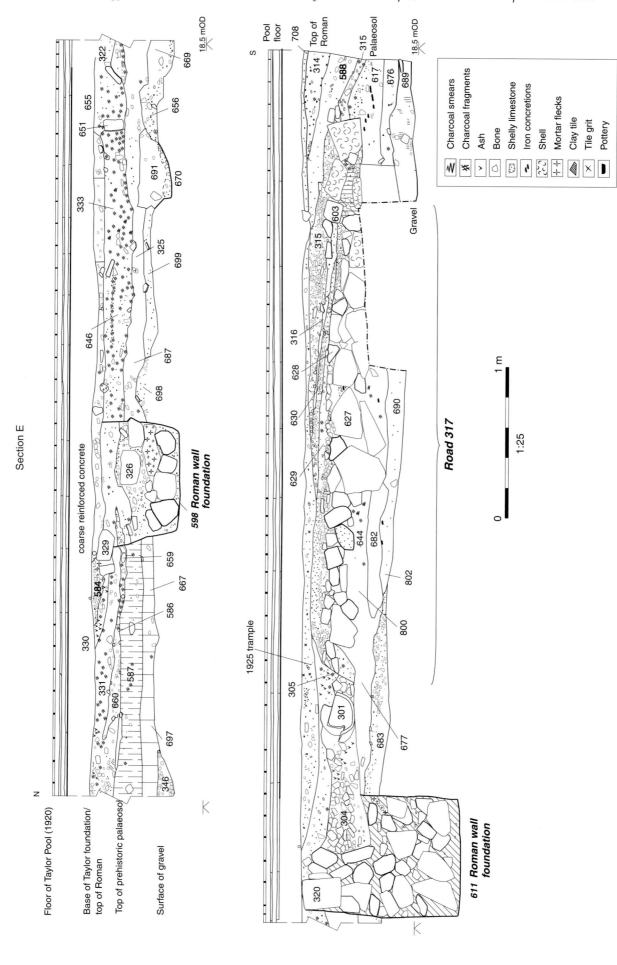

Figure 3.4 Bath Spa Excavations: Section E showing footings of Wall 611 of south range of Building D with road surfaces to the south.

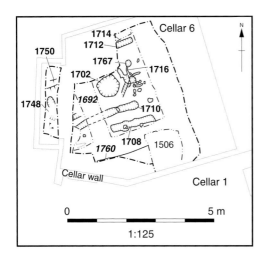

Figure 3.5 Bath Street Excavations: Plan of possible garden features under Room VII of Building D.

century so it may indicate that the layer belongs to the first half of the 2nd century. The presence of glass and painted plaster in layer 1752 suggests building activity going on in the vicinity at an early date, but the nearest known such activity is the baths and temple, unless it is regarded as deriving from Building D, which would place the garden in Period 3. There appears to be no evidence of any early buildings close by to which such a garden might belong. The phasing of these features must inevitably remain uncertain. In addition to the bedding trenches, a small area to the south-west in cellar 4 produced evidence of spade marks in the surface of the palaeosol and some small postholes or possible bedding pits.

Early Building

In the subsequent period of redevelopment (Period 3.1) large quantities of the materials used for the floor and wall foundations, make-up layers and deliberate infill of the culvert trench [1280] for the construction of Building D appear to have been derived from a building of 1st–early 2nd century date that had been demolished. It is clear that no earlier building stood on this actual site, but it is worth considering here the character of this material and what it can tell us about the phase of early

Figure 3.6 Bath Street Excavations: Photo of garden features under Room VII, Building D.

Roman activity in Bath. It may also help to shed some light on the nature of Building D. The impression is that a high proportion, if not all, of the building materials and occupation debris used in the foundations of Building D came from a single source, forming a coherent group. The character of these materials suggests that this was a high status building (Betts and Davenport this volume; for full reports see site archive). The material evidence for this building can be divided into two groups: structural elements and occupation detritus.

The demolished building materials comprised architectural stonework, mortar fragments, painted plaster, limestone and tile *tesserae*, Pennant slabs and large quantities of clay tile and brick. It is likely that much of the rubble and building stone used in the foundations of Building D was recycled from the same source and the occurrence of fragments of painted plaster actually within wall and floor foundations indicates that much of this derived from walls demolished elsewhere.

Architectural fragments included column drums, capitals and bases, attached half columns, springers and a cornice fragment possibly from an arch (Fig. 3.19), indicating that the demolished building was of some size and grandeur. The wear and weathering on this stonework also suggests that it had been standing for some time, and was perhaps amongst the earliest structures to be built in Roman Bath.

The majority of the plaster was painted red or white, whilst a small quantity exhibited other colours including narrow lines in green, grey-green, black and red/pink, or wider bands. This suggests that the most common form of decoration was as plain painted panels enclosed by thin lines of another colour or separated by wider bands of colour. The walls may also have had areas of imitation marbling suggested by traces of black paint or black brush-strokes on a red ground. (A report on the painted wall plaster by Lesley Zienckewicz and Cynthia Poole can be found in the site archive).

A large quantity of ceramic tile and brick was found in the infill of F1280 as well as dumped in the make-up layers and to a lesser extent the wall foundations of Building D. The ceramic building material comprised roofing tile, both *tegulae* and *imbrices*, box flue tile, both combed and relief patterned voussoir tiles, wall tiles and bricks. Stone building materials included red and grey Pennant roofing slabs, tufa fragments, a few pieces of Pennant paving and a small quantity of *tesserae* made from white-cream limestone and dark grey-black limestone and sandstone. Lead off-cuts and dribbles were probably waste from plumbing for a bath building.

Occupation debris was found in large quantities in the culvert trench and to a lesser extent in make-up layers elsewhere in Building D. This included Samian ware and other pottery dated consistently to the late 1st–2nd centuries AD, glass and occasional iron fragments. Organic material included a few leather off-cuts. Animal bone, together with a variety of shellfish, predominantly oyster but including mussels and cockles, was found in the culvert trench fill. Waterlogged plant macrofossils were also present and included both economic and environmental indicators (see below).

Although objects of other materials were not prolific they include a typical range of personal items including hair pins (Fig. 3.12, 2 & 3), one with an unusual carved bearded male head (Fig. 3.12, 4), a boxwood comb (Fig. 3.13, 10), a glass bead (Fig. 3.12, 8), ceramic counters and a bone counter (Fig. 3.12, 5), a shale armlet (Fig. 3.12, 11), as well as a pipe clay figurine (Fig. 3.13, 1) of a draped male figure, possibly Mercury. There is also a lozenge-shaped piece of bone inlay (Fig. 3.12, 6). Five copper alloy coins were all of 1st or 2nd-century date, identified as two asses/*dupondii* and three *sestertii*, one of which was possibly of Domitian.

EARLY ROMAN ENVIRONMENT

This picture of the environment incorporates the evidence from the charcoal and wood reported by Gale (reports in site archive), waterlogged plant macrofossils reported by Pelling (report in site archive), the pollen assessment by Tinsley (see site archive) and the archaeological sequence itself. The information characterises the local environment for this specific plot of ground immediately prior to major Antonine development *c* AD 150–160, which expanded into areas not previously utilised for building. The archaeological record of this area prior to the construction of Building D suggests that there was little more than waste ground to either side of the ditch with occasional shrubs or trees and no doubt frequent weeds growing along the edges of the features. However, there may have been a formal garden further north and the area between this and the ditch may have also contained some sort of garden of less formal character.

Evidence for trees and shrubs growing in the vicinity of the ditch has come from the analysis of the waterlogged and carbonised wood. Gale notes that some of the wood was in the form of roundwood ranging from 2 mm to 25 mm in diameter, and must have derived from twigs and small branches of trees that had been growing in the area of the ditch just before Building D development started. These included elm (*Ulmus* sp.), hazel (*Corylus avellana*), ash (*Fraxinus excelsior*), elder (*Sambucus nigra*), alder (*Alnus glutinosa*), blackthorn or cherry (*Prunus* sp.), probably field maple (*Acer campestre*) and box (*Buxus sempervirens*). It is probable that trees and shrubs, growing along the banks of the ditch and overhanging it, as suggested by the large elm root found in the side of the ditch and by the presence of hazel nutshells, were the source of much of this roundwood. In addition to the elm root in the north side of the ditch, there is archaeological evidence that two large trees (2341, 670) were growing south of the ditch. A layer of charcoal (648), predominantly of oak, overlies the root hollow 670 and may represent remains of the burnt out tree stump. In contrast 2341 was left to rot, perhaps indicating that this tree had died earlier in the period before development started.

In addition to the waterlogged material there was also frequent charcoal in the fill of the culvert trench. The species identified by Gale were field maple, alder, hazel, ash, the hawthorn/*Sorbus* group (Pomoideae), blackthorn (*Prunus spinosa*), oak (*Quercus* sp.) and willow (*Salix* sp.) and/or poplar (*Populus* sp.), all represented by narrow roundwood as well as heartwood in the case of oak and ash. Gale would normally interpret such material as fuel debris from firewood – either gathered from the vicinity of the culvert or possibly derived from loppings of brushwood associated with a local activity/craft. However in view of the evidence for bonfires at this site at the start of construction activity it seems likely that much of this charcoal derived from trees and shrubs growing on the plot and cleared at the end of Period 2 to make way for the construction of Building D.

Gale concludes that charcoal and waterlogged wood recovered from the culvert probably originated from different sources and/or activities conducted close to the site. This suggestion is based on the absence of artefactual wood in the charcoal, in contrast to woodworking remains and natural deposits in the waterlogged samples. Whereas the waterlogged wood probably represents residues from both natural deposits and wood working activities (discussed below), the charcoal is interpreted as the remains of the disposal of (mostly) scrubby waste materials by burning.

Of the waterlogged material reported by Pelling, the large amounts of wood fragments and seeds/buds from trees, particularly *Acer campestre* may be interpreted as indicating the presence of trees on the site, rather than as branch wood brought in for fuel or wattle fencing. *Alnus glutinosa* (alder) is a tree species of damp ground and may have been growing in the lower, wetter parts of the site. The scrubby species, *Sambucus nigra* (elder) and *Rubus fruticosus* (blackberry) are common in urban areas, while *Crataegus monogyna* (hawthorn) is a common scrubland species and also used for hedging. These species suggest the presence of scrubland and trees within the site or its immediate vicinity.

Gale observes the particular interest of twigs of box, suggesting that these derived from a living specimen rather than artefactual remains. Although recorded at the rural settlement of Farmoor, Oxfordshire (Lambrick and Robinson 1979, 87, 127) it is rarely found in archaeological contexts of this date in Britain. In Italy box was favoured as a decorative garden plant and it was probably used in a similar manner at more prestigious settlements in Britain. Farmoor was not a high status site. It also occurred a Frocester (Price 2000, 258). Other occurrences may be noted at the pottery production site at Blackbird Leys, Oxford (Challinor 2003, 254–47), and from within a lead coffin (grave 5) in a late Roman cemetery on Roden Downs, Berkshire (Hood and Walton 1948, 47).

Table 3.1   Quantification of pollen and spore types from Culvert Trench 1280.

Species	2315 (upper)	2315 (lower)	2324	2326
Pinus		1		
Quercus		1	1	
Ulmus		1	1	
Alnus	1		2	1
Corylus		1	1	
Poaceae	2	7	17	4
Cereal			3	
Lactuceae	1	15		
Plantago major			1	
P. lanceolata			4	
Rumex			2	
Centaurea		1		
Apiaceae			1	
Brassicaceae			2	
Filipendula			1	
Calluna				2
Pteridium	5	5	3	5
Filicales	1	2	2	1
Total	10	34	41	13
Trichuris egg cases				5

Pollen samples were taken from the dumped deposits within the culvert trench. As all these layers were imported material the pollen is likely to have derived from a variety of catchments as well as the immediate area of the excavation. There is generally better preservation than in the palaeosol and a greater number of species represented as shown in Table 3.1.

Pollen spectra from ditches can be difficult to interpret because the pollen may be derived from a variety of sources such as secondary pollen from the erosion from the ditch sides (not a serious problem in this case as the trench was rapidly backfilled soon after recutting), airborne pollen from the surrounding vegetation and pollen already incorporated in the fill material (which could include both earlier ditch silts thrown back in and material brought in from an outside source of unknown origin in the city). The assemblage from deposit 2324 (Fig. 3.3) within the Culvert trench was dominated by pollen of grasses and ruderal species (weeds), such as ribwort plantain and cabbage family, typical of grazed ground or possibly meadow. It is possible therefore, that this ditch fill includes remains of hay or stable waste. The assemblage is fairly similar to those described by Greig (1982) as typical of ditch fills on urban archaeological sites. Greig attributes this type of assemblage to the presence either of hay or dung, or to locally growing "weedy" communities in the urban area. The presence of elm (*Ulmus*), alder (*Alnus*), hazel (*Corylus*) and oak (*Quercus*) in samples from context 2315 coincides with the evidence of trees growing on site, whilst pine (*Pinus*) may represent air-borne pollen of trees growing outside the city. The grass and weed pollen could have derived from the immediate vicinity, whether the area was garden or waste ground adjacent to the ditch, though the presence of cereal suggests that some pollen came from outside the immediate area. Similarly heather (Calluna) may have been brought in as bedding for animals or a roofing material and became incorporated in sediments brought onto the site from outside the immediate area.

As a result of the limited survival of early Roman deposits only five bulk samples were taken from contexts of this period, one from a posthole fill and the remainder from layers. Only one sample from layer 648 produced cereal grain and occasional weed seeds, though all samples contained charcoal fragments. The small number of samples and the sparsity of plant macrofossils preclude any analysis of the carbonised plant remains of this period.

Seven waterlogged samples from the culvert ditch fill were assessed and two of these were subsequently fully analysed. Wild herbaceous species from these deposits derive from a range of habitats, which include arable and/or ruderal habitats, damp ground or aquatic environments and grassland. Such species provide evidence of the environment in the immediate vicinity of the site as well as the environmental resources exploited by the inhabitants. Weeds of arable or ruderal habitats could have entered the site either with arable crops or in some cases could have been growing within the site. In view of the virtual absence of crops amongst the seed, it is likely that many of the weeds were actually growing on or close to the site. *Adonis* sp. (Pheasant's Eye) is the only species that can be regarded as an exclusively arable weed and is regarded as an introduction. *Silene alba* (Red Campion) is also an introduced weed. Both species may have arrived with cereal remains from some distance and entered the site with occupation material from the demolished building, though in view of the lack of cereal grain (only two grains of carbonised barley were recorded) it is tempting to speculate that they were associated with the garden identified some distance north of the ditch. It is known from military sites such as the 3rd century AD South Shields granary, Tyne & Wear (van der Veen 1988) that grain supplies were imported into Britain even late in the Roman period, and this activity is likely to have been a major source of weed introduction. While the majority of the ruderal species may have grown on disturbed soils within the site, some provide a more specific indication of conditions. *Conium maculatum* (hemlock) and *Hyoscymus nigra* (henbane) are commonly found in damp nitrogen rich ruderal habitats, particularly within farmyards or on midden heaps, and suggest the presence of some rotting vegetation within or around the culvert. The damp ground or aquatic species including *Ranunculus* subgen *Batrachium*, *Mentha* sp. and *Sparganium erectum*, prefer shallow muddy water rather than a free-flowing stream. *Eleocharis palustris* is a damp grassland species, which requires its roots to be in water for

at least part of the year. *Carex* sp. (sedges), *Juncus* sp. (rush), *Ranunculus acris/repens/bulbosus*, *Hypericum* sp. and *Apium graveolens* are all likely to have been growing on damp ground alongside the ditch and suggest quite muddy, marshy conditions.

The grassland species mostly have an association with calcareous or at least circum-neutral soils and suggest local grassland conditions, presumably on slightly higher, dryer ground. *Rumex acetosella* gp (sheep's sorrel) is more usually associated with acid soils and therefore suggests the exploitation of grassland some distance away. Such species might enter a site with animal dung, suggesting that animals may have had access to graze the area of the present site.

The waterlogged deposits at the Spa site have produced some interesting insights into the vegetation of the area prior to the construction of the temple complex. Some light tree and scrub cover is indicated in the immediate vicinity and the low lying ground within the site and alongside the ditch is likely to have been wet and muddy, with areas of disturbed or waste ground where weeds could take hold. Open grassland is suggested for better drained, higher ground beyond the site with species representative of both calcareous and acid soils.

MATERIAL EVIDENCE

The finds reported in this section include those found in Period 2 contexts together with those from Period 3.1, which represent in their entirety residual 1st and early 2nd century material that derived from Period 2 activity or structures. A very high proportion of this material was deposited at the very beginning of Period 3.1 with a high proportion found in the culvert trench F1280. The authors regard this material as originating from a single source: the Period 2 unplaced building, discussed in this section.

Early Roman Pottery
by Lisa Brown

Introduction

The excavations produced an assemblage of 3634 sherds of Roman pottery weighing 42.364 kg from stratified Roman deposits (Periods 1–3), which was fully recorded, quantified and analysed. The fabric type series has been linked, as far as was possible, to the typology for Bath devised by Paul Bidwell and Alex Croom (Bidwell and Croom 1999 and forthcoming) and to the National Roman Fabric Reference Collection (Tomber and Dore 1998) (Table 3.2). Full details of the fabrics, forms and the stratified assemblage may be found in the site archive.

The Roman pottery assemblage is largely of late 1st and 2nd century date and the greater part of this assemblage appears to have been deposited on the site during the early to mid 2nd century AD. Contexts assigned to prehistoric Period 1, summarised in Table 3.3, produced 33 sherds (260 g),

Table 3.2 Pottery Fabric codes, descriptions and comments.

Finewares

Code	Name	Comments Dating
ARG CC	Argonne colour-coated ware?	The orange fabric and matt black slip correspond well with the example published in the National Roman Fabric Reference Collection (Tomber and Dore 1998) but the source of wares matching this description remains the subject of debate (Symonds 1990). Mid C2 onwards
KOL CC	Cologne colour-coated ware	Claudio-Neronian to mid C3
CNG CC2	Central Gaulish cream colour-coated ware 2	
MOSBS	Moselkeramik Black-slipped ware	produced at Trier in the Mosel valley and distributed in Britain from AD 180–250. Post-Roman deposits only
OXF RS	Oxfordshire red-slipped ware	240-end C4
NFO CC	New Forest metallic colour-coated ware	Post-Roman deposits only. 260-end C4
CC Misc	Colour-coated miscellaneous,	unsourced

Oxidised wares

SVW OX1	Severn Valley oxidised ware 1	(Malvernian)
SVO OX2	Severn Valley oxidised ware 2	Unsourced
OXW2	Oxidised ware fabric 2	Sandy orange fabric with rare large red inclusions. (Bidwell 1999, 69)
OXFWH	Oxford white ware	In production from 2nd century at Oxfordshire Group 3 kilns (Young 2000). One mortarium sherd from Ditch 1280 and a non-mortarium vessel from a post-Roman deposit
OXFWS	Oxford white-slipped ware	Mortarium sherds from post-Roman deposits only. 240–400 + (Young 2000)
OXFRS	Oxford red-slipped ware	Single sherd from a post-Roman deposit. 240–400 + (Young 2000)
FIWW	Fine white-firing ware	
GRWW	Gritty white-firing ware	
FIORW	Fine orange-firing ware.	
MEORW	Medium coarse orange-firing ware	
COORW	Coarse orange-firing ware	
FLA	Flagon fabric A	Fine, soft orange fabric with soft ferrous inclusions. May have white/cream slip
FLB	Flagon fabric B	Orange fabric with frequent calcareous inclusions, sometimes under-fired to soft buff. May have a cream slip
FLBB	Flagon fabric	Highly fired flagon fabric B, often with grey core and voids within fabric
FLC	Flagon fabric C	Hard fabric with granular surfaces. Outer surfaces range from dark red to mid-grey, orange, red or grey core. May have thick cream slip
FLWW	Flagon fabric	Varies from white to pink with small red inclusions and from soft to highly fired

Reduced wares

Code	Name	Comments
BB1 SED	South-east Dorset black-burnished ware 1	
BB1 SW	South-west black-burnished ware 1	
SAV GT	Savernake Grog-tempered ware	Swan 1975. Claudian-mid C2
CRW	Coarse reduced ware	Category comprises a range of grey-firing fabrics
TNC	Terra nigra copy	
FIRW	Fine reduced ware	Hard, smooth light grey ware with darker grey surfaces, few or no visible inclusions
SMICRW	Sandy micaceous reduced ware	Holbrook and Bidwell 1991, fabric 151, Belgic ware
FMICRW	Fine micaceous reduced ware	Holbrook and Bidwell 1991, fabric 125
SANDRW	Sandy reduced ware	Light or mid-grey fabric with darker surfaces, soft black inclusions (Bidwell and Croom 1999)
GRANRW	Granular reduced ware	Grey micaceous fabric with medium quartz and small soft black inclusions. Mid to dark grey surfaces, sometimes burnished (Bidwell and Croom 1999)
SOB GT	Southern British ('Belgic') grog-tempered ware.	Dark grey or reddish-brown soft, 'muddy' fabric containing abundant ill-assorted inclusions of dark grog, most 2 mm or under
LST	Limestone-tempered ware	including oolitic ware
HARSH./ LRSH	Late Roman shell-tempered ware	produced at Harrold in Bedfordshire and perhaps other sources, W exported across the east and south Midlands from the early 4th century. (Tyers 1999). Single sherd from a post-Roman deposit

Table 3.3 Summary quantification of Period 1 Roman pottery assemblage.

Contexts 346, 358, 359, 542, 544, 587, 617, 685, 2345

Fabric	No.	Wt	Form
CRW	2	10	Rim 2
GRANRW	1	3	
SANDRW	1	3	
SMICRW	1	3	
FMICRW	4	23	
MEOR	1	3	
FIOR	1	3	
SEVOX1	2	3	
SEVOX2	1	3	
FLA	1	5	
FLC	3	18	
FLWW	6	54	Flagon fragment
Total	**33**	**260**	Mean sherd weight 7.8 g

Table 3.4 Summary quantification of Period 2 primary Roman pottery assemblage.

Fabric	No.	Wt.	Forms
BB1SED	1	7	
CRW	7	65	Necked jar
GRANRW	9	11	Butt beaker (copy)
SAVGT	4	44	
SMICRW	19	165	Platter copy
FMICRW	5	47	Flat-rimmed bowl
COOR	1	114	Lid
MEOR	2	14	Cup rim flagon (Fishbourne type)
FIOR	24	85	
SEVOX2	2	9	
FLA	11	61	Multiple ring necked flagon
FLC	1	4	
FLWW	6	13	Multiple ring-necked flagon
TN copy	6	44	Platter copy (terra nigra type)
KOLCC	1	2	
Total	**102**	**713**	Mean sherd weight 7 g

all of early Roman date, suggesting that these were lying on the surface of the deposits rather than within them. (However, analysis of the stratigraphy has shown the palaeosol surface remained exposed to some extent during the early Roman period allowing artefacts to be incorporated and the separation of the early Roman pottery into Periods 1 and 2 is artificial). The Period 2 deposits, representing the earliest Roman activity on the site, produced only 102 sherds (713 g), all of which could be placed within the mid to late 1st century AD. Most of the early Roman pottery recovered from the Spa site was, however, residual within 2nd century culvert trench deposits assigned to Period 3.1, but is thought to derive from an early building demolished to make way for Building D.

The primary Period 2 assemblage

The small Period 2 assemblage, summarised in Table 3.4, may all date to the 1st century and includes two fine grey ware copies of *terra nigra* platters resembling in form, but not fabric, a type found in Exeter (Holbrook and Bidwell 1991, fig. 53, no. 25.1). A flagon with multiple ring-neck in fabric FLWW is probably an Exeter product and a similar vessel in fabric FLA was probably supplied by a local kiln during the Flavian period. A cupped-rim flagon in red sandy ware with cream slip has a close parallel from a period 1 deposit at Fishbourne (Cunliffe 1971, fig. 94, no.107). Only two body sherds of Severn Valley ware were present in the Period 2 assemblage. The most common Period 2 coarse ware, SMICRW (Exeter 151), probably originated in the south-west, possibly Exeter, during the mid 1st century and its popularity declined during the 2nd century. Black-burnished 1 (BB1) from Dorset is not thought to have reached Bath in any quantity until the Trajanic period (Holbrook and Bidwell 1991, 92) and its absence within Period 2 deposits, apart from

a single small sherd, lends some weight to the case for an early Roman phase at the site.

The Period 2 assemblage, however, lacks almost entirely the 1st century imported fine ware and specialist ware element (eg Lyon ware, *terra nigra*, Pompeian-red ware, amphorae and mortaria) that elsewhere in early Roman assemblages from Bath provides likely evidence of a military presence. A single Cologne colour-coated sherd was present and this could date from the Claudian, but more likely, the Flavian period. The late 1st and 2nd century Spa assemblages do, however, include notably large proportions of flagons. Flagon wares (FLA, FLB, FLC, FLWW) account for 17.6% of Period 2 fabrics and 14% for all Roman periods on the site by sherd count.. Large proportions of flagons within early Roman deposits, and a corresponding decrease in quantities of the form in the later Roman period, add weight to the argument for a military origin for the town (Croom and Bidwell forthcoming).

The major feature assigned to Period 2, drainage ditch 2355, did not produce any pottery that can be assigned to it with certainty. Context 2318 may be a fill of this ditch, but equally it could be assigned to feature 1280 and the pottery does not clarify the matter. Only 16 sherds of pottery were found in it and all may be of late 1st century date, although some of the associated samian ware may be as late as Hadrianic. A butt beaker copy in fabric GRANRW, one of only two examples of the form from the Spa site, is significant in that the form is very uncommon in Bath.

The Residual Period 2 Assemblage

The largest component of the quantified assemblage, 65% by count and 68% by weight, was recovered from deposits relating to the infilling of Period 3.1 culvert trench 1280, details of which have been presented in the next section. The combined evidence indicates that the culvert trench was filled during the mid 2nd century, but that the fill incorporated much earlier material, including late 1st and early 2nd century pottery.

The large stratified pottery assemblage from culvert trench 1280 (and related deposits) has been selected for detailed presentation on a context by context basis. (The detailed Roman Pottery report by Brown can be found in the site archive). This group forms the basis of the illustrated catalogue (see below and Figs 3.7–3.10) but a small additional group of well-preserved, large sherds from layer 1583 (limestone rubble floor foundation) has also been

illustrated (Fig. 3.10, 122–127). The combined assemblage from deposits associated with the construction of Building D has been described in some detail but not illustrated due to the relatively poor preservation of sherds and absence of unusual forms. The remainder of the pottery from stratified Roman deposits is summarised for this period in Table 3.5.

Assemblage from Building D foundations

This assemblage was recovered from construction features and layers of Building D and as such does not represent activity in Building D but is derived from earlier occupation, probably associated with

Table 3.5 Summary quantification of Period 2/3.1 and Period 3.1 Roman pottery assemblage.

Fabric	No.	Wt.	Forms
BB1SED	350	4319	Cooking pot 1&2, bead-rim jar, flanged bowl 1, flat-rimmed bowl, straight-sided dish, lid
BB1SW	54	793	Cooking pot 1, bead-rim jar, flat-rimmed bowl, chamfered bowl, straight-sided dish
CRW	442	6392	Cooking pot 2, necked jar, bead-rim jar, narrow neck jar, carinated bowl, flat-rimmed bowl, flanged bowl, shallow dish, straight-sided dish
GRANRW	24	470	Narrow neck jar, flaring rim jar, necked bowl, straight-sided dish, lid
SAVGT	30	1004	Bead-rim storage jar, storage jar, flanged bowl
SOBGT	5	35	
LST	5	18	Necked jar
COOR	4	97	Handle
MEOR	23	430	Beaker, jug
FIOR	140	1597	Necked bowl, cordoned bowl, flanged bowl, bead-rim bowl, straight-sided dish, carinated beaker, roughcast beaker, indented beaker
SANDRW	71	126	Flaring rim jar, necked bowl, flat-rimmed bowl
FMICRW	410	4375	Necked jar, short-necked jar, bead-rim jar, bead-rim bowl, shallow bowl, shallow flanged bowl, carinated bowl, necked bowl, flat-rimmed bowl, straight-sided dish, jug, globular beaker, bag beaker, cup, lid
SMICRW	144	6503	Rusticated beaker, chamfered cup, carinated bowl, cordoned bowl, flat-rimmed bowl, flanged bowl, necked bowl, shallow bowl, shallow dish, platter, short-necked jar, necked jar, carinated jar, narrow-neck jar
FIRW	5	29	Beaker
SEVOX1	4	29	Curved-sided bowl
SEVOX2	17	247	Curved-sided bowl, shallow dish, flanged bowl, lid
OXW2	3	12	
GRWW	34	864	Flagon, cup-rim jug, handle, flanged dish
FIWW	13	109	
FLA	249	1988	Ring-necked flagon, multiple ring-necked flagon, pulley-wheel rim flagon, jug, handle, curved-sided dish
FLB	4	40	
FLBB	2	31	Jug
FLC	155	1440	Ring-necked flagon, multiple ring-necked flagon, pulley-wheel rim flagon, handle
FLD	1	4	
FLWW	25	349	
CCMISC	22	263	Flaring rim bowl, roughcast beaker, indented roughcast beaker
ARGCC	11	27	Roughcast beaker
CNGCC2	7	37	Roughcast beaker
KOLCC	3	13	Roughcast beaker
TN Copy	3	37	Terra nigra platter copy x 2
AMPHORAE	11	786	Southern Spanish, Gaulish
MORTARIA	19	426	*Gallia Belgica*, south Wales, Shepton Mallet
Prehistoric	7	77	
Total	**2298**	**27011**	Mean sherd weight 12 g

the early, demolished building. The assemblage comprised 607 sherds weighing 5803 g. The majority of contexts contained few sherds, and only context assemblages of more than 10 sherds are summarised in the detailed report on the web site. The assemblage from Building D is composed largely of utilitarian wares – cooking pots, flat-rimmed bowls and straight-sided dishes in coarse reduced wares, including black-burnished wares. Flagon wares and other fine wares are uncommon and only one beaker sherd was identified. This is in direct contrast to the assemblage from culvert trench 1280 (see below). The mean sherd weight was fairly low, averaging 9.7 g, and sherd groups were moderately abraded except in the cases of layers 2094 and 2098 which contained heavily abraded assemblages with a particularly low mean sherd weight. The pottery within several of these groups, including 2094 and 2098, appears to be 2nd century or earlier in date and is residual material.

The composition of the residual assemblage found in Period 3.1, dominated by the culvert trench 1280 group, is unusual in that it deviates from the general preponderance of coarse wares and functional vessels that characterise most Roman domestic assemblages. Although it is difficult to account for this phenomenon on the basis of the ceramic evidence alone, it is possible that the assemblage reflects a specialised function of the building (or one part of it) with which it may have been associated, the debris of which was used to backfill culvert trench 1280. Within the Spa assemblage for this period (not taking into account samian wares) 65% of classifiable vessels are table wares (flagons, beakers, cups, platters and bowls) and 55% of fabrics are at the fine end of the scale. The latter figure includes fine grey wares such as FMICRW, found in the Spa assemblage to have been used largely for the production of eating and drinking vessels, rarely jars. FMICRW represented almost 18% by sherd count of the residual assemblage, in contrast to a mere 6% of SMICRW, which had been the predominant coarseware within the small Period 2 assemblage.

In contrast to the fine wares and fine grey wares, SMICRW, BB1, coarse reduced ware (CRW), granular reduced ware (GRANRW), southern British 'Belgic' grog-tempered ware (SOBGT) and Savernake grog-tempered ware (SAVGT) form under half the total residual assemblage and, within this coarse ware group, storage and cooking jars are less common than bowls and dishes. SMICRW (Exeter fabric 151) has been noted as a significant supplier of coarse wares to other sites in Bath during the pre-Flavian and Flavian periods (Croom and Bidwell forthcoming) and some proportion of these wares from culvert trench 1280 may be residual pieces of late 1st century date. The range of forms is broader than for most other fabrics, and includes decorated, carinated bowls, cups, dishes and platters as well as necked and narrow-neck jars. Production of this fabric probably ceased in the second half of the 2nd century, when it was overshadowed by the wide distribution of FMICRW and BB1.

Savernake grog-tempered wares, probably from Wiltshire, represent only just over 1% of Period 3.1 wares, despite the fact that this ware is relatively prolific on Roman sites elsewhere in Bath. It was used mainly in the manufacture of cooking and storage jars and the dearth of the type at Spa is almost certainly a reflection of the more general phenomenon of the predominance of table wares within the fill of culvert trench 1280. Only two storage jars, both in SAVGT, were present in the residual assemblage, all from culvert trench 1280. Five body sherds of the total of seven SOBGT sherds from the site came from culvert trench 1280. Significantly, BB1SED and BB1 SW together account for less than 19% of the total for this period at a time when these Dorset and south Somerset sources were developing into major coarse ware suppliers to the Bath area. BB1 forms deposited during Period 3.1 included cooking pots with upright or everted rims, bead-rim jars, flat-rimmed bowls, straight-sided dishes, lids and, amongst the latest types, flanged dishes with a high flange, dating to *c* AD 160–200. Utilitarian vessels in CRW and GRANRW included, in addition to the latter forms, narrow-neck jars and necked jars and bowls.

Severn Valley wares (SEVOX1 and OX2) formed only a minor source of coarse wares to the site. Only 7 and 19 sherds respectively were present in the quantified assemblage, 21 of them from Period 3.1 deposits. The only forms represented in these fabrics were curved-sided bowls, shallow dishes and a possible lid. The tankard and jar forms more commonly found in the Severn Valley ware export areas (Webster 1993) were altogether absent, perhaps another reflection of the unusual composition of the culvert trench 1280 assemblage.

The mix of sources for fine wares and table wares from culvert trench 1280 was wider than had been the case for Period 2 deposits, although this reflects in part the much larger size of the assemblage. Continental imports included North and Central Gaulish and Cologne roughcast beakers, *Gallia Belgica* mortaria from the Oise/Somme region and Gaulish and southern Spanish (Baetican) amphorae. Nonetheless, continental imports formed only a very small element of the table ware assemblage, which was dominated by British products. The occurrence of flagons in particular in the fill of culvert trench 1280 was very high. Approximately 20% of the residual assemblage was made up of fabrics used mainly in the manufacture of flagons, including local Bath wares FLA and FLB and Exeter ware FLWW. Fabric FLA was the dominant flagon fabric from the residual deposits and classifiable vessels in this ware included ring-neck, multiple ring-neck and pulley-wheel rim flagons, two jugs and a curved-sided shallow bowl. Fabric FLC may have been produced in Gloucester or Wiltshire and was imported to the Bath area during the 2nd century (Bidwell and Croom 1999, 71). A single Verulamium ware sherd, fabric FLD, from fill 874 of culvert trench 888, is probably of Flavian date.

In addition to the continental examples, beakers occurred in fine and medium orange wares and colour-coated wares of uncertain source. Most examples in these wares are roughcast or indented beakers but some fragments were too fragmentary to identify precisely. A small number of globular and bag-shaped beakers with simple out-turned rims in fabric FMICRW may be Exeter products. A globular beaker with barbotine dots (No. 28) in fine micaceous grey ware is an uncommon type for the site but the form is common elsewhere in southern England, including in Neronian and Flavian deposits in the London area (Davies *et al.* 1994). The source of the Spa example is uncertain but it may be an Exeter product (Fabric 125) as this fabric was commonly used to produce imitations of London wares into the Antonine period and beyond, long after the south-eastern prototypes had ceased to circulate (Holbrook and Bidwell 1991, 165). FMICRW appeared in Exeter at the end of the fortress occupation but seems to have ceased production as late as the end of the 2nd or beginning of the 3rd century.

The range of bowls and dishes in FMICRW recovered from Period 3.1 deposits reflects the south-eastern ('Belgic') influence in the form of London derived imitations such as carinated bowls with rouletting, grooves and cordons imitating samian forms and two compass-inscribed sherds from fills 2321 and 2328 of culvert trench 1280, probably dating to the first half of the 2nd century (ibid., fig. 64, nos. 31.1, 32.1). BB1 imitations, including flat-rimmed bowls and straight-sided dishes, formed another element of the 2nd century FMICRW range.

The condition of pottery from Period 3.1 deposits in general and culvert trench 1280 in particular was better than that of all other period groups. The mean sherd weight was 12 g in contrast to between 7 g and 8.7 g for the other assemblages. A relatively high proportion of large fresh sherds was noted, particularly in the case of contexts 873, 885, 2306, 2323, 2326 and 2328. Contexts 2321, 2322 and 2328 produced significant numbers of conjoining sherds, suggesting that large vessel fragments were broken during deposition.

Illustrated Catalogue (Figs 3.7–3.10)

1. **Roughcast beaker**, FIOR, colour-coated with clay pellet {Exeter group 1], 2305.
2. **Flat-rimmed bowl**, BB1SW, burnished lattice decoration, 2305.
3. **Ovoid jar with flaring rim**, SANDRW, burnished, 2305.
4. **Ring-necked flagon**, FLA with white slip, 2306.
5. **Ring-necked flagon**, FLC with white slip, 2306. Hadrianic + .
6. **Spouted strainer**, FMICRW, crudely hand-made, 2306.
7. **Lid**, GRANRW, partly burnished, 2306.
8. **Small globular jar with out-turned rim**, SMICRW, burnished, 2306.

9. **Carinated bowl copying samian Drag 29**, FMICRW, rouletted decoration, 2308/2311.
10. **Flat-rimmed bowl**, FMICRW, 2308.
11. **Flat-rimmed bowl**, BB1SED, burnished lattice decoration, 2308.
12. **Shallow bowl or lid**, SMICRW, 2308.
13. **Miniature necked jar**, SMICRW, 2308.
14. **Beaker**, FMICRW, 2308.
15. **Beaker**, FMICRW, 2308.
16. **Roughcast beaker**, CNG CC2, 2308.
17. **Beaker with cornice moulded rim**, FIOR with red slip, source uncertain, 2308.
18. **Beaker or miniature pot with carinated shoulder**, FIOR, mica coated but does not conform to Braives mica-dusted type, 2308.
19. **Beaker base**, MEOR, 2308.
20. **Multiple ring-necked flagon**, FLA, 2309.
21. **Double bead-rim flagon**, GRWW, 2309. 1st century.
22. **Narrow-necked jar**, CRW, 2309.
23. **Flat-rimmed bowl**, SANDRW, 2309.
24. **Flat-rimmed bowl**, FMICRW, burnished, 2309. Vitreous deposit adhering to outer surface.
25. **Bead-rim bowl**, BB1SED, burnished lattice decoration, 2309.
26. **Globular beaker with barbotine dots**, FMICRW, silvered surface, 2309.
27. **Small beaker**, FMICRW, 2309.
28. **Bead-rim jar with elongated bead**, BB1SW, 2309.
29. **Bowl with sharp, carinated shoulder**, FMICRW, 2309.
30. **Mortarium**, probably south-west England or south Wales, orange-brown fabric, quartz trituration grit, [Shepton Mallet ?], 2311.
31. **Flat-rimmed bowl**, BB1SW, burnished lattice decoration, 2311.
32. **Necked jar**, SMICRW, 2311.
33. **Bead-rim bowl**, BB1SED, 2311.
34. **Wide-mouthed bowl**, SEVOX2, 2311/2328.
35. **Curved-sided dish**, FLA, 2315.
36. **Flat-rimmed bowl**, BB1SED, burnished lattice decoration, 2315.
37. **Narrow-neck jar**, CRW, 2315.
38. **Necked bowl**, GRANRW, 2315.
39. **Carinated bowl/dish**, FMICRW, 2315.
40. **Plain-rimmed bowl with groove**, FMICRW, 2315.
41. **Mortarium**, Oise/Somme? Holbrook & Bidwell (1991) fabric FC3, quartz and flint trituration grit, 2317.
42. **Segmental bowl**, flange missing, SEVOX2, 2317
43. **Lid**, FMICRW, 2317.
44. **Lid**, BB1SW, burnished, 2317.
45. **Rim of wide mouth jug**, FLC, 2317.
46. **Rusticated jar**, CRW, 2317.
47. **Imitation of samian Drag 29 or 30 bowl**, FMICRW with metallic grey slip and rouletted decoration, 2317.
48. **Chamfered cup**, SMICRW, 2321.

49. **Imitation of samian Drag 29 or 30 bowl**, SMICRW with metallic grey slip, roulette and barbotine decoration, 2321.
50. **Cordoned bowl**, SMICRW, burnished, Drag 29 copy, 2317/2321.
51. **Bead-rim jar**, BB1SED, burnished acute lattice decoration, 2321.
52. **Short-neck jar**, SMICRW, 2321.
53. **Cooking pot**, BB1SED, burnished chevron on neck, 2321.
54. **Cooking pot**, BB1SED, burnished, 2321.
55. **Lid**, FMICRW, 2321.
56. **Lid**, FMICRW, 2321.
57. **Lid**, BB1SED, burnished linear decoration, 2321.
58. **Shallow bowl/dish**, possibly a lid, FMICRW, 2321.
59. **Flat-rimmed bowl**, FMICRW, 2321.
60. **Flagon with pulley-wheel rim**, FLA, white slip, 2321.
61. **Flagon**, GRWW 2321.
62. **Flagon with pulley-wheel rim**, FLC, white slip, 2321.
63. **Ring-necked flagon**, FLC, white slip, 2321.
64. **Flagon with pulley-wheel rim**, FLA, white slip, 2321.
65. **Bag-shaped beaker**, FMICRW, metallic grey slip and barbotine dot decoration, 2321.
66. **Mortarium with roll rim**, Oxfordshire product, probably from Littlemore workshop, AD 100–147/170, 2322.
67. **Handled dish**, FLA, 2322.
68. **Flat-rimmed bowl**, burnished acute lattice decoration, 2322.
69. **Lid**, SMICRW, 2322.
70. **Lid or shallow bowl with grooved rim**, FMICRW, 2322.
71. **Lid**, FMICRW, burnished, 2322.
72. **Necked jar**, FMICRW, metallic grey slip, 2322.
73. **Butt-beaker copy**, FMICRW, burnished surface, 2322.
74. **Cupped rim jug / flagon**, GRWW, 2322.
75. **Ring-necked flagon**, FLA, white slip, 2322.
76. **Flagon rim**, FLC, 2322.
77. **Roughcast beaker**, unsourced colour-coated ware, clay pellets, 2322.
78. **Roughcast beaker with cornice rim**, ARG CC, 2322.
79. **Roughcast beaker base**, KOL CC, 2322.
80. **Cup**, SMICRW, incised wave decoration, 2322.
81. **Bead-rim jar**, BB1SW, burnished acute lattice decoration, 2322.
82. **Cooking pot**, BB1SED, 2322.
83. **Necked jar with neck cordon**, CRW, 2322.
84. **Bowl rim**, FMICRW, rouletted decoration. A similar form in the same fabric has been recovered from a Period 6 deposit at Walcot Street (Croom and Bidwell forthcoming), 2323
85. **Base** FMICRW, 2323.
86. **Handled jug or jar**. FLBB, hard-fired, 2323.

87. **Flat-rimmed bowl**, BB1SED, burnished acute lattice, 2324.
88. **Bowl**, FMICRW, rouletted decoration, 2324.
89. **Shallow, necked bowl**, SMICRW, 2324.
90. **Shallow S-shaped carinated bowl**, FMICRW, 2324.
91. **Carinated dish**, CRW, 2324.
92. **Beaker**, FMICRW, metallic grey slip, 2324.
93. **Beaker**, FMICRW, 2324.
94. **Jar with flaring rim**, SMICRW, 2324.
95. **Ring-necked flagon**, FLWW, 2327.
96. **Cup-rim flagon or jug**, FLA, 2327.
97. **Small bead-rim globular jar or beaker**, FMICRW, 2327.
98. **Copy of black-burnished ware cooking pot**, CRW, burnished lattice decoration, 2328.
99. **Flanged bowl**, BB1SED, burnished lattice decoration, 2328.
100. **Narrow-necked jar with cordon at neck**, SMICRW, 2328.
101. **Large necked jar**, CRW, 2329.
102. **Flat-rimmed bowl**, BB1SED, burnished diagonal line decoration, 2329.
103. **Flat-rimmed bowl**, BB1SED, burnished diagonal line decoration, 2329.
104. **Flat-rimmed bowl**, BB1SED, 2329.
105. **Shallow bowl / dish**, SEVOX2, 2329.
106. **Plain-rimmed dish**, SEVOX2, 2329.
107. **Lid**, FMICRW, 2329.
108. **Ring-necked flagon**, FLC, white slip, 2329.
109. **Pulley-rim flagon / jug**, SMICRW, 2329.
110. **Bowl rim**, SMICRW, 2329.
111. **Roughcast beaker with cornice rim**, CNG CC2, 2329.
112. **Small beaker**, FMICRW, 2329.
113. **Bead-rim jar**, BB1SED, 2329.
114. **Necked, cordoned bowl**, FIOR, 2329.
115. **Necked, cordoned bowl**, SMICRW, 2329
116. **Necked bowl**, FMICRW, 2329.
117. **Necked jar**, SMICRW, 2329.
118. **Cooking pot**, SMICRW, burnished lattice decoration, 2329.
119. **Jar with short flaring rim**, GRANRW, 2329.
120. **Cooking pot**, BB1SW, 2329.
121. **Cooking pot**, BB1SW, 2329.
122. **Mortarium, Gillam form 255** (*Gallia Belgica*, probably Oise/Somme), Holbrook and Bidwell fabric FC5, AD 140–200, 1583.
123. **Narrow-necked jar**, GRANRW, 1583.
124. **Narrow-necked jar**, SMICRW, 1583.
125. **Wide mouth bowl**, SEVOX2, 1583.
126. **Short-necked jar**, FMICRW, 1583.
127. **Short-necked jar**, FMICRW, 1583.

Samian ware (Fig. 3.11)
by Felicity C. Wild

The site produced about 4 kg of Samian ware, from some 274 vessels, mostly in small pieces, of which 44 (16%) were decorated forms. Some 126 vessels (46%) were from South Gaul, 146 (53%) were from

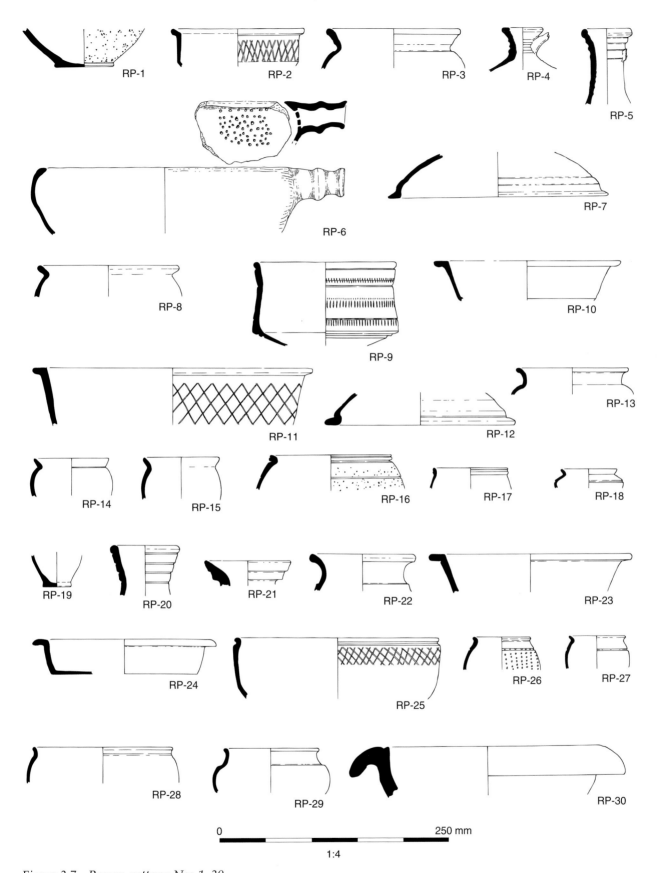

RP-1
RP-2
RP-3
RP-4
RP-5
RP-6
RP-7
RP-8
RP-9
RP-10
RP-11
RP-12
RP-13
RP-14
RP-15
RP-16
RP-17
RP-18
RP-19
RP-20
RP-21
RP-22
RP-23
RP-24
RP-25
RP-26
RP-27
RP-28
RP-29
RP-30

0   250 mm

1:4

Figure 3.7   Roman pottery: Nos 1–30.

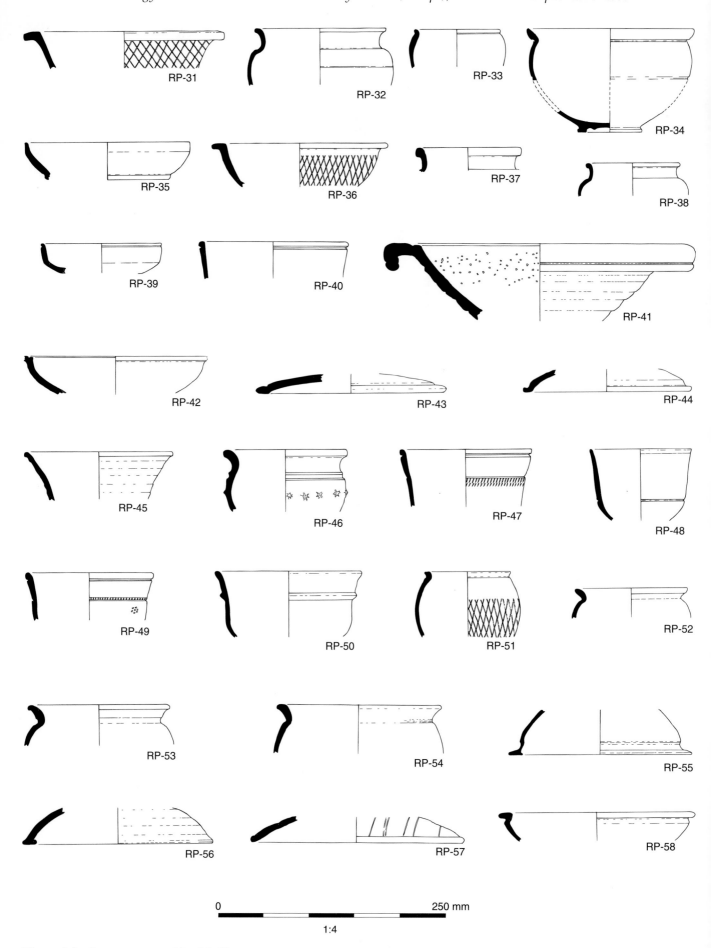

Figure 3.8   Roman pottery: Nos 31–58.

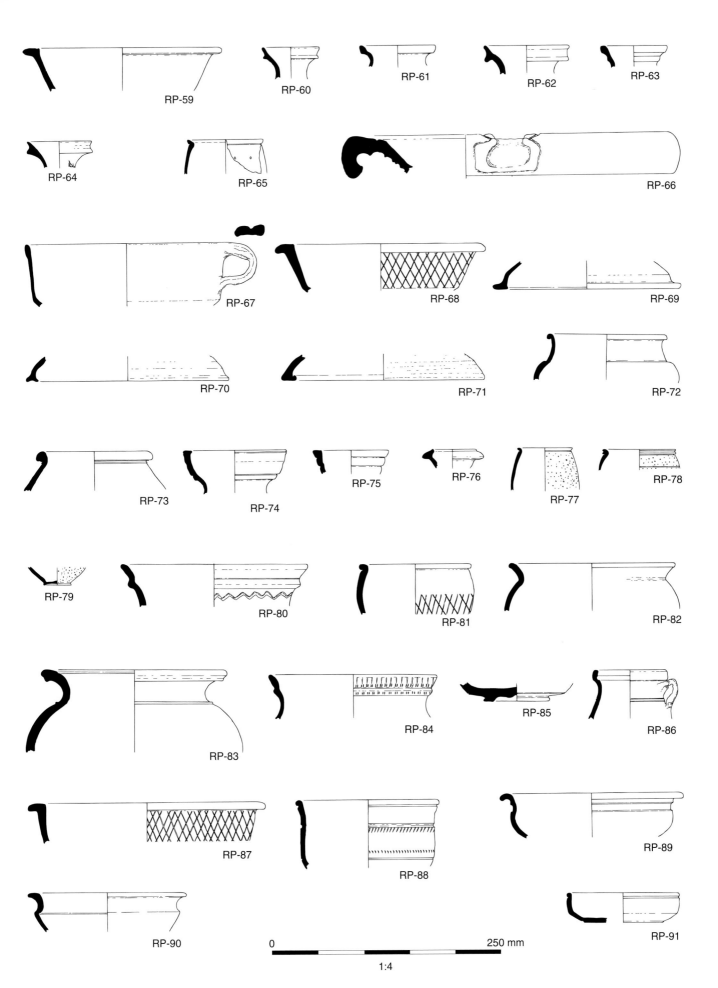

Figure 3.9   Roman pottery: Nos 59–91.

43

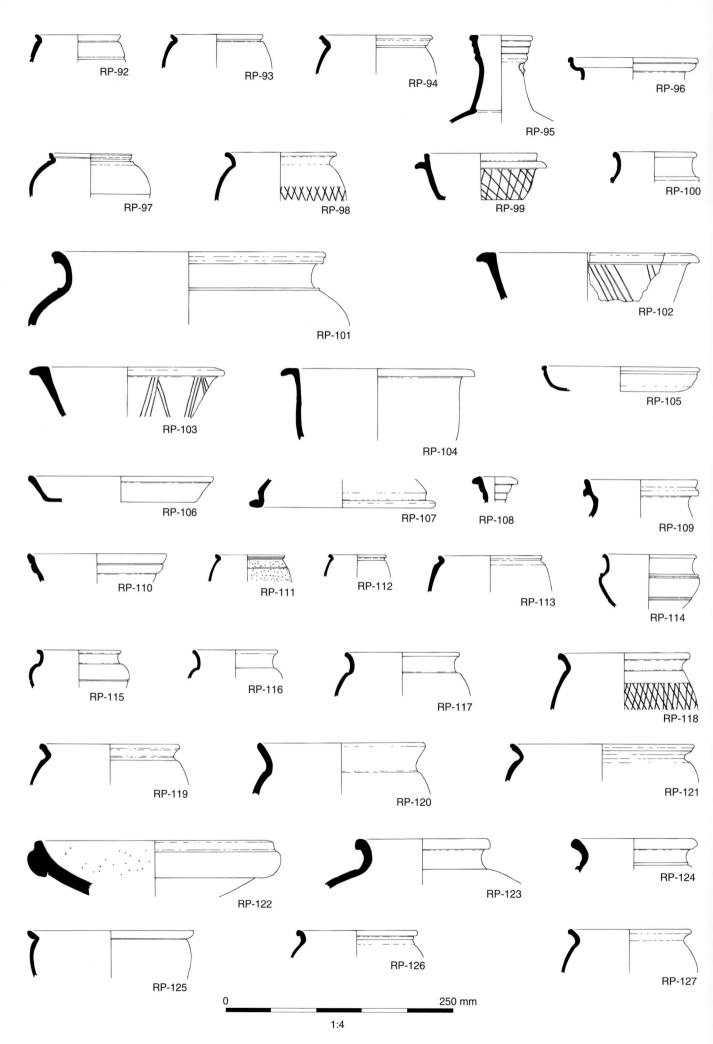

Figure 3.10   Roman pottery: Nos 92–127.

Central Gaul, including 37 in the fabric of Les Martres-de-Veyre, and two (0.7%) from East Gaul. There was a small but significant group from Period 2 contexts; the bulk of the material was found in Period 3.1 contexts. All the material found residually in post-Roman contexts was of the same date and types as found in Periods 2 and 3. In the discussion of the decorated ware the following abbreviations are used:

O   Oswald 1936–37
Rogers   Rogers 1974
S&S   Stanfield and Simpson 1958

Period 2: Early Roman

Period 2 contexts (including those classified as 2/3.1) produced 30 sherds from a maximum of 19 vessels, all South Gaulish apart from three vessels of Central Gaulish origin. Additionally three vessels technically assigned to Period 1 as they were found in the prehistoric palaeosol are included here (shown in square brackets in Table 3.6) as this soil continued as the early Roman ground surface with Roman debris being trampled into the soil during Period 2. Forms are quantified in Table 9 by kiln site as number of vessels.

The earliest material was of Neronian date, including stamp no. 4, of Niger, *c* AD 50–65. The characteristic pre-Flavian forms are lacking, though in so small a group, this may be no more than coincidence, as one example of form 24/25 came from a Period 3.1 context. The bulk of the material, however, was probably Flavian. The latest pieces in the group are the two from Central Gaul. These are in the fabric of Les Martres-de-Veyre and of Trajanic-Hadrianic date (however both are from 2318, which has been tentatively designated as the early ditch fill, though it could be interpreted as belonging to Period 3.1).

Table 3.6   Quantities of samian ware vessels from Period 2 (including 2/3.1) and Period [1].

Forms	South Gaulish	Central Gaulish	CG (Les Martres-de-Veyre)
15/17 or 18	1	~	~
18	4	~	~
18/31	~	[1]	1
27	5	~	~ [1]
29	2	~	~
30	1	~	~
35/36	1	~	~
36	1	~	~
37	1	~	~
42/36?	~	1	~
78	1	~	~
Unid	3	~ [bowl]	1
Total	20	2 + [2]	2 + [1]

Decorated ware (Fig. 3.11)

1. (Not illustrated). **Form 29, South Gaulish**, showing plain, straight gadroons in the lower zone. Such gadroons were common in the Neronian-early Flavian period, cf Modestus (Knorr 1919, Taf. 58C), Meddillus (Knorr 1952, Taf. 40C) and Pass(i)enus (Mees 1995, Taf. 157, 1). There is nothing here to suggest a particular potter. Neronian or early Flavian. (2099)

2. **Form Knorr 78, South Gaulish**, showing festoons with spirals. An example from La Graufesenque (Hermet 1934, pl. 92, 18) shows similar festoons, though with a different pendent motif. The spindle was used by many potters in the Flavian-Trajanic period.
    It was used with similar, though not quite identical, festoons on form 29 by Vitalis (Knorr 1919, Taf. 84C) and on form 37 by Biragillus (Mees 1995, pl. 14, 1) and Mercator (ibid., Taf. 137, 3,4). A Flavian or Flavian-Trajanic date seems likely. (678)

Residual Samian found in Periods 3.1–3.2

Period 3 contexts produced 324 sherds from a maximum of 234 vessels (Table 3.7), almost equally divided between South Gaulish and Central Gaulish apart from two vessels of East Gaulish origin assigned to Period 3.1, but in Period 3.2 Central Gaulish accounted for nearly two thirds (62%) of the vessels. Most of the samian ware from the site (64%) came from contexts assigned to period 3.1, and ranges in date from the Neronian or early Flavian period to the middle of the 2nd century AD. Forty-one percent of the material is South Gaulish, 58% Central Gaulish and 1% East Gaulish. The fragmentary state of the material and high proportion of earlier pieces is entirely consistent with material dumped from elsewhere as make-up for the construction of Building D. Forms are as follows:

The Central Gaulish ware is almost entirely Hadrianic or early Antonine in date, with very little that need post-date AD 150. The latest pieces are no. 18 below and the rosette stamp (stamp no. 9). Of the two East Gaulish pieces, stamp no. 8 is among the earlier products of East Gaul, and there is no reason to think that the other sherd need be much later. Among the plain wares as a whole, the earlier forms 27, 18/31 and 18/31R outnumber forms 33 and 31, and late Antonine forms, such as 31R, are absent altogether. Stamps nos 1–3 (*c* AD 135–155, 125–145 and 115–140) and 7–9 are all from contexts assigned to this period. In all, the material suggests a date of construction for the building of around, or shortly after, AD 160.

Decorated ware (all residual from Period 3.1 contexts) (Fig. 3.11)

3. **Form 37, South Gaulish**. Small scrap showing a chevron wreath above a zone of gadroons. The chevron wreath was a common feature on work

Table 3.7   Quantities of samian ware vessel types from Periods 3.1 and 3.2.

Forms	South Gaulish		CG (Les Martres de Veyre)		Central Gaulish (other)		East Gaulish	
Phase	3.1	3.2	3.1	3.2	3.1	3.2	3.1	3.2
15/17R	2		1					
15/17 or 18	4							
15/17R or 18R	1							
18	22	5	3	1				
18 or 18R	4	1						
18 or 18/31	3	2	2					
18/31	1		1		17	5		
18/31R					5			
18/31 or 31					2	2		
18/31 or 18/31R			2		1			
18/31, 31 or R variant					8	3		
18/31R or 31R							1	
22	1							
24/25	1							
27 (& 27 g)	17	1	3		8	5		
29	7							
30	3	1				1		
30 or 37	2		1					
37	7		3	1	16	2		
33			1		7	3		
33a	1				1			
35	1*	1						
35 or 36	3							
36	2							
38					1	1		
40 or 32?							1	
42	1?				1			
67	1?	1						
81					1			
Curle 11		1			1?			
Curle 15			1		1			
Ritt. 12 or Curle 11	3							
bowl	1	1	1		2	1		
cup	2		1					
beaker								
Unid	4	1			5	1		
Total	94	15	20	2	77	24	2	0

* joins with Period 3.2 vessel.

in the style of Calvus. A sherd in the Museum of London (Mus. no. 5228G) with Calvus's large rosette ovolo shows both the chevrons and gadroons. It is not clear what lies above the chevron wreath on the present sherd, but it is probably not an ovolo. *c* AD 70–85. (2177)

4. **Form 37, South Gaulish**, showing panel decoration typical of the Flavian-Trajanic period, with boar (O.1670) and panel of leaftips. There is no basal wreath. The bowl has been carelessly finished, with a patch of grit adhering to the slip in one place. There are traces of a trifid bud beneath the boar, but its detail is obscured by the grit. Crucuro made use of similar panels of leaftips (Mees 1995, Taf. 57, 1, which also lacks a basal wreath) and also the boar (ibid., Taf. 56, 6). *c* AD 80–110. (2181)

5. **Form 29, South Gaulish.** Seven fragments, including two of base, with poorly impressed decoration, showing festoons in the upper zone and a row of vertical leaf motifs in the lower. The general connections of the bowl suggest that it is likely to come from a group of potters at La Graufesenque, dominated by Mommo and Niger, sharing a common mould-making workshop. The bud was used as a frieze, rather than as a pendant, as here, on a bowl stamped by Albus i, another member of the group. Other bowls show its use as a pendant between festoons or medallions, though on the lower zone of form 29. It is difficult to tell the precise form of the leaf in the lower zone here, as it is so badly impressed, but it is probably that used on a form 29 from La Graufesenque stamped by

the potter(s) signing their work Niger And...,
who were also associated with the group. *c* AD
60–75. (2322, 2327, 2329)

6. **Form 29, South Gaulish**, showing gadroons in
the lower zone, above a basal wreath of trifid
buds. The bud has been recorded on work in
the style of Iustus, who used similar gadroons.
It occurs as a wreath beneath gadroons, as
here, on a form 29 from Vechten stamped by
Vanderio (Knorr 1919, Taf. 80D). *c* AD 70–85.
(2308)

7. **Form 30, South Gaulish**, with leaf-scroll decoration in the style of Masclus, who used similar
heart-shaped leaves, the twisted tendril and
tendril-binding (Mees 1995, Taf. 106, 1,2; 107,
2,3). *c* AD 50–70. (1729)

8. **Form 30, South Gaulish**, showing panel decoration with corner tendril and upright row of
trifid buds. The ovolo is a blurred version of
that used by Germanus (Dannell et al. 1998,
RR), though Germanus is not known to have
used these motifs. A bowl in Germanus's style
from Verulamium (Hartley 1972, D31) shows
the ovolo and an identical scheme of decoration, though with Germanus's usual bud and
tendril. Although unlikely to be by Germanus,
this is presumably the work of an associate or
contemporary. *c* AD 65–80. (1041)

9. **Form 37, South Gaulish**. The very distinctive
single-bordered ovolo with large-beaded border has been recorded at La Graufesenque on a
form 37 with zonal decoration (Hermet 1934, pl.
81,8) and on form 30, without the beaded
border, with a scroll containing the same leaf as
here (ibid., pl. 6, 22). It has not yet been
associated with any named potters, but its use
on form 37 suggests a date *c* AD 70–90. (2329)

10. **Form 37, South Gaulish**. Three joining fragments showing part of an animal type above a
palisade of lanceolate leaves (Hermet 1934, pl.
13, A7). The palisade, also used by potters such
as Censor and Crucuro, was commonly used by
Frontinus at the base of the decoration (Mees
1995, pl. 60, 5; 63, 6) and has frequently been
recorded on bowls in his style from first-
century sites in Scotland, eg at Inchtuthil
(Hartley 1985, D17, D20). *c* AD 70–90. (2317)

11. **Form 37, Central Gaulish**, in the fabric of Les
Martres-de-Veyre, showing the ovolo (Rogers
B28) with wavy-line border used by the potter
X.2. A bowl from London (S&S, pl. 5, 59) shows
the ovolo with his characteristic cup motif
(Rogers U61) between double arcades, as here.
c AD 100–120. (2322)

12. **Form 37, Central Gaulish**, in the fabric of
Les Martres-de-Veyre, showing a basal wreath
(Rogers G366 or 365) surmounted by a wavy-
line border. The wreath is well known from Les
Martres, and was similarly used, with a wavy-
line border on the upper side only, by X.2 (S&S,
pl. 4, 38 etc.) and by X.12 (S&S, pl. 41, 485).
Beneath the decoration are traces of a cursive

signature, probably reading SCAN[or SCAM
[(retr.). It appears to have been cut into the
mould after firing and is presumably part of the
name of the man who owned the mould,
though it might refer to the mould-maker
himself if he had left the mould to dry out
beyond the leather-hard stage before signing it.
No potter is known with a name starting like
this. *c* AD 100–120. (2098)

13. **Form 37, Central Gaulish**, in the fabric of Les
Martres-de-Veyre. Panels show the pedestal
(Rogers Q65), panel of leaf-tips and fine-beaded
lines over a mask (O.1270A), and the warrior
(O.167). The style is that of Rogers's potter X.13.
A bowl in his style from Cirencester (S&S, pl. 46,
539) shows the pedestal, mask and beaded
borders with rosette (Rogers C280) at the junc-
tions. Another, from London (S&S, pl. 47, 549),
shows the panel of leaf-tips. The warrior is also
listed as one of his types. *c* AD 100–120. (2322)

14. **Form 37, Central Gaulish**, with fabric slightly
burnt. The ovolo fits Rogers B14 for size,
though the tongue is clearly corded in the Z
direction, like B6. Both were used by X.13. It is
presumably identical to that on a bowl from
London (S&S, pl. 48, 567) where it is surmounted by a bead-row, as here, and also
shows the dot rosette (Rogers C280) at the top
of a vertical border. *c* AD 100–120. (2322)

15. **Form 37, Central Gaulish**, showing the ovolo
(Rogers B7), seven-dot rosette (Rogers C280)
and the festoon (Rogers F8) used as an arcade.
All three motifs were used by X.13, X.14 and
Attianus. The fabric is probably that of Lezoux
rather than Les Martres-de-Veyre, suggesting a
date *c* AD 125–150. (2308)

16. **Form 37, Central Gaulish**, with ovolo (Rogers
B7) as on no. 15 above, showing a freestyle
hunting scene with the panther (O.1542) at-
tacked by a hunter. The hunter, chipped at
the edge of the sherd, cannot be identified with
certainty (possibly O.1076?) though the spear
appears to be a bead-row, the impression badly
smudged. Connections appear to lie with the
Sacer-Attianus group, who used both ovolo and
panther. Sacer produced similar hunting scenes
(S&S, pl. 84, 16, with the panther; pl. 82, 1, with a
(different) spearman). *c* AD 125–150. (1787)

17. **Form 37, Central Gaulish**. Two sherds in the
style of Docilis. One shows his ovolo (Rogers
B24) and panels with the Hercules (O.774) and
baluster (Rogers Q5). Both types occur together
on a signed bowl from Colchester (S&S, pl. 91,
1). The other shows the Mars (O.151), which
also occurs on the Colchester bowl, and his
trifid bud (Rogers G256). There is no certain
evidence that the two sherds came from the
same bowl, but it is possible. *c* AD 130–150.
(2324, 2308)

18. **Form 37, Central Gaulish**, showing the ovolo
(Rogers B103) used by Advocisus and a freestyle hunting scene with large and small stags

running to right (O.1720, O.1732). Although Advocisus produced similar hunting scenes (cf S&S, pl. 113, 14), there is no evidence that he used the stags. Oswald notes O.1732 on work in his style. Another bowl in his style (S&S, pl. 113, 19) shows a large stag similar to O1720, running to left. Rogers illustrates a freestyle bowl with same ovolo for Priscus I/Clemens (Rogers 1999, pl. 88, 12), who used O.1732, but this is unsigned and the potters are also of later Antonine date. The good craftsmanship and clear detail here suggest the work of Advocisus. *c* AD 160–190. (1608)

Small finds from the fill of the culvert trench 1280 (Figs 3.12–3.13)
by John Clarke

The assemblage discussed here comes from the fill of the culvert trench F1280 deposited during the mid 2nd century AD. All the material has been brought from another source as make-up during the construction of Building D and is thought to derive from a building demolished in the locality (see above) to make way for Building D. The complete list of small finds and their descriptions can be found on the web site. Descriptions of those illustrated appear below.

0   100 mm

1:2

Figure 3.11   Decorated Samian: Nos 1–18.

Only two coins were recovered – a probable sestertius, possibly of Domitian (no.12) in a very worn state and a penny of George V (no. 13). The latter is clearly intrusive and must have been accidentally introduced during the excavation. The number of lead offcuts, dribbles etc. (nos 15–25) is consistent with an area that included a bath suite and its associated plumbing. The spindle whorl (no.14) is not closely dateable, but other artefactual evidence places it in the 2nd century. The iron possible lace end (no. 26) is a type more usually of medieval date and of copper alloy, so may be intrusive.

The fragment of pipe clay figurine (fig 3.13, 1) is an interesting addition to the two dog figurines from the Roman Baths and Beau Street excavations (Bircher 1999, 99–100), three Venus fragments, mother goddess and bird from Aldridge's and reclining female figure from Nelson Place (Bircher forthcoming). These figurines were produced in the Allier region of Central Gaul in the 1st and 2nd centuries and are, if not in a burial, indicative of religious and ritual activity. This brings the total of these figurines found in Bath to nine, of what is a relatively rare artefact in Roman Britain.

The five pottery counters, one of samian ware (no. 27) and four of grey wares (nos 28–31) are of 1st/2nd century date and may reflect the social aspects of the demolished building. Four samian ware and one grey ware counter were found during the Beau Street excavations and dateable to the mid- to late 2nd century (Bircher 1999, 99–101). For a fuller discussion of pottery counters, see Crummy 1983, 93–94. The four stamped samian ware bases (nos 32–35) are of 1st/2nd century date, as are the stamped mortaria rim sherds (nos 36 & 37).

The bone counter of Crummy Type 2 (Fig. 3.12, 5) is of a type that appears in the 1st century and continues throughout most of the Roman period (Crummy 1983, 91). The piece of bone inlay (Fig. 3.12, 6) may have come from a box or from a piece of furniture or a box. It is rough on the back to facilitate gluing. Fragments of bone inlay occur quite widely, see for example pieces in variety of shapes from Kingscote (Timby 1998, 171–74 & figs 83, 4.28–4.61 & 84, 4.69–4.87) and more particularly pieces recovered from cremation in the cemetery at Brougham (for example cremations 276, 286 and 307: Cool 2004, 222 & fig. 4.225, 4a–4i; 230 & fig. 4.234, 4a–4r; and 243–44 & fig.250, 9b–9v). The bone hair pins (Fig. 3.12, 2–3) are of Crummy Type 2 (Crummy 1979, 21) and in Colchester this type appears in contexts of pre-Flavian and later date, c 50–200. The pin head in the form of a bearded male head (Fig. 3.12, 4) is unusual and no close parallels have been found. A copper alloy example from Colchester is similar, but the face is unclear due to corrosion, though the back has grooves like the Spa item (Crummy 1983, 30–32, fig. 31, no. 503), and is dated 60/1–c 125. A bone example of a female head, again with hair indicated by grooves, is from a modern pit (ibid. 25–26, fig. 23, no. 445). A bone moustached male head from South

Shields is dated 2nd–3rd century (Allason-Jones and Miket 1984, 86, no. 2.536).

The glass bead (Fig. 3.12, 8) could date from AD 150 to c 450 (Crummy 1983, 34, fig. 34, nos 1346–49), but given the other dating evidence from this context, the earlier date is more likely. The boxwood comb (Fig. 3.13, 10) is of interest mainly because preserved organic remains are rare in Bath. This type of wood is ideal for use as a comb, as it does not splinter, so will not catch the hair and it can be thinned to a fine, dull point, so will not harm the scalp. Wooden combs were a new type of artefact for Roman Britain and their distribution spread quickly from Fishbourne to the Antonine Wall. For a fuller discussion, see Pugsley 2001.

This assemblage comprises a fairly typical range of artefacts, but with a notable absence of copper alloy, a fact reflected from the site as a whole, from which only 12 objects were recovered. The dating of the finds to the 1st and 2nd centuries correlates well with the pottery evidence and with that gained from the excavations of 1986.

Illustrated Artefacts

Ceramic pipe clay figurine (Fig. 3.13, 1)

1   **Pipe clay figurine fragment**. Part of the torso of a draped male figurine, possibly Mercury, with the right shoulder and stump of the arm surviving. The figurine was hollow, and inside has prints showing where the pipe clay was pressed into the bivalve mould. The figurine has fractured around the side seam. Length: 85 mm, max. width: 48 mm, thickness: 13 mm. Context 2322, SF 6100.

Bone (Fig. 3.12, 2–7)

2   **Pin**, Crummy Type 2, complete, with two widely spaced grooves below the conical head. Length: 124 mm. Context 2329, SF 6082.

3   **Pin**, Crummy Type 2, broken, with two close grooves below the conical head. Length: 34 mm. Context 2329, SF 6083.

4   **Pin head** in the form of a bearded male head, with a tall, oval head dress or hair style. The front has two horizontal grooves, with more grooves radiating up from the lower one to the edge. Another groove runs around the top for the extent of the radiating ones. A groove encircles the shaft just below the chin and above the break. Stained a very dark brown. Henig (pers. comm.) has pointed out that the high hairstyle would normally be female and it may originally have been intended as such, the notching for the beard being added subsequently. He suggests as an alternative interpretation that the head represents a theatrical mask with a high onkos. Length: 21 mm. Context 2309, SF 6067.

5   **Counter**, with concentric grooves and lathe centre indentation on the obverse. Crummy

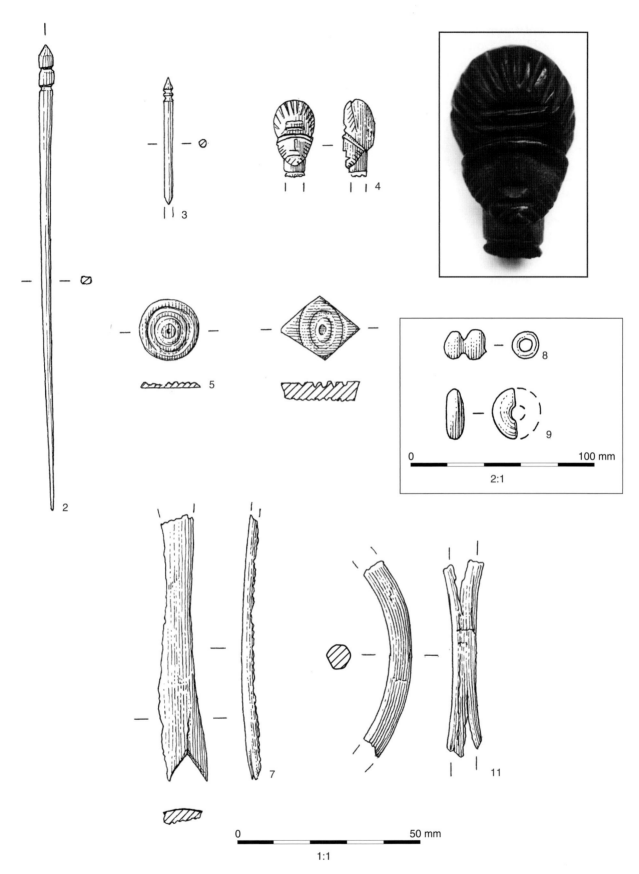

Figure 3.12   Roman small finds: bone pins (2–4) (including detailed photograph of pin head 4), bone counter (5) and inlay (6), bone fragment (7), glass beads (8–9) and shale bangle (11).

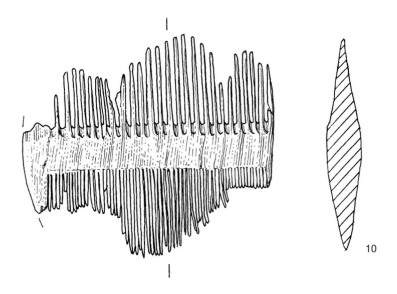

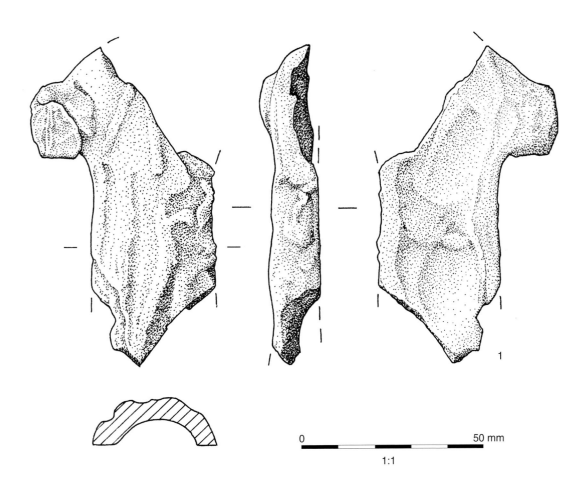

Figure 3.13   Roman small finds: wooden comb (10) and pipe clay figurine (1).

Type 2 counter. Diam: 17 mm. Context 2328, SF 6079.

6   **Bone inlay**, consisting of a lozenge-shaped piece with an oval ring-and-dot motif occupying most of the upper surface. A strip of inlay, in which the edges impinge to varying degrees on the outer ring of the design. Length: 21 mm, width: 16 mm, thickness: 5 mm. Context 2324, SF 6077.

7   **Forked object**. Irregular strip, notched at one end. Possibly scrap from bone working. See Crummy 1983, 150–3, figs 185 and 186, nos 4333–47. Length: 70 mm; breadth: 11 mm; width: 3 mm.. Context 987, SF 6027.

Glass (Fig. 3.12, 8–9)

8   **Glass bead** of opaque green, probably part of a longer segmental bead. Length: 6 mm, diam: 4 mm. SF6074. Context 2308.

9   **Disc bead** in opaque blue glass, half only. Possibly late 4th century. Diameter: 7 mm; width: 2 mm. Context 348, SF 6032.

Wood (Fig. 3.13, 10)

10   **Boxwood comb** with fine teeth on one side, coarse on the other. Part only. The central rib is flat and the surviving terminal is a plain curve. Length: 68 mm, max. width: 58 mm, thickness: 12 mm. Context 2322, SF 6076.

Shale (Fig. 3.12, 11)

11   **Plain, oval-sectioned armlet**, not closely dateable. Length: 51 mm; width: 7 x 6 mm. Context 2098, SF 6066.

Ceramic Building Material (Figs 3.14–3.17)
A summary of the report by Ian M Betts

A large quantity of building material was recovered, comprising 3994 fragments weighing 527.86 kg. A high proportion of this is of Roman date (post-Roman material is referred to in the relevant sections) and most is in good condition allowing tile types to be positively identified in the majority of cases.

Fabric type

The fabric divisions used are those in the Bath type series (Betts 1999a). Roman fabric types identified are fabrics 1, 2, 3, 4, 5, 7, 8, 9, 16, 17, 18, 23. Descriptions of all of these fabrics can be found in the full report in the site archive. No local kiln sites have been positively identified for the Bath region, but most of the fabrics are thought to be relatively local. Fabric 8 appears to be Museum of London fabric type 3019, which is believed to come from the Hampshire area in the early 2nd century. Examples have been found in London and suggest that the

material is coming from a major supplier with an extensive trade network across the south of England.

Of particular significance is a scatter of overfired roofing tile fragments (both *tegulae* and *imbrices*) found in Period 3.1 and 3.2 contexts. One of these had a fragment of clay attached to the top surface suggesting that it may have derived from some sort of tile and clay built kiln structure, possibly representing evidence of tile manufacture somewhere in the locality. Unfortunately, these fragments are too overfired to identify their fabric type with any certainty. A further overfired imbrex tile (either fabric 2 or 16) was found in context 1049. It is possible that a temporary kiln was constructed on site to manufacture bricks and tiles for Building D in the subsequent period, but no evidence of such a structure has been found. It is therefore not possible to say whether the overfired fragments are construction waste from Building D or demolition debris from the unsited earlier building.

Tile types

Roofing tile (fabric types 1, 2, 3, 4, 5, 7, 9, 16, 17, 18)

Both *tegulae* and *imbrices* are present, indicating the presence of buildings with ceramic tiled roofs. Six *tegulae* have nail holes, a characteristic that does not normally appear until around AD 160 in London (Betts 1991; Pringle in prep). No *tegulae* were complete though it was possible to estimate the top breadth for some at *c* 328 mm and *c* 298 mm. The imbrex roofing tiles are all of normal type, although two are slightly unusual in having knife trimming on their bottom edge. One imbrex has what appears to be keying on the tile end. This would have been to aid the attachment of mortar where the tiles overlapped on the roof. There are no complete *imbrices*, although one example has a breadth of approximately 172 mm.

Brick (fabric types, 2, 4, 5?, 7, 8, 16, 17)

Very few bricks survive intact. One complete example measured 212 mm square by 45–50 mm thick and two partially complete examples were 192 mm wide x 40–49 mm thick and 308 mm wide x 46–54 mm thick. Pedalis bricks used as hypocaust pilae measuring 300 mm square were also recorded from context 1191 and larger bricks 400 mm wide were used in the associated flue lining. Other brick fragments occur in the variety of thicknesses (26–54 mm), which suggests that a range of brick types is represented. More unusual is what appears to be a brick, 34 mm in thickness, with a combed surface (context 905, fabric 16). The side and what appears to be the base have been knife trimmed. The purpose of this brick is uncertain, although it may also, like the more typical examples, have been used as flooring.

Wall tile (fabric types 2, 7, 9, 17, 18)

There are two distinct types of wall tile based on the type of keying present, which aided the attachment of a mortar or plaster covering. The first type (fabrics 2, 7, 17, 18) has knife scoring on the sanded underside and the second type (fabric 9), has combing on the upper surface. Both scored and combed examples (made with a normal sized five-toothed comb; Fig. 3.16) come from a single source, while a second variety of combed in a distinct fabric and with a different style of combing was clearly made at a different production site. Box tiles with the same type of combing also came from this source. At least one tile has a clay nib attached to the upper surface (Fig. 3.14, 4), which was presumably meant as an additional aid to keying and is comparable to a wall tile from the Tramshed site (Betts forthcoming).

Box-flue tile (fabric types 2, 3, 4, 7, 16, 17)

There are three types of box-flue tiles present: scored, combed and relief-patterned (also known as roller-stamped). This keying was normally applied to the front and back faces of the tiles whilst the two sides, into which vent holes were cut, were left plain. The scored keying was applied with a sharp knife in a lattice pattern (Fig. 3.15, 6) but in some cases what appears to be a blunt ended tool (or possibly part of a comb) was used to form a wavy pattern running down the length of the tile. One of the lattice scored pieces has part of a round vent hole in the adjacent plain side. In London and other sites in south-east England lattice scored keying seems to be an early Roman feature, which was superseded by combed and roller stamped keying during the early 2nd century.

The vast majority of box-flue tiles found at the Spa have combed keying in a variety of patterns, added with different sized combs containing from four to 19 teeth. Part of the combed surface of one flue tile has been cut away suggesting that it may have been placed on the hypocaust floor with the cutaway allowing heat up into the flue tiles stacked above. A relief-patterned tile from Angmering has cutaways for this purpose (Betts *et al* 1994, 8–10).

There are five box-flue tiles with keying applied by a wooden roller. These have been keyed with four different roller-stamps (dies 25, 53, 54, 56) all of which are already known from various other sites in the West Country (ibid., 98, 117–120). The roller stamped tiles found at the Spa (Fig. 3.17) come from two different kiln sites. The first kiln site used a fine micaceous clay (fabric 16) to produce the box-flues keyed with dies 25 and 53. This tilery also supplied the flue tiles to other sites in and around Bath including the Tramsheds site (die 25) and the suburban villa at Oldfield Boys School (die type uncertain). The second kiln site produced the flue tiles (fabrics 2, 4) keyed with roller-stamp die types 54 and 56. Both examples of die 56 are on flue tiles with square or rectangular vent holes. A box-flue tile with die 56 was also used in the suburban villa at Lower Common, Bath.

Both these sources were supplying roller stamped tiles over a fairly wide area probably during the 1st and early 2nd centuries, as tiles decorated using dies 53 and 56 were found at Shakenoak villa in Oxfordshire, where the earliest bath-house is dated *c* AD 120. Die 54 on the other hand was found at Shaw, Berkshire, associated with pottery of AD 65–85, although the tile may be later in date.

Half-box flue? (fabric type 16)

What may be the flange of a half-box flue was found residually in Period 5 (Fig. 3.15, 10). These were a short lived type which were used in Roman Britain in the 1st century but were largely superseded by ordinary box-flue tiles in the Flavian period (Black 1996, 62).

Voussoir (fabric types 2, 3, 4, 7, 16)

Voussoir tiles are of crucial importance because they indicate the presence of a vaulted roof structure. However, small fragments of voussoir tile are very difficult to distinguish from box-flue tiles. There are, however, two features that help in their recognition: their size and the presence of keying on adjacent sides. No complete voussoirs survive, though three sizes appeared to be present. The majority of the Spa voussoirs are smaller than those used at the Great Baths, presumably because they were used to span smaller floor areas. All the voussoirs have combed keying, but unlike those used at the Great Baths, the top surface has been keyed along with the other three surfaces. Similarly in Canterbury, Kent there are voussoir tiles with keying on all four faces (Betts *et al* 1994, 11).

The Spa voussoir tiles are all keyed with combs with from six to 19 teeth. At least some of the Spa examples may have had vents, as there is one example with part of a round vent hole. Vent holes in combed tile faces are normally parts of voussoirs. None of the Great Baths examples have vents although these are a feature of voussoirs used elsewhere such as at Beauport Park, East Sussex (Brodribb 1987, 80).

Markings

Graffito

A possible wall tile (context 588, fabric 2) has part of a name (...LLV...) neatly inscribed in the top surface before firing. Not enough letters survive to show exactly which name is represented. It is still of great interest as it may well represent the name of a Bath tile maker.

Signature marks

Signature marks made by the tips of the fingers on the tile surface, believed to represent the individual marks of the tilemakers (Brodribb 1987, 99), are present on 71 tiles. Eight different marking types are present (Fig. 3.16, 1–8), most commonly semi-circles of between one and four lines and also loops made with one or two fingers (Fig. 3.16, 5–8). These are all on *tegula* and brick with the exception of two semi-circular marks on wall tiles. A total of 44 definite and 27 probable examples were found on spa tiles.

Tally marks

Tally marks normally in the form of knife cut lines in the tile edge or the flange top of *tegulae* are much rarer and only one definite and one possible example were found at the Spa. The definite example on a *tegula* flange appears to be three diagonal knife cuts, whilst the possible example comprises a single diagonal line on the tile edge.

Imprints

Most Roman sites in Bath produce a few tiles with paw prints and the Spa is no exception. There are six examples of paw prints, two each of finger marks and probable claw marks and what may be part of a shoe impression.

Illustrated Ceramic building materials

Fig. 3.14

1   *Tegula* partially complete with square nail hole added prior to firing. Context 2324.
2   **Wall tile** with side notches crudely pushed in. Context 2076.
3   **Wall tiles** with combing covering all surface and with clay nib. The two tiles are arranged

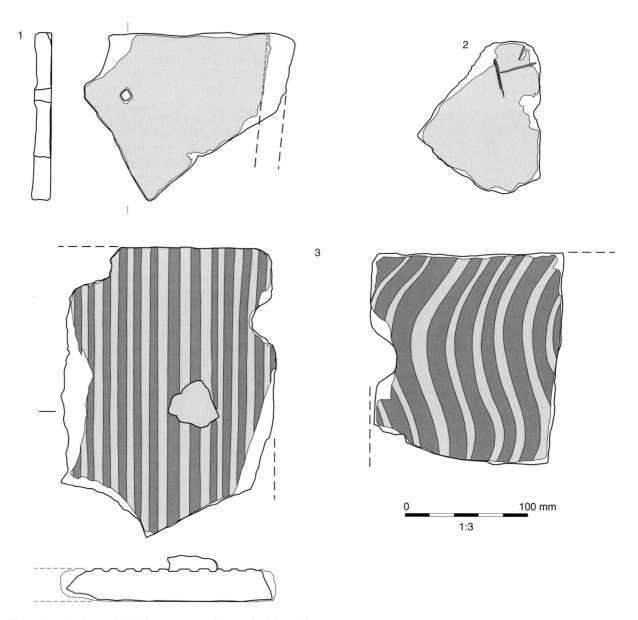

Figure 3.14   Ceramic Building materials: tegula (1), wall tiles (2–3).

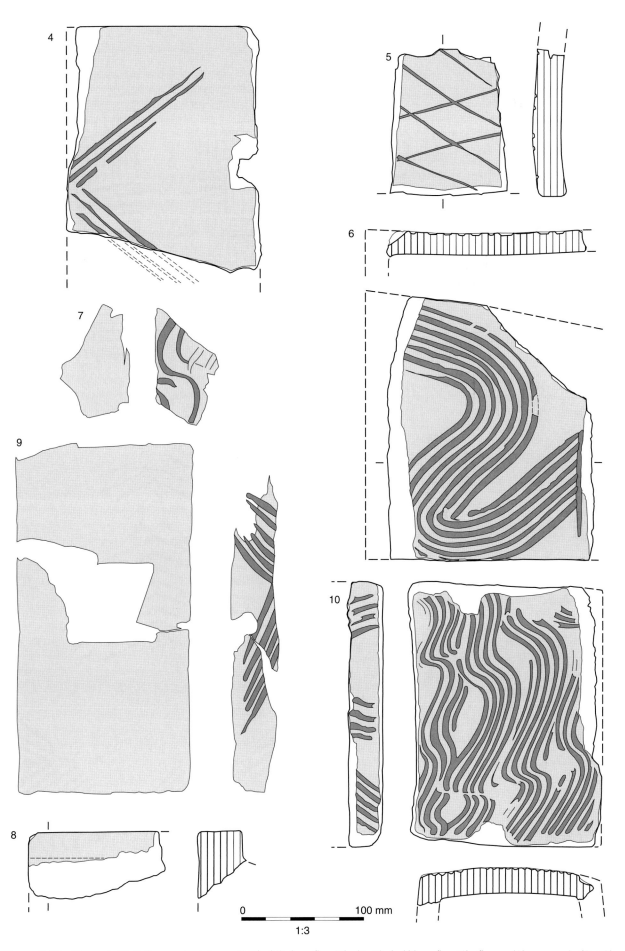

Figure 3.15   Ceramic Building materials: wall tile (4), box-flue tile (5–7), half box-flue tile flange (8), voussoir (9–10).

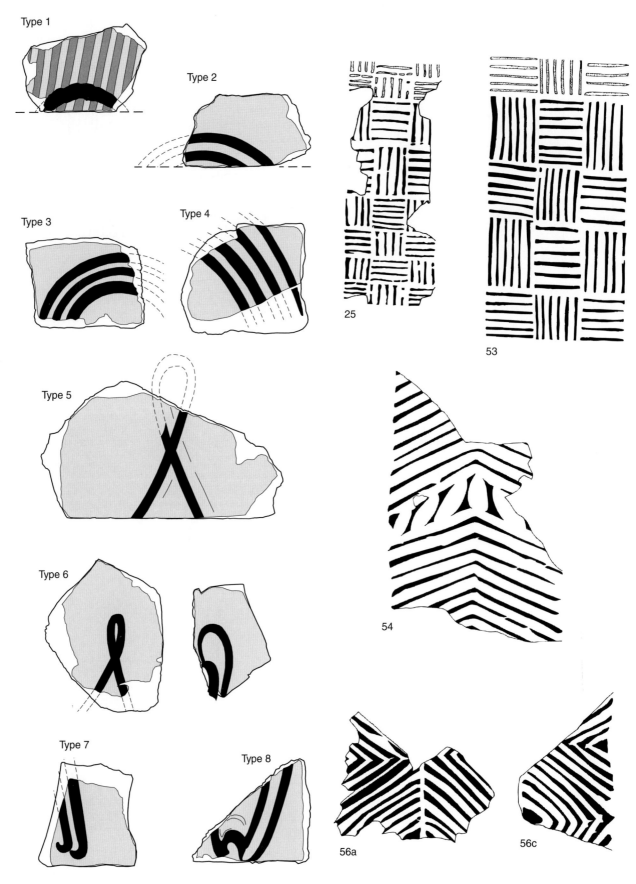

Figure 3.16 Ceramic Building materials: Signature marks – Types 1 (Context 549), 2 (Context 806), 3 (Context 1810), 4 (Context 737), 5 (Context 1659), 6 (Contexts 1001, 1059), 7 (Context 835), 8 (Context 1138).

Figure 3.17 Ceramic Building materials: Relief-pattern tile designs found on the Spa site – dies 25, 53, 54, 56.

side by side as they would be in use. Contexts 316 and 647.

Fig. 3.15

4   **Wall tile** with partial combed keying. Context 2076.
5   **Box-flue tile** with knife cut lattice scored keying. Context 916.
6   **Box-flue tile** with wavy keying and part of a round vent hole. Context 916.
7   **Box-flue tile** with partially complete plain side showing the position of two vent holes. Context 723.
8   **Possible flange from a half-box flue.** Context 905.
9   **Voussoir tile**, side face, size type 1. Context 864.
10 **Voussoir tile**, top face believed to belong with the side faces of size 1. Context 2322.

Discussion of the stratified groups

Period 2

The only ceramic building material in substantial features came from the road and the ditch, but it can be argued that these layers were deposited at the start of Period 3.1 rather than in Period 2 and therefore could be part of the debris from the early demolished building. The material comprised predominantly ceramic roofing tile (*tegulae* and *imbrices*) with smaller quantities of wall tile, box-flue tile and brick. Tiles from at least three separate production sites can be identified (fabrics 2, 9, 16) although the location of these tileries is still unknown. Other fabric types (fabrics 3, 7, 17) containing various quantities of quartz sand are also present. Some of these may represent variations in clay used at the tilery producing tiles in fabric 2, whilst others may originate from other kiln sites.

The tiles in fabrics 2, 9 and 16 are also present in the earliest phase of the Tramsheds site dated from the 1st to the mid 2nd century (Betts in prep). The kiln site supplying the tiles in fabric 9 made both roofing and wall tiles, both of which were found in Period 2. The wall tiles, many of which were found associated with the road, can be identified by the notches in the tile sides situated near each top corner and by combed keying covering all the top surface. This was applied with a large comb with broad shallow teeth or, in the case of a possible example from context 588, with a knife. The latter has part of a graffito made with a stylus or similar sharp-pointed instrument. This has been examined by R S O Tomlin (Wolfson College, Oxford) who reports that the tile reads: [. . .] LLV [..]. This is "probably part of a personal name ending in '-llus'. There are too many possibilities ranging from conventional cognomina like 'Gallus' and 'Marcellus' to diminutives in '-illus', to make any guesses".

Wall tiles were set vertically with their combed side facing into the room and were then covered with a mortar or plaster finish. They formed a continuous wall jacketing allowing all the interior walls of the room to be heated. To allow the circulation of hot air the tiles were separated from the wall by circular ceramic objects known as spacer bobbins. Both were held in place by iron clamps or nails, which fitted through the gaps left by the notches in the tile sides and passed through the centre of the bobbins into the solid wall behind. Surprisingly, no spacer bobbins have been ever been found in Bath, suggesting that they may have been wood rather than ceramic.

These wall tiles are important as they must have formed part of a hypocausted masonry structure, almost certainly a bath building. In London wall tiles seem to have been used in major public buildings in the city (Betts 1995, 214) and it is possible that the same situation prevailed in Bath. Wall tiles were used in Roman Britain from the late 1st century to the early 2nd century, although by the Hadrianic period box-flues had become all but universal (Black 1996, 67; Black per comm).

Residual 1st–2nd century tile found in Period 3.1

A large quantity of ceramic roofing tile, brick, box-flue tile and wall tile was found in Period 3.1 contexts. Practically all of it came from the culvert ditch fill and most of the remainder came from wall foundations and make-up layers for the floors of Building D, implying that all of this material derives from an earlier demolished structure, or structures. A number of the roofing tiles found in the wall foundations have mortar on their broken edges indicating reuse. A partially complete *bessalis* brick was recovered from one of the foundations (context 326).

The group found in make-up layers for the courtyard of Building D (contexts 2177–2179 and 2181) included box-flue tiles, (but no wall tiles) which indicates that these derive from a hypocausted building, or bath house. This may have had a partially tiled and stone roof as the box-flues were found with both ceramic roofing tile and grey Pennant stone roofing. All the box-flues have combed keying made with combs with from seven to *c* 17 teeth. These are probably early 2nd century in date as there is evidence in London that combing replaced knife scored keying at certain tileries during this period (Betts 1991; Pringle in prep).

A similar group of material in the top of the culvert trench produced numerous fragments of *tegulae*, *imbrices* and combed box-flue, suggesting it may have derived from the same building as the material in the courtyard make-up. This would seem to have been a bath house as there are a number of voussoirs from a vaulted roof. A few fragments of brick are also present in the culvert trench fill, probably remains of the hypocaust floor, along with a box-flue with relief-patterned keying. The keying pattern is die 53 already known from Bath, Cirencester, Gloucestershire and the villa at Shakenoak,

Oxfordshire. At Shakenoak tiles of this type were probably used in the earliest bath-house at the villa dated to around AD120 (Betts *et al* 1994, 117–8).

Also from the ditch are four tiles with knife scoring in their sanded base and a further tile with scoring on the smoothed upper surface. These are probably 1st century box-flue tiles, although some of the thicker fragments could be wall tiles. Wall tiles with scored keying are certainly present in the wall foundations of Building D (context 321, fabric 18) and in make-up layers (contexts 1169, 2076 (Period 3.2), fabric 2), which occur in and over F1280 to the south-west of Building D. There is also a combed wall tile from the same tilery as most (if not all) of the scored examples in context 2076. Both scored and combed wall tile have also been found on the Tramsheds site (Betts forthcoming).

A number of fragments of red and grey coloured Pennant sandstone were found in the make-up layers, together with a slightly finer grained sandstone probably from the same quarry source.

Residual 1st–2nd century tile found in post-Roman contexts

A roller stamped box-flue with die 56 (Period 5 context 972) was probably brought in from the demolished building, as postulated for other roller stamped tile found in the make-up layers (Period 3.1) for Building D. The small number of wall tiles found in Period 4 and 5 contexts may have derived from the same source and were probably incorporated into later deposits as pits cut through the make-up layers of Building D. The presence of a possible half box-flue tile (fabric 16) in context 905 may be explained in the same way. This was a short-lived type, which were used in Roman Britain in the 1st century but was largely superseded by ordinary box-flue tiles in the Flavian period (Black 1996, 62).

Architectural fragments (Figs 3.18–3.19)
by Peter Davenport

The drawn items are identified by catalogue no. on the figures.

Column capitals

No. 32 (Fig. 3.18) **Capital fragment, approximately a quadrant**, also broken top and bottom. Part of the upper surface survives and has a low flat boss. The plain abacus tops a cavetto/shallow cyma which is bracketed by a double fillet. Each pair is made up of a sharp edged and battered fillet under a more rounded one. Below these is a cyma separated from the column drum by a round fillet and a groove. Lathe turned. Context 996, SF 6162.

Height 245 mm; abacus height 60 mm; mouldings 179 mm; shaft diameter *c* 350 mm.

Broadly similar to the column cap A1 (Blagg 1999, 79) but quite different in detail. It is also from a different size of column. While not the same as capitals from any other site in Aquae Sulis, it does share the usual bipartite grouping of mouldings seen on them.

No. 2 (not illus.) **Upper part of a capital**, small fragment. Part of the top survives as a flat surface. It is well-finished, almost certainly lathe turned.

Abacus height 60 mm; mouldings 33 mm survive; shaft diameter 300–400 mm (the piece is too small and fragmentary to be sure for this dimension to be sure) Context 2304.

The abacus is of the same size as No. 32 (SF 6162) above and the fillets are also identical. The drum size is a very broad estimate and this may well be a fragment of the same capital.

No. 8 (not illus.) **Upper part of a lathe turned capital** rather similar in design and size to No. 32 (SF 6162). The abacus edge is broken off but the upper surface is still recognizable.

Height 165 mm; abacus height *c* 50 mm; mouldings 115 mm survive. Context 2304.

The differences from No. 32 are extremely slight in the areas that survive and would result from the lathe turning process being controlled by an approximate rather than a particularly nice template. This is presumably a part of or more likely a companion to capital No. 32.

No. 18 (not illus.) **Part of a column cap at the junction with the column shaft**. A different moulding profile to the other fragments, broken off in all directions. A simple fillet is separated from the shaft by a thin groove and similarly from the cyma above it. From here on the moulding is missing. Context 996.

These turned capitals, typical of the buildings from Aquae Sulis, are essentially in a Roman Doric tradition and are therefore likely to cap proportionately shorter columns than the Corinthian columns of the Temple of Sulis Minerva. However, we should not expect Vitruvian or Palladian proportions to have been followed particularly closely.

Column bases

No. 1 — (Fig. 3.19) **Attic base with a length of drum attached**. Bottom torus is mostly missing. The full height of the block still survives but only as a sector of about 74 degrees.
Height 500 mm; base 250 mm; shaft diameter 500 mm
Context 2312.
This base is well made and presumably lathe turned. By size it belongs to the same group as Nos 3, 7 and 22, larger than that represented by A13 (Blagg 1999, 80) and is slightly different from them both in profile, notably in that the lower torus projects beyond the upper.

No. 30 — (not illus) **Upper torus and cavetto of an attic base**, fragment. The profile of this piece matches No. 1 rather than the other pieces, strengthening the case that there are two larger column types represented here (three with A13 from Blagg 1999, 80).
Context 2312.

Nos 3, 7, 22 — (Fig. 3.19) **Column bases**. Four fragments from three different bases.
One of the profiles is taken from two fragments making up a nearly complete base. The diameter is therefore directly measurable. They are close enough in size and design to certainly come from the same building, but vary enough to be clearly not the same column. These are lathe turned but on the basis of the variation were judged by eye and not cut to a template. No 3 has a medial groove in the lower torus cf No. 29, the others not surviving in this area.
Base height 260 mm (best preserved); shaft diameter 500 mm
Context 2312.

No. 28 — (not illus) **Attic base of a column**, detached flake, giving an almost complete profile. It is similar in profile and size to the bases described above.
Base height *c* 260 mm; shaft diameter *c* 500 mm
Context 2312.

No. 29 — (not illus) **Torus and fragment of filleted cavetto above**, chip. The torus has a medial groove. This appears to be the bottom torus and part of the intermediate cavetto of an attic base. Compare No. 3 above.
Context 2312.

No. 31 — (not illus) **Lower torus of an attic base**, fragment, no medial groove, but matches dimensions and proportions of the others described above.
Context 2312.

Attic bases are used almost to the exclusion of other styles in Bath and examples are known from the Baths and Temple as well as sites in Walcot Street. In Bath the two tori are usually separated, as here, by a filleted groove (eg from the King's Bath, Cunliffe and Davenport 1985, fig. 44). Two further fillets either side of the cyma separate it from torus and the shaft. The examples from the Spa site are not all from the same size of column. Fragment A13 (Blagg 1999, 80) for example is 305 mm in diameter at the shaft base. The three fragments here are about 500 mm at the base and from the evidence of the best preserved, have a medial groove in the lower torus. Attic bases are, in strict Vitruvian terms, meant to go with Ionic or Corinthian columns but in provincial Roman contexts are as often paired with Doric/Tuscan style capitals.

Column fragments

Nos 5, 6, 10–12, 14–15, 19–21 — (Fig. 3.18) **Column drums**, ten fragments. In size they seem to fall into two groups. Nos 10–12, 14, 15, 20 and 21 have diameters between 166 to 234 mm. The fragments are small, only in one case more than a quadrant, so the dimensions are imprecise. Nonetheless they are distinct from the other three pieces which are from a large column or columns with diameters ranging from 350 to 500 mm. In addition these smaller drums seem, where enough survives to be measured, to be a standardized height of 430 mm or very close to 1.5 Roman feet.
Context 2304.

Nos 31–33 — (not illus) **Column**, three fragments. Two are broken on all faces except the column face and one of these (33) has a combed or scored face. The third has part of the joint face surviving on one end (32). The diameters seem to be in the larger range.
Context 2312.
The largest of the smaller column pieces has a rectangular dowel

hole in the base, which could allow it to be the base of the column, or a joint in a column. As it is the largest diameter of these pieces, it is perhaps a base drum. The varying sizes would allow the reconstruction of a column about 2.34 metres high (or about 8 Roman feet) with a visually more than acceptable *entasis* or at least a reduction in diameter (Fig. 3.19). The multiple of 10 diameters is high but not inappropriate for smaller columns. Alternatively, 5 drums at 1.5 Roman feet would give a height of 7.5 feet (just over nine base diameters). Such columns would serve for a peristyle, a *compluvium* court or a porch.

The larger fragments could similarly be part of a column tapering from one dimension to the other and a shaft height of about 3.5 metres (12 Roman feet or 7.1 base diameters) would accommodate these fragments. Such columns are from a high status building. The attic bases Nos 3, 7, 23 and the cap SF6162 would suit this column and indeed probably come from it. An odd feature is the scoring or grooving on the shafts of both these sizes of column. It is made by roughly vertical, parallel but irregular, relatively fine and shallow scoring in short lengths. As far as can be seen, it is confined to the middle parts of the column shaft, not occurring on any of the largest diameter, or base fragments, nor near the capitals. It does not look decorative, but it is equally hard to see it as keying for plaster. It seems most likely, however, that the effect is meant to be a kind of rustication, which was popular in Rome in the first century. One fragment has a red staining or colouring (different from the iron staining apparent on many of these fragments from the conditions of burial) in a patch about 300 mm across and the scoring appears to be scratched through this. This strongly suggests that the scoring is secondary, and that the columns were originally coloured.

No. 16 (Fig. 3.18) **Column drum fragment**, less than a quadrant a with a band of moulding near its top end. The lower end of the fragment is vertically scored. The top end is broken off, but a joining face survives as the base. The moulding is a torus above a rounded fillet with a flat narrow fascia separating it from a small cyma kicking into the shaft. The moulding is very sharp and has tiny fillets either side of the lowest torus. Lathe turned.

Height 308 mm; height of moulding 72 mm; diameter 283 mm
Context 996, SF 6163.

The moulding and the entasis of the column show that it is a fragment from just below the capital. It is of the same size range as capital A1 and base A13 (Blagg 1999) rather than the other bases and capitals from these contexts. Similar below-capital moulding bands are known from the baths and are typical for Doric/Tuscan columns, but there are none with the same moulding pattern (Cunliffe 1969, pl. LXXV). The shaft has scoring like that on the column fragments above to within 150 mm of the moulding.

No. 17 (Fig. 3.18) **Column drum fragment with an integral bracket**. The bracket has a large, single cyma reversa on the underside, like a scrolled corbel, with recessed side facets. The upper surface is plain and slopes slightly to throw off water. The sides of the drum are scored. The upper joint of the drum survives, but the lower face and rear are broken off.

Height 243 mm; shaft diameter 420 mm; projection of bracket 235 mm.
Context 996, SF 6159.

The bracket would fit the larger column we have reconstructed from the fragments and would be in the upper half of the shaft. This kind of bracket is common on columns fronting on to a street or a public space, often used to display statues, trophies or support lamps or torches. The small size of the bracket would only allow a small statue of a person, about half size, as would the head room implied by its likely position on the column. The weathering slope makes it unlikely that the bracket was meant to support a beam to a lower, adjoining colonnade.

Attached half columns

No. 4

(not illus). **Attached, half round column**, section of. One half of the block survives in plan and the upper portion has been broken off. The flat part of the block to which the half column is attached is finely finished and returns on the surviving side.

Height 180 mm; column diameter 360 mm; distance from recess edge 120 mm; depth of recess 63 mm Context 2312.

The finished return face suggests either a pilaster or raised panel backing the column. It may more probably represent an opening or recess flanked by the half column. A slight return suggests either a blind recess or a rebated or ordered opening. The column diameter implies a shaft height of 2.5–3 metres, which is a more than domestic scale for an opening, flanked by columns. A door seems more likely than a whole façade with windows or recesses between a range of half columns. Another possibility is that the block represents a respond to a column or pier with attached column across a corridor or portico.

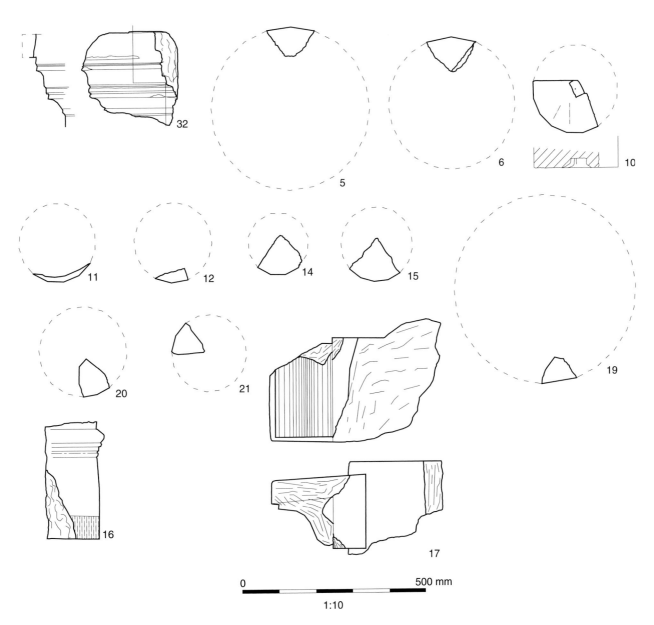

Figure 3.18 Architectural fragments: capital fragment (32), column fragments (5–6, 10–12, 14–15, 19–21), column drum fragment (16), column drum fragment with an integral bracket (17).

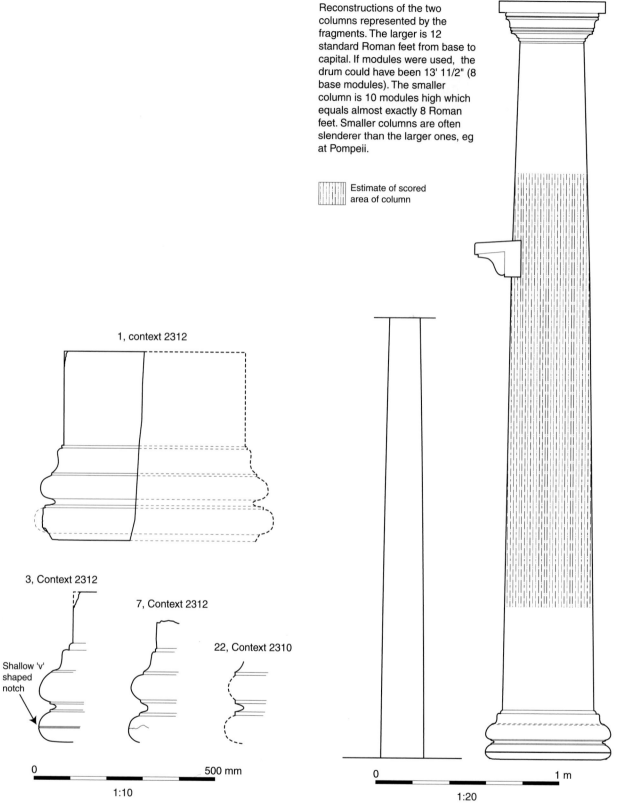

Reconstructions of the two columns represented by the fragments. The larger is 12 standard Roman feet from base to capital. If modules were used, the drum could have been 13' 11/2" (8 base modules). The smaller column is 10 modules high which equals almost exactly 8 Roman feet. Smaller columns are often slenderer than the larger ones, eg at Pompeii.

Estimate of scored area of column

1, context 2312

3, Context 2312

7, Context 2312

22, Context 2310

Shallow 'v' shaped notch

0   500 mm

1:10

0   1 m

1:20

Figure 3.19   Architectural fragments: Column base profiles and column reconstructions.

No. 24   (not illus) **Attached, half round column**. Similar to No. 4 but the return face at right angles to the face with the attached half col- umn is complete and 500 mm long; 280 mm of the rear face also survives and suggests that this was part of a freestanding pier

with an attached column. It had been split in half and was used in the footings of Building D.
Context 2312.

No. 25   (not illus) **Attached, half round column** fragment very similar to Nos 4 and 24 with minor dimensional differences. The column diameter was less, suggesting the block was from higher up the wall.
Context 2312.

These three blocks suggest a building with a row of piers with attached columns. No. 4 may be a pier with a return or a blocked arch with a recess or opening in it. This is most likely to have supported arches, and thus an "arcade". Whether the arches sprang from the level of the capitals of the attached half columns or, as at the Colosseum, were included under the architrave is unknown. However, the latter arrangement would have an arch key stone at about 3 metres with the spring at about 2 metres, a scale, but not design, similar to that in the corridor south of the Circular Bath in the Roman Baths, of approximately the same date.

Other fragments

Nos 26 and 27   (not illus) **Blocks**. These two blocks were not kept but are described in the site records as "springers". They were wedge shaped and were 300 mm by 260 mm × 130 mm. The angle was not recorded nor is it known which edges were measured, so the radius of the arch to which they presumably belonged cannot now be estimated. If the larger measurements are the plan size and the smallest the maximum height, the stones might have been suitable for an arch like that posited above.
Context 996.

No. 13   (not illus). **Part of a small cornice**, a simple cyma with a quadrant at top and bottom. The block is complete in profile but has been broken across its length. The upper surface slopes slightly. It is very worn and it is not clear if the quadrants were originally more angular fillets.
Height 91 mm; width 157 mm; projection from wall face 93 mm
Context 958.
The slope on the top surface of the block and the resultant angles of the bedding faces make it clear that this is a cornice and not a wall base or jamb moulding. The small size implies a string course rather than a full cornice. The wear does, however, seem to demand that the block had been used secondarily somewhere before being discarded. It was found in a medieval rubbish pit so could have come from either Building D or the unlocated earlier building.

Discussion

A question arises as to how these lathe turned bases and capital were actually made. Even a colonnette in Bath stone weighs about 100 kilos and spinning a roughly shaped block at even a low speed requires the control of some fairly fierce forces. The larger blocks here could have weighed more than double or treble that in complete form. We must envisage some very heavily built and large lathes turned by animal/slave or perhaps water power. A reciprocating or pole lathe would not have been adequate due to the great inertia of such a rotating block. Blagg addresses these problems and points to a reference in Pliny which can only refer to the turning on the lathe of huge columns from the Temple of Hera on Lemnos (Blagg 2002, 13–15). Vitruvius also makes it clear that columns were shaped out in the quarry (Book X). It is usually assumed that the Romans quarried stone on Combe Down. A Saxon charter covering this area dated 970 has one of its boundaries as Quarry Field. This almost certainly refers to a Roman quarry and there are old workings here (Whitaker 2000).

Economic Plant Remains
by Ruth Pelling

A range of species and species types was present, including both cultivated and wild plants, which may represent food debris. Several fruit species were identified, of which *Vitis vinifera* (grape), *Ficus carica* (fig) and *Olea europaea* (olive) are Mediterranean in origin. While grape and fig are common Roman finds, and grape was cultivated in the later part of the Roman period (Brown *et al.* 2001) the find of olive is unusual, especially at this early date. Olive has been found from Roman contexts in London (Willcox 1977) and mid-late 2nd century York (Hall and Kenward 1990), but finds from smaller provincial towns are rare. Given the context and the presence of the other imported fruits, the stone of *Prunus avium* (cherry) may be of the cultivated variety, regarded as a Roman introduction to Britain. In addition to the Mediterranean fruits, fruit and nuts of British species are also present and may have derived from food debris. This is particularly so of *Corylus avellana* (hazel nut) represented by broken fragments of nut shell suggesting the extraction of the nut. *Fragaria vesca* (wild strawberry) and *Rubus fruticosus* (blackberry) may have been deliberately collected and consumed, although they could have been growing in the vicinity. Seeds of these species and of *Ficus carica* are commonly found in sewage deposits, for example from the military latrine at the Roman fort of Bearsden, Scotland (Dickson and Dickson 2000, 251). However in view of the association of this material with fine table wares the seeds are perhaps more likely to have derived from discarded food.

Two possible condiments are represented. *Linum usitatissimum* (flax) has been cultivated in Britain since the Neolithic and is used for oil, as flavouring or for fibre. The presence of seeds suggests its culinary use in this instance rather than its cultivation for fibre. *Coriandrum sativum* (coriander) is another Roman introduction, originally of Mediterranean or Near Eastern origin. *Coriandrum sativum* was probably initially imported as seed for consumption by the Roman army, although it may have been locally cultivated by the end of the 1st century AD. It has been found in other early Roman sites including Colchester from a shop burnt during the Boudiccan revolt in AD 61 (Murphy 1984), Bearsden (Dickson and Dickson 2000, 243) and more recently from the Roman military site of Alchester in Oxfordshire (Robinson 2000). While these Roman introductions were all common by the later Roman period as the diet of the Romano-British population became more Romanised, even on quite low status settlements, evidence for such a level of Romanisation in the earlier Roman period would be consistent with a military presence and the import of foodstuffs.

Mammal and Bird Bone
by Lorrain Higbee

The analysis of the bone is based on material from Period 3.1–3.2 and has disregarded the very small quantities of bone from Periods 1, 2 and 3.3. At the time of analysis it was not clear that a more logical grouping of bone would have been Periods 1–3.1, representing bone relating to the period prior to the construction of Building D. The quantity of bone from Period 3.2 is very small and unlikely to have had any significant impact on the final interpretation of the bone assemblage. Approximately three quarters of the bone assemblage was recovered from the culvert trench F1280. As with other finds the bone from Period 3.1 relates to an earlier demolished building that was in use during Period 2 and not to the use of Building D, in the foundations of which it was incorporated.

The animal bone that can be assigned to primary Period 2 contexts of the 1st and early 2nd centuries AD is very small in quantity. The bone found in the palaeosol (assigned to Period 1) is taken to be Roman in date in view of the fact the soil continued as the early Roman ground surface and the lack of evidence for prehistoric activity on the site. The bones are from the core domestic species, cattle, sheep/goat,

Table 3.8   The mammal and bird bone from Periods 1–3. The number of specimens identified to species (or NISP) by period for the Roman assemblage. Figures in parenthesis are 'non-countable' bones after Davis (1992).

	Period				
Taxon	1	2	3.1	3.2	3.3
Cattle	1	4	48 (5)	5	
Sheep/Goat	5	5	145 (13)	4	
Sheep	1	1	13 (2)	2	
Pig	3	10	96 (13)	14	3
Horse			3 (1)		
Dog	(1)		2		
Red deer			2		
Hare			7 (1)	1	
Chicken	2	3	91 (1)	2	2
Chicken/Pheasant			3		
Pheasant			1		
Duck			1		
Goose				1	
Pigeon c.f. wood/rock pigeon			2		1
Corvid c.f. crow/raven			2	1	
Cattle/Horse sized	(1)		(24)	(2)	
Sheep/pig sized			(11)	(1)	(1)
Total	12	23	416	30	6

pig, chicken and dog found in the later phases and quantities are summarised in Table 3.8.

Occurrence and relative importance of species

A complete list of the species identified from all periods is given in Botanical section of the archive report. In common with most archaeologically recovered animal bone assemblages from Britain the majority of identified fragments from Bath Spa belong to the three main livestock species. Cattle, sheep and pig together account for *c* 74% of the total number of specimens identified to species (or NISP) in the Roman period. A number of other mammalian species have also been identified; together they account for only *c* 3% of the total NISP and include horse, dog, red deer, hare. Bird bones are more common, accounting for *c* 23% of the total NISP although this is largely due to the large number of chicken bones which alone account for 21% of NISP. Less common bird species include pheasant, duck, goose, pigeon and crow/raven. Most but not all of these less common species probably represent food items whilst the presence of corvids is not considered to be related to anthropogenic action.

Looking more specifically at the relative importance of the three main livestock species by NISP and minimum number of individuals (or MNI), sheep is the most abundant species accounting for *c* 50% of NISP and 57% of MNI in the Roman assemblage. Pig is the second most abundant species accounting for *c* 34% NISP and *c* 28% MNI, whilst cattle accounts for only *c* 16% NISP and *c* 14% MNI.

The importance of cattle in the Romano-British economy and diet is well known (King 1978; 1984; 1999; Grant 1989) thus the Bath Spa assemblage, with its high frequency of sheep from the Roman period, is a little unusual. This aberration from the expected is even more surprising when comparison is made to other Roman assemblages from Bath. At the Hat and Feather Yard, Walcot Street (Higbee n.d.1) the proportion of cattle shows a sharp increase over time from 40% NISP in the Flavian periods (2–4) to nearly 70% NISP in the late Roman periods (7/8) and MNI frequencies show a similar trend. Cattle are also the most common species by NISP in the Tramsheds, Beehive Yard (Higbee n.d.2) and Nelson Place (Lovett n.d.) assemblages. King (1978) suggests that the dietary preference for beef was imported to Britain by central European legions of the Roman army, thus military sites, which are likely to be more Romanised, would have higher proportions of cattle and to a lesser extent pig than say rural civilian sites which are more likely to continue the native Iron Age tradition, that is a dietary preference for mutton. Urban settlements, such as Bath, would therefore be intermediate between the two. The basic sequence of site types with increasing proportions of cattle and pig suggested by King (1999, 180), is as follows: rural settlements, villas, secondary urban centres, urban sites, legionary sites. With the exception of its high frequency of pig, the Bath Spa assemblage does not conform to King's suggested pattern for an urban settlement which we know from other evidence to have been highly Romanised. However, it is possible that a combination of factors have skewed the results, such factors might include the location of the excavation area within the urban centre, differential disposal patterns between feature types (since 76% of the mid-late Roman assemblage was recovered from the various fills of the Period 3.1 culvert trench F1280), and small sample size. Of these factors the last two are considered to be the most significant.

Sheep

Body part distribution

Most parts of the mutton carcass are represented, notable exceptions being the total absence of skulls and horn cores. The most common skeletal elements in the Roman period are pelvises, mandibles and first/second molars (or m1/m2's). The pelvis is considered of high meat value and as such represents domestic waste; other common elements of high meat value are the humerus, radius and tibia. Mandibles and loose teeth on the other hand are considered primary butchery waste, and it is surprising that other waste elements, such as those from the limb extremities (eg carpals, tarsals, metapodia and phalanges) are under-represented. These absences or under-representations cannot be accounted for by recovery methods or preservation, both of which have been shown to be favourable (Higbee, archive

Faunal report). It seems likely therefore that the majority of primary butchery waste was deposited elsewhere, skulls (minus the mandible) and feet were probably left attached to the hide during the process of skinning and taken to a different location for processing. The proximity of industrial and craft activities within urban centres, particularly those using different parts of the same raw material, is likely, and horns and metapodia may have been detached by the tanner to pass on to a horn- or bone-worker. It seems reasonable to conclude that only small quantities of butchery waste were deposited and that the majority of bone waste represented is kitchen/table waste of domestic origin.

Butchery

Butchery marks were recorded on 17% of sheep bones and chop marks made with a cleaver are more common than knife cuts. The quantity of information from this period is insufficient to interpret carcass utilisation patterns.

Ageing

The age information available from epiphyseal fusion of the post-cranial skeleton can be found in the site archive. The data are limited but suggest that a significant number of sheep were culled as lambs or in their second year of life. The mandibular wear stage data (see site archive) confirms the results obtained from epiphyseal fusion. Thirteen percent of mandibles are from lambs aged only 2–6 months, there is an even spread of mandibles from wear stages C–E and these represent lambs aged 6–12 months and young sheep aged between 1–3 years; there are very few older sheep represented. This indicates that a little over a quarter of sheep survived into their second year of life. The kill-off pattern for this period suggests that sheep were primarily managed for the production of lamb and prime mutton.

The kill-off pattern for Roman sheep varies somewhat from the regional and national pattern. On a regional level the kill-off pattern is similar to that recorded from Roman Exeter (Maltby 1979, 45), where a significant proportion of sheep were killed in their first year. It contrasts, however, with the kill-off pattern recorded from Roman Winchester (Maltby 1994, 96), where most sheep selected for slaughter were over three years of age, suggesting that wool production was of some importance.

Pathology

Abnormal attrition was noted on the teeth of two sheep. In both cases inter-dental attrition was recorded between the fourth premolar (or p4) and first molar (or m1), the result of over-crowding and a reflection of genetic characteristics and/or a susceptibility to environmental stress (eg malnutrition).

Biometry

Only one long bone was suitable for withers (or shoulder) height estimates and this gave a withers height of 0.57 m. This compares well with those previously recorded from Roman Bath.

Cattle

Body part distribution

All parts of the beef carcass are represented with the exception of skulls and horn cores. This could be a product of small sample size but the fact that these elements were also absent from the sheep body part distribution for this period suggests that similar factors are at play. Pelvises and third molars are common; long bones of high meat value are also relatively common as are bones from the upper part of the foot (eg metapodials), but all other elements are under-represented. This basic pattern suggests that most meat was procured as dressed joints. In the Roman phase the foot appears to have been detached lower down compared to the medieval assemblage, hence the greater number of metapodials.

Butchery

Butchery marks were common on cattle bones and were recorded on 53% the Roman assemblage. Chop marks are more abundant than cut marks. These were generally observed at major joints and in the mid-shaft region of long bones, and relate to dismemberment and reduction of the carcass. One scapula bore the characteristic marks of having been cured. These marks include trimming around the glenoid, removal of the processes coracoideus and spina, and nick marks along the margo thoracalis. Differences in the combination of butchery marks on Roman scapulae have been used to suggest that different curing process were employed (Dobney *et al* 1996, 27). For example, scapulae with trimmed glenoid cavities and spinae are thought to represent cold-smoked (ie brined) joints, whilst scapulae with little or no evidence for trimming of these areas are thought to represent hot-smoked joints. The Bath Spa example would therefore represent a cold-smoked joint; this process preserves the meat for longer than hot-smoking. A large collection of scapulae bearing this type of evidence have recently been recorded from Roman phases at the Hat and Feather Yard (Higbee n.d.1) where it was suggested that the waste may have come from a single shop or vendor. This type of butchery has been noted at a wide variety of Roman sites up and down the country (Maltby 1985; 1989) as well as on the continent (Lauwerier 1988), many of which have a military connection. However, the presence of processed scapulae in non-military contexts suggests that standard military butchery practises were taken up by professional butchers serving the domestic market (Grant 1987; Maltby 1989).

Ageing

Epiphyseal fusion data for the mid-late Roman period is limited but suggests that the majority of cattle were culled at the optimum age for prime beef.

Pathology

One pathological specimen was recorded: a small area of eburnation (or surface polish) was noted on the acetabulum (hip joint) of a pelvis. This pathological condition represents joint disease that may have been triggered by trauma or stress to the joint.

Pig

Body part distribution and butchery

All parts of the pork carcass are represented. The most common skeletal elements in the Roman period are mandibles and tibiae, whilst other common elements include the major meat bearing bones from the fore and hind limb. All other body parts are under-represented suggesting that, like mutton and beef, most pork was procured as dressed joints.

Butchery marks were noted on 26% of pig bones. Cut marks are more common than chop marks on Roman pig bone. The higher incidence of cut marks on Roman pig bones reflects two distinct processes: skinning marks are seen on skull and foot bones and cut marks on the posterior lingual surface of mandibles caused by removal of the tongue, presumably for consumption.

Ageing and sexing

Epiphyseal fusion data show that most pigs survived into their first year but a significant proportion was culled early in the second year of life and only a small proportion survived into their third year of life. The information available from tooth eruption and wear is of limited analytical value. Pigs are primarily meat animals and are usually killed at a relatively young age in most societies.

Approximately 88% of the canines/alveoli that were assessed for sexual differences belong to males. Males tend to be aggressive once they reach sexual maturity, so it is not surprising to find high numbers of young males sold to supply the urban meat market.

Other less common mammals

A small range of other mammalian species accounted for only *c* 3% of NISP. Horse, dog, red deer and hare were identified. Of these species hare is the most common and the majority of bones from this species were recovered from the various fills of culvert trench F1280. Butchery marks were noted on a radius and pelvis. The type and location of these marks suggest that they relate to dismemberment. Also of note are the two red deer bones, a metatarsal and radius, both of which were recovered from culvert trench fills. The metatarsal is from an immature animal and the radius bears extensive butchery marks. Chop marks were noted on the lateral proximal part of the shaft just below the articular surface and relate to disarticulation of the joint. Cut marks were noted on the medial distal shaft and much of the shaft was pitted with shallow scoops, evidence that the venison was filleted off the bone.

Birds

Bird bones account for *c* 23% of NISP in the Roman period with most bird bones belonging to chicken.

Domestic birds

Of the domestic bird species, chicken is the most common accounting for *c* 89% of all bird. Similar high frequencies of chicken have been recorded from a number of other Roman sites in Bath. All parts of the chicken carcass are represented suggesting that whole birds were procured, perhaps still in their plumage. It is of course highly likely that chickens were kept by individual households for their eggs and were slaughtered once they become less productive. Unfortunately it was only possible to establish the sex of a few bones. It is clear however, that the majority (93%) of chickens were adult.

Both duck, most probably mallard, and goose account for a very small fraction of the domestic poultry consumed and all of the bones from these two species are from adult birds.

Wild birds

Pheasant, pigeon and crow (or raven) are present. These species have previously been recorded from other sites in Bath. Some, such as pheasant and pigeon, probably represent food items whilst crow is considered incidental finds.

Summary and Conclusions

Analysis of the Bath Spa assemblage has shown that preservation and recovery are good, and that the assemblage is dominated by domestic livestock species. Sheep is the most abundant species, at 50% of NISP and 57% of MNI, followed by pig as the second most abundant species and thirdly cattle. It has been suggested above that the results from the assemblage might be skewed by a combination of differential disposal patterns and small sample size.

The age structure of sheep supplied to 2nd century Bath suggests that there was great demand for lamb and prime mutton; indeed three quarters of the sheep from Bath Spa were less than two years old when selected for slaughter. The kill-off pattern established for cattle and pig indicates that the majority were slaughtered at the optimum age for the production of prime beef and pork. Pigs are primarily meat animals and this is reflected in the

relatively young age at which the majority were slaughtered. Maltby (1994, 89–90) has suggested that Roman towns may have had an organised procurement strategy, particularly with regard to beef, and that this might have resulted in the preferred acquisition of animals of a particular age for the urban meat trade.

Butchery techniques include evidence for the curing of shoulders of beef in the Roman period. Very little primary butchery waste was present, indicating that most meat was procured as dressed joints. This is consistent with the suggestion that professional butchers were operating within the town and fits with some of the butchery evidence noted above.

Not all of the animal based protein consumed within the town was provided by the three main livestock species; chicken formed a significant part of the diet and it would seem that further variety was provided by the occasional bit of venison, hare, duck, goose, pheasant, pigeon, and both marine and freshwater fish (see Humphrey and Jones below).

Fish Bones
by Alice Humphrey and Andrew K. G. Jones

Deposits dated to the Roman period produced low concentrations of fish bones and all were recovered from Period 3.1 contexts (Table 3.9). In view of the fact that all associated ceramic material is dated to 1st-early 2nd centuries AD the fish bone is also regarded as being representative of Period 2, brought in from another site, rather than having any relevance to the construction of Building D in Period 3.1

Few fish remains were recovered from the Roman occupation. The majority of bones recovered were from large fish, although this may be a result of recovery bias as the sample includes only 4 bones recovered by sieving and 12 recovered by hand. The fish represented include two marine fish, bass, *Dicentrarchus labrax*, and a large member of the sea bream family, Sparidae. Freshwater fish are represented by a single large pharyngeal bone of a cyprinid fish, almost certainly a chub, *Leuciscus cephalus* and a single eel, *Anguilla anguilla* vertebra.

Table 3.9 Numbers of fish bones from Period 3.1 contexts.

No. of contexts		9
Leuciscus cephalus (L.)	chub	1
Anguilla anguilla (L.)	eel	1
Dicentrarchus labrax (L.)	sea bass	2
Sparidae	sea bream family	1
Pleuronectidae	flatfish	1
Unidentified		10
Total		**16**
Average number of bones per context		1.5

An unidentified flatfish vertebral spine completes this small assemblage.

Overall this assemblage demonstrates that both inshore marine and river fish were reaching the site in the Roman period. However the general paucity of fish remains, especially when compared to the 11th century assemblage, indicates that fish were not important in the diet and economy of *Aquae Sulis*. It is interesting to note the similarities between the assemblage from Bath and contemporaneous assemblages from York (O'Connor 1988). Here both cyprinid and eel bones were recovered as were flatfish and sparid remains. It was suggested that because sparid fishes are common in the Mediterranean and were often preserved and transported in amphorae throughout the Roman world it is possible that they were imported to York. The sparid bone from Bath Spa may also have arrived in similar fashion, as indeed may the two large bass vertebrae. However, it is important to note that both bass and sea breams are common in the waters of the English Channel.

While fish remains in Roman deposits are rare, there is some evidence for exploitation of the freshwater and migratory fish. There is also the intriguing possibility of the importation of some Mediterranean species.

GENERAL DISCUSSION

Although a variety of features can be assigned to this period, this patch of ground remained undeveloped until the mid 2nd century. The overall characteristic of this area was probably that of a little used plot supporting scattered trees and overgrown with shrubs and weeds along the banks either side of the drainage ditch. Much of the area was damp and boggy. Wood recovered from the culvert trench indicates that a variety of trees and shrubs was growing in the area immediately prior to the redevelopment of the site, in addition to the elm rooted into the side of the ditch. The occasional post holes or small pits may indicate that parts were fenced off or put to some marginal use, perhaps grazing, or formed some kind of garden. Some suggestion of a formal garden layout was found on the northern edge of the excavation. Although early buildings are known to have existed to the north-west at the Citizen House site (Greene 1979) and to the south of this plot of ground (Cunliffe 1969) they appear to have been sufficiently distant to ensure that virtually no occupation debris became incorporated into layers which accumulated at this time. Of the little activity represented, several features appear to relate to the very end of this period, being infilled with the primary make-up layers for Building D, and may relate to preparatory work on site prior to actual commencement of building. The area may have remained undeveloped for such a long period because of the boggy soil conditions, the open ditch being a preliminary attempt at drainage and indicative of the difficulties faced in draining the area.

The activity represented in this period is sparse and sporadic and many of the deposits and features may have been generated only shortly before Period 3.1. Very few artefacts were deposited during Period 2, though the small pottery assemblage does suggest a distinct group of late 1st century material. The lack of imported fine wares typical of sites elsewhere in Bath is not surprising considering the character of this plot; however the large proportion of flagons in this period (with a corresponding decrease in later periods) adds weight to the argument for a military presence in Bath.

Large quantities of building and occupation debris of 1st and early 2nd century date, but deposited during the construction of Building D in the next phase, are thought to derive from a single source, probably a building close to the site.

Early Building
by Peter Davenport

The architectural fragments (Figs 3.18–3.19) described above were all recovered from the footings, wall core and make up layers of Building D, erected around AD 150–160, and were associated with much painted plaster and ceramic building material, both of which were consistent with a mid-late 1st to early 2nd century date (Zienkiewicz, site archive, and Betts, this volume). Associated pottery gave a *terminus post quem* for the deposition of the fragments of the late 1st–2nd centuries AD (Brown above). It seems quite clear then, that they originally belonged to a building of that general date which was demolished and its components broken up and recycled into Building D as hardcore after a comparatively short life. Indeed, the stone fragments had been very carefully smashed up precisely for this purpose. That they did have an existence in an earlier building and were not just spare parts in a mason's or builder's yard is attested by the wear and weathering apparent on the surfaces and the existence alongside them of the plaster and ceramic building material.

Two questions in particular present themselves: what kind of a building was it? and where was it? It might also be asked why it was demolished so soon. The last question is the easiest to address. It is becoming clear that there was a major re-organization of the area around the baths in the mid 2nd century. The vaulting and first extension of the baths seems best fitted into this period (although the evidence is slight), the Temple Precinct outer colonnade or portico was completed at this time (Davenport 1999, 63) and roads were realigned and built over at this time (ibid.). In addition, although it is undated, a building under the Roman Hot Baths recorded by Irvine in 1864 (Cunliffe 1969, 151–154) was replaced by the new baths suite, probably around this period, and the new building contained similar recycled architectural mouldings in its foundations. One of the realigned roads identified (Davenport 1999, 44) seems to run alongside the west side of Building D and may well link up to the gravelled lane recorded by Irvine under the Royal United Hospital (now City of Bath College, Gainsborough Building). This lane seems to belong to the later building phase (Irvine Papers). If this is so then that early building was replaced at this general period. Consequently it seems likely that, wherever the building was that supplied these fragments, it fell victim to an extensive Antonine replanning scheme for the centre of *Aquae Sulis*.

The fragments tell us that the building was large and monumental. It contained much expensive cut ashlar, large columns, which must at this date imply a public building, smaller ones suggesting expensive architectural treatment of doors and/or windows and the possible existence of a peristyle. The ceramic building material indicates that the building was heated, with pilae hypocausts and wall flues. Voussoir box tiles suggest vaulted ceilings in the heated rooms, as do also a few pieces of tufa. The wall plaster, which has a wide range of colours arranged in panels defined by painted lines and filled with flat areas of colour, adds to the impression of a very well appointed building.

It is tempting, though strictly unproven, to associate Building D with the Antonine completion of a scheme, involving the building of at least the western range of the Temple Precinct, and perhaps further work on the main baths, and the construction of the baths uncovered in 1864–7. The latter involved the destruction of what seems to have been a building with at least two wings with corridors, perhaps around a courtyard, extending over an area more than 30 m by 23 m. A block with an attic pilaster base, inverted and embedded in the foundations of the overlying building, was very reminiscent of the reuse of the blocks under consideration (Scarth 1864, 136). No more is known of this building, but it must be a candidate for the source of the stonework described above. The source was not on the Spa excavation site, as there was clearly no masonry building on the site before Building D.

The early date and elaboration of the building represented by the stonework is significant. Its high degree of Romanisation would be surprising at this date were it not for the known existence of the early phase Roman Baths and Temple, and construction at the legionary fortresses at Exeter and Caerleon. These latter are, of course, military and the baths here are often assumed to be military in origin (*pace* Henig 1999). This raises the question of whether such a building is evidence of an administrative military presence at Bath at this time. Finds from the excavations at Hat and Feather Yard, Walcot Street (Beaton forthcoming) suggest the presence of military men and their pay in the mid-late 1st century and some sort of military administration is probably indicated by the inscriptions referring to a *centurio regionarius* (Cunliffe 1969, 199) and from Combe Down referring to a *principia*, some kind of military, or at least official, administrative building (RIB 179). The Combe Down one records the repair "from the ground" of a building which had fallen into this state of disrepair before the early 3rd century.

It can therefore be hypothesized that the building under Irvine's baths was the (or a) military administration headquarters or regional office, built in the mid-to-late 1st century to a suitably high standard, and demolished when the administrative structures became fully civilianized in the middle years of the 2nd century. This change from military administration to civilian could have been the occasion for the comprehensive demolition of a relatively recent, expensive and elaborate building and the erection of new, equally grand structures in the context of a related replanning of the town centre. The fragments of plan suggest a fairly standard building of at least two wings with a corridor, but while this suggests the possibility of a courtyard, *principia*, type of building, little more can be said.

The quality of the building materials has already been noted. Some unusual characteristics have been recorded amongst the artefacts regarded as occupation debris from this building. The collection of pottery deviates in character from the normal Roman domestic assemblage dominated by coarse wares and functional vessels (Brown above). The material from the culvert trench may reflect the specialised function of the building from which it derives. Approximately 65% of the vessels are classified as table wares and over half the fabrics fall at the fine end of the scale. The table ware assemblage was dominated by British products, containing only a small proportion of continental imports. There was a particularly high occurrence of flagons, a feature already noted in relation to the Period 2 pottery and thought to reflect a military presence. In contrast to the material dumped into the culvert trench, the pottery incorporated in the construction levels of Building D is composed largely of utilitarian wares – cooking pots, flat-rimmed bowls and straight-sided dishes in coarse reduced wares with few fine wares present. This difference may reflect the functional aspects of different areas within the demolished building.

The imported fruit and spice remains suggest that the diet was one of an unusual level of Romanisation at this early period, which is in keeping with a military or administrative presence. By contrast the animal bone is atypical as the high proportion of sheep bone might be considered more typical of native dietary preferences and is at variance with other sites, especially those in the Walcot Street area of Bath. Henig has suggested that viewing the bone purely from an economic viewpoint may be misleading and the dominance of sheep may relate to religious practices and that the sacrifice of sheep may be appropriate in the worship of Mercury. A further religious association is indicated by the pipe clay figurines of the draped male figure found in the most recent excavations and a dog from the 1989 excavations. These figurines are always associated with religious or ritual activity.

Chapter 4: Spa Period 3: Middle to Late Roman

OVERVIEW

Period 3 has been subdivided into three phases representing the phase of development during the Antonine period which resulted in the construction of a large masonry building referred to as Building D (Period 3.1) (Fig. 4.1), its subsequent use (Period 3.2) and demise (Period 3.3). Period 3.1 is equivalent to periods 3–5 in the 1989 excavations. The building occupied the site for the latter half of the Roman period and though there has been much destruction of the archaeological deposits in later periods, there is nothing to suggest it was ever replaced by any later Roman buildings. Parts of Building D were first excavated in the 1988 and 1989 excavations in Bath St and Beau St, where separate areas were designated as Buildings D, E and F (Davenport 1999, 42–5). Dating evidence based on the pottery and ceramic building material broadly converge to suggest that construction occurred about AD 150–160 and Period 3.1 is taken to be a short lived phase confined roughly to this decade. The majority of the Roman structures and stratigraphy exposed in the excavation can be assigned to Period 3.1. They form part of a building of at least two wings (a west and south range) arranged around a courtyard to the north-east with streets to the south and west.

When post-excavation analysis of the site began Periods 3.2 and 3.3 were more hypothetical than real, as at that early stage there appeared to be very few contexts that could be attributed to these later phases because of the destruction by 19th-century structures of all of the building above its contemporary ground level. Therefore, no contemporary occupation deposits survived and there was very little evidence for structural changes to the building.

The ceramic dating showed that many of the layers around the exterior of the south-west corner of Building D were of late 2nd- to 3rd-century date, leading to their interpretation as resurfacings of a road skirting the south and west sides of the building and referred to below as the southern road. These account for the bulk of the deposits assigned to Period 3.2 and, though contemporary with the use of Building D, add little to our understanding of its function.

Period 3.3 is characterised by deposits of demolition debris, mainly within the disused hypocausts, which indicate that robbing of the structures, at least within the building, was happening before the accumulation of dark earth deposits over the site in the 5th century or later. Such robbing could have taken place as early as the 4th century, if the building was subject to a major change of function as seen in the buildings excavated on the Bellott's Hospital site

and in the outer Temple Precinct (Cunliffe and Davenport 1985, 184).

GEOARCHAEOLOGY OF THE MID 2ND-CENTURY ROMAN DEPOSITS
by David Jordan

The mid 2nd-century Roman deposits represent a wider range of activities than seen previously, including the recutting and filling of the large early Roman ditch, the laying of new working surfaces and the construction of substantial buildings. The truncation of the whole site by Georgian and later buildings, especially the baths and cellars, and the relatively restricted range of surviving later Roman deposits means that the interpretation of the Roman site in Period 3, by stratigraphy or by geoarchaeology, is similarly restricted. Some geoarchaeological analyses were carried out, nonetheless, and some further conclusions are drawn.

The later Roman strata are generally more granular, coarser, stonier, more calcareous and lighter in colour than those deposited earlier. These differences are due partly to post-deposition decay and partly to the choice of parent material made by the Roman occupants and thus to the nature of the activity that they undertook. The downward percolation of calcareous groundwater and fine matter from the medieval and later deposits above has contaminated the strata with calcium carbonate, organic matter and other precipitates, found deposited on fissure surfaces and, probably (though not visibly) incorporated into the strata.

The fills of the main culvert trench, which on ceramic evidence are of a very restricted date range, are varied but show little evidence of gradual accumulation and differentiation *in situ* once deposited. Rather they appear to have been deposited quite rapidly since they show no evidence of internal sorting or of reworking, though the angle of rest of the stones suggest that the filling took place over days, weeks or months rather than hours. The culvert trench fills represent the redeposition of occupation deposits, which are almost entirely unrepresented elsewhere on the site, in contrast to almost all of the other mid 2nd-century strata, which are surfaces constructed of mortar, cement, terrace gravel and building debris or walls made largely of stone – deposits which record only a small range of activities. Three of the culvert trench fill strata were analysed in detail and found to be mostly quite stony, granular and calcareous with abundant traces of mortar and other building debris. Magnetic susceptibility was moderate (20–35 SI) with one

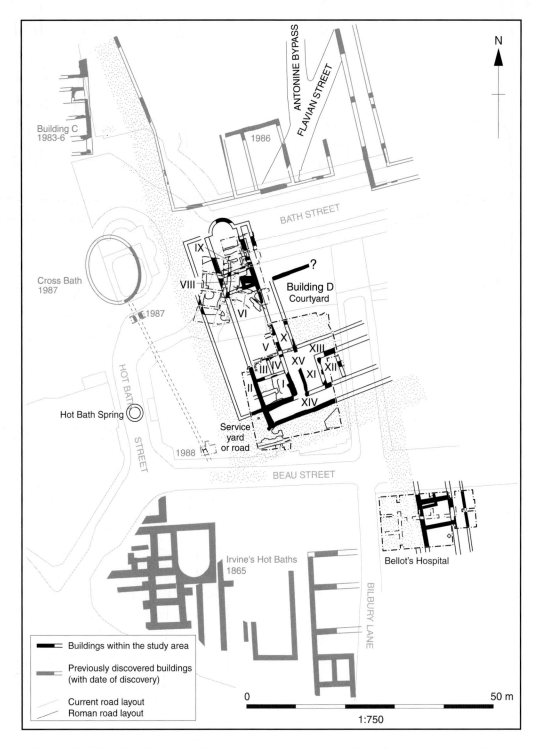

Figure 4.1   Plan of Building D and associated Roman structures and roads in the south-west quadrant of the city.

exception (873) which was much more susceptible (125 SI). However, similar variations of susceptibility were found throughout culvert trench strata, most of the lower susceptibility associated with volumes of building rubble and the high susceptibility with burnt debris and charcoal. Much less frequent were volumes of organic urban soil with moderate or high susceptibilities and with any burnt matter or charcoal finely incorporated into the stratum matrix.

This gave the impression that the burnt debris and charcoal had not had time to become incorporated into a soil before the whole stratum was redeposited in the ditch and thus that activities on the site did not, during the mid 2nd century, include the gradual formation of granular "garden" soils of the kind so common in more recent urban strata. In this context the identification of a possible garden and tree or shrub plantings in Period 2 is interesting, suggesting that the rich, organic soils which would have allowed such a garden to flourish are more likely to have been prepared especially for the purpose rather than being a natural product of urban occupation of the site.

The feature fills and layers reflected many of the characteristics of the culvert trench fills, dominated by building debris and representative much more of construction and demolition than of occupation. Particularly striking is the degree to which these depositional processes and the parent materials involved appear relatively unmixed, suggesting that there had not been a prolonged period of gradual deposit evolution and reuse but, rather, that deposits had simple origins with relatively few steps from parent material to final deposit. Thus the apparent simplicity of the archaeological narrative derived from the excavation is supported by a more detailed analysis of the deposits themselves. There really does appear to have been relatively little going on at this site in the 2nd century and later, other than the construction and demolition of which we have stratigraphic evidence. It may be that the missing layers, removed by the medieval pits and the later buildings, contained abundant occupation evidence but why, if this is the case, is there so little evidence of intensive occupation within the strata which do survive? The presence of two apparently well developed granular soils derived from such debris suggests that there was some occupation nearby but it is interesting that so little evidence survives, other than as domestic ceramics.

STRATIGRAPHIC AND STRUCTURAL EVIDENCE

Period 3.1: Antonine *c* AD 150–160

Construction of Building D (Figures 4.1–4.9)

The 1998–99 excavations revealed part of the plan of a substantial building possibly built around a courtyard. The excavations revealed most of a NNW-SSE orientated range of rooms, flanked on the east and west sides by corridors. This is interpreted as a the west range of a large building. Evidence was also recovered for a south range, flanked north and south by corridors. In the angle between the two wings it is suggested that there lay a courtyard.

It became clear that the footings revealed in the 1989 excavations, and interpreted as three separate buildings (Davenport 1999, fig. I.3, buildings D, E & F), formed, with the 1998–99 discoveries, parts of a single building complex, here called Building D. In the eastern area of the Spa excavations the walls had been heavily damaged by Manners' foundations and could only be traced intermittently. No contemporary floor surfaces survived (Fig. 4.2). The dating evidence of the 1989 excavations suggested that the buildings within the Beau Street baths were dated to the Antonine period. However conflicting evidence

of a 4th-century AD date was recovered in the Bath Street cellars. As the new excavations have shown Buildings D, E and F to be part of a single complex, the date of construction is discussed further below and an attempt made to resolve the conflicting evidence.

The Period 2 drainage ditch [2355] was recut as a preliminary to construction work on Building D. The recut formed a deep and steep-sided trench [200, 808 = 1280], probably greater in depth than the original open ditch [2355] (Figs 3-2–3.3). A stone-lined culvert [2349] was constructed in a narrow trench [2350] cut into the base of 1280 to carry the flow of water below the proposed building (Fig. 4.3). The culvert [2349] was constructed of rectangular tabular limestone blocks laid on edge along the sides in two courses, capped with similar tabular blocks, frequently forming a double capping layer (Fig. 4.4). One block had a hole cut through it, possibly to allow groundwater to drain into the culvert, but more likely indicating re-use. The culvert was below the level of the natural gravel aquifer, so it will have drained groundwater from the local water table, as well as water from a source to the north-east from which it originates. It appears to run from the area of the King's Bath spring, but the silty clay (2356), which had accumulated within it, was not typical of spring water sediments and had the appearance of eroded Lias clay. It is difficult to judge the length of time this culvert was actively in use and accumulating sediment, as it produced only a single sherd of Roman pottery (which could not be more closely dated) and a few bones. The silt (2356) within the culvert was sampled for environmental evidence, which is reported by Pelling, below. The impression in excavation was that the organic remains were of the sort one might expect in a storm water drain, with small twigs, nut shells and pieces of stem, and this is borne out to some extent by the analysis. The culvert may have been designed to take run off from the Temple Precinct area or surplus cold water from the baths.

The culvert was sealed with Lias clay (2320, 2347). Gravel layers (2317, 2321–2, 2327, 2329, 2344) were spread over this to form a firm base for the foundations of walls constructed across the trench. Several short gullies, each about 1–2 m long, were dug apparently to drain run-off from the building site, rather than having any structural function, during this preliminary construction phase. Three [880, 1211, 1374] were set along the north lip of the ditch approximately at right angles to it at intervals of 2–3 m and one [2363] was observed on the south side (Fig. 3.1). Only gully 880 produced a few pieces of pottery of 2nd-century date, clay tile, bone and oyster shell. Two gullies [1374, 2363] were filled entirely with dumped layers relating to later construction work. It is clear that 880 was not only infilled at this time, but also had in fact been cut through some of the preliminary make-up layers (852, 881–2) for the floor of Room I of Building D, thus firmly placing this in the construction phase

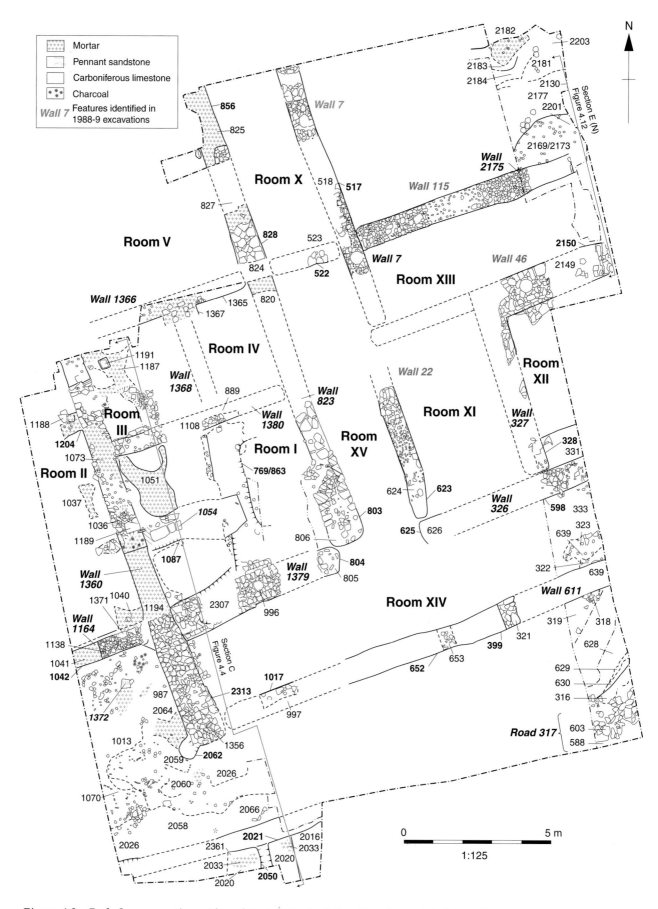

Figure 4.2   Bath Spa excavations: Plan of Period 3.1: Building D and associated deposits.

Figure 4.3   Bath Spa excavations: Stone culvert 2349 in trench 2350 cut into the bottom of trench 1280.

rather than prior to it. By extension the other gullies, which could otherwise have been of Period 2 or 3.1, can be assigned to this phase. A severely truncated feature [255] found on the south lip of the ditch in the 1989 excavations and described as a water channel is likely to have been another of these drainage gullies. An elm tree growing in the side of the earlier ditch must have been cut down at some point during these preliminary activities.

A high density of artefacts and occupation debris was recovered from the contexts within the culvert trench, and this has been discussed above in relation to the Period 2 demolished building. Waterlogged wood was frequent (Fig. 4.5), especially in layer 2327, and Gale's analysis shows this to be a mixture of wood derived from trees or shrubs growing on the site immediately prior to the new development and waste timber relating to construction activities. (The report on the wood can be found in the site archive.) The analysis of the Samian ware shows that material from the construction phase of Building D ranges

from early Neronian or Flavian through to early Antonine in date. There is very little that need post date AD 150 and Building D is likely to have been constructed around, or shortly after, AD 160. This dating is supported by the analysis of the other pottery, which all dates consistently to the late 1st-2nd centuries AD (Brown Above Chapter 3) and also the clay tile (Betts below).

Some evidence for recutting of the culvert trench was found in the 1989 excavations. (Davenport 1999, 23). There, the pre-culvert ditch was not recognised and the culvert trench was seen to have been recut at least once and probably twice. Nothing of this kind was found in the 1999 excavation and it is difficult to reconcile the different sets of evidence, only a few metres apart. One possibility would be to reject the evidence for recutting and accept that construction and fill in all parts of the trench were contemporary: however, as one of the authors was present during the 1989 excavations and published the 1999 report it is difficult to accept this. The second possibility is to

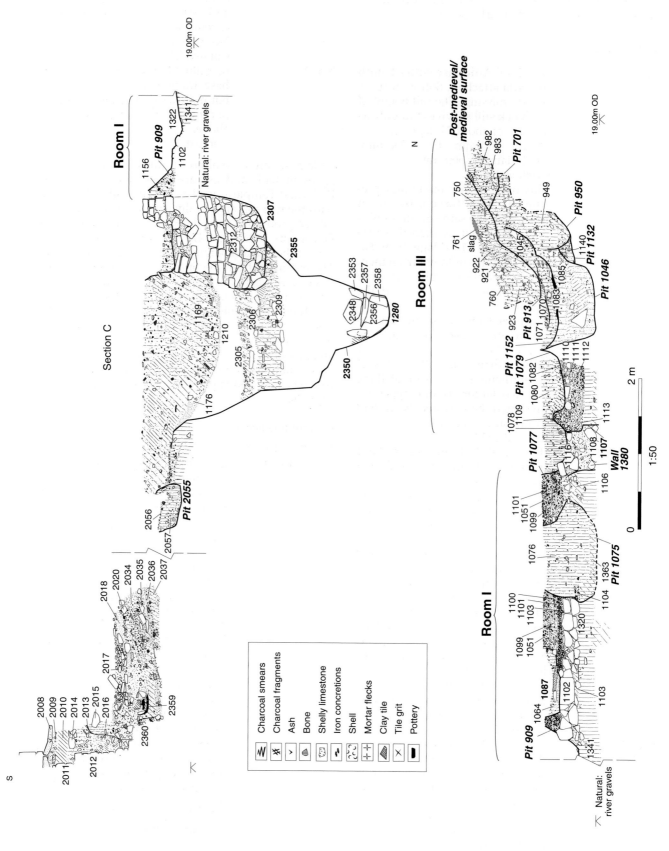

Figure 4.4   Bath Spa excavations: Section C; south–north section through Rooms II and I of the West range of Building D. (See Fig. 4.2 for location.)

Figure 4.5   Bath Spa excavations: Waterlogged timbers in base of culvert trench 1280.

accept the evidence for recutting in this eastern section of ditch and to explain it by assuming a different local history for this part of the ditch. The vital area where the two 'histories' met was obscured by a later wall inserted into the culvert, so this explanation cannot be (and could not have been) tested. All that has to be explained is a localised recutting of the culvert trench in an area separated from the 1998 observations by a wall footing. There appears to be little significant lapse of time, if any, between the infilling of the culvert trench, the filling of the re-cut trench, and the construction of all parts of Building D, all of which appear to be dated around AD 150–160. What we may actually be seeing here are simply changes on a building site during work in progress. Another scenario is that the culvert trench was filled in for ease of access during construction of the west range, but areas were subsequently re-excavated where it was necessary to put in deep foundations for walls of the south range.

In the 1989 report referring to the period 3 deposits, which are broadly contemporary with Period 3.1 here, it was suggested that the area north of the culvert trench 'was planned as a work yard of some sort…Activity over a fairly short time span seems to have been continuous' (Davenport 1999, 29). This interpretation would fit very well with this part of the site being used as the main working, preparation and store area during construction of the building complex. Some of the wood analysed from the culvert trench appears to be waste from wood working activities in the form of chippings from mature timbers of oak, ash, elm and maple and suggests that timber preparation was occurring on site. The carpentry waste generated appears to have been disposed of in a manner typical of the average builder, by being swept into the nearest hole!

In the narrow strip in the north-eastern area (Fig. 4.2), deposits which could relate to a general work yard include a mortar spread (2182) and three successive circular areas of *in situ* burning (2183, 2200, 2201) on the surface of earlier gravel layers,

forming maroon patches between 0.3 and 0.8 m in diameter. Similar features were found in the adjacent 1989 excavations (Davenport 1999, 26). These areas of burning were not formally constructed hearths, but may be explained as nothing more than bonfires, a means of disposing of the small trees and shrubs that were apparently growing on this plot of ground and had to be cleared before construction work started. Some of the wood found in the culvert trench was round wood, which had probably fallen off local trees and shrubs, possibly as the vegetation was cleared for construction. Some of this was probably burnt in a series of bonfires and much of the debris both from the bonfires and unburnt twigs and branches were conveniently swept into the trench. This interpretation is supported by the charcoal samples from the lower layers of the culvert trench examined by Gale (below, see also full report in the site archive) which were dominated by small roundwood suggesting the clearance of scrubby growth prior to building work. The only feature of any size encountered in this north-eastern area was a linear hollow [2191] which was 1.9 m wide by over 4 m in length and extended eastwards from the squared terminal represented by pit 133 in the 1989 excavations (Fig. 3.1). The function of the trench is unclear, but it was clearly contemporary with the construction activity of Building D. It was filled with a series of dumped layers of yellowish brown sandy clay, limestone rubble, river gravels and grit and dark tips of occupation with much charcoal and clay tile (2177, 2181, 2179), which appear to have derived from the same source as debris infilling the culvert trench (Fig. 4.13). It was subsequently completely masked by the make-up layers for what is thought to be the courtyard of Building D.

Once the culvert was completed, sealed with clay and the lower part of the trench lined with gravel, construction of the Building D commenced over the whole area of the development. Evidence was found for two wings of Building D – a West Range aligned NNW to SSE and a South Range aligned ENE to

Figure 4.6   Bath Spa excavations: Footings of wall 1360 (context 2312) of Building D built into top of trench 1280.

SSW. The similarity of construction methods for all the foundations and the distinctive use of broken architectural fragments in the massive foundations [806/226=823, 996/1137/2304=1379, 2312=1360] for all the walls constructed across the culvert trench confirm that almost all the wall foundations in the excavated areas were contemporary, forming a single major complex (Figs. 4.6 – 4.8).

Figure 4.7   Bath Spa excavations: Footings of wall 1360 (context 2312) of Building D incorporating reused architectural fragments.

Figure 4.8   Bath Spa excavations: Wall 1379 (context 996) of Building D built into partly filled culvert trench 1280.

West range

The layout of Building D is most straightforward in the western half of the excavation, where the West range was revealed. The extensive remains of the West Range were exposed running for 20 m within the main excavation (Fig. 4.2) and continuing in the cellars of 7–7a Bath Street for a further 12 m to form a total length of *c* 45 m before joining with the apsidal ended wall originally identified as Building D (Davenport 1999, fig. I.3) (Fig. 4.9). Two large walls [1360; 823] aligned NNW-SSE and set 6 m apart were linked by cross walls [1379, 1380, 1366, 1760, 1663] creating a series of rooms sometimes with further walls [1692, 1368] subdividing the spaces (Figs 4.1 & 4.9).

Wall 1360 extended for some 40 m from the southwest corner of the building to a point in the Bath Street cellars, although only fragments of the west wall (1650 & 1796) were found in the 7–7a Bath Street excavation (Fig. 4.9). More substantial footings were found in the Spa excavation (Fig.4.2).

Wall 823 was traced over a slightly shorter distance. Its remains in the Bath Street excavations (1815, 1667, 1705, 1674, etc) were more substantial than those of the west wall (Fig. 4.9). In the Spa excavations its south end (806), like that of the west wall was built over the filled culvert trench.

The south ends of both NNW-SSE walls [1360 and 823] were constructed over the infilled culvert trench 1280, and had substantial footings (2313=1360 and 806=823) which included a number of large archi-tectural fragments (Fig. 4.7). They were 1.2–1.3 m wide at the base with approximately three roughly

laid courses of limestone blocks, some set on edge, topped with a level course of rectangular blocks on which a narrower foundation *c* 1.1 m wide was constructed of squared rectangular limestone blocks, at least ten courses high before the wall proper commenced. It was in the lowest courses that a variety of broken architectural fragments, including column base, drum, architrave and other mouldings occurred (Fig. 4.5; see Davenport above Chapter 3 and Figs 3.20–3.21). As it was not completely excavated, it has not been possible to verify whether the foundations of wall 46, also built over the culvert trench and exposed in the 1989 excavations, had any architectural fragments built into its foundations, but all other characteristics of its construction and dating evidence are consistent with it being contemporary with the walls of Building D. In addition, the pottery dating this wall was the richest and clearest collection of mid-Antonine ceramics from the site.

Outside the culvert trench the foundations were invariably narrower, *c* 0.75–0.8 m wide and con-structed of carefully laid angular limestone rubble with courses of large blocks pitched on edge, levelled with small stones and separated from the next by a layer of mortar. This basic pattern was observed in all the foundation trenches (this method is very similar to that observed by Irvine in the footings of the bath building revealed in 1864 south of Beau Street; Scarth 1864, 136; Cunliffe 1969, pl. LXXXb). It is likely that much of the stone was reused, based on the presence of occasional burnt stone and a low density of wall plaster and clay tile incorporated in the foundations. In a few cases the uppermost layer of the foundations survived as a layer of harder, cream-white mortar, which apparently formed the bedding layer for the wall proper.

Dateable Roman pottery recovered from the wall foundations comprised types in use from the late 1st century through to the early 3rd century AD, with the emphasis generally on 2nd-century types. The samian ware ranged in date from Flavian to Antonine with the main emphasis on the Hadrianic-early Antonine period.

Following construction of the wall foundations, the culvert trench was filled in with dumps of occupation debris (the artefacts from these have been discussed above in relation to the earlier demolished building). The soil analysis confirms the rapid infill

of the ditch: this may have take place over the course of a few months at most and more likely just a few days. Once the wall foundations constructed over the culvert were completed it would be most convenient to get the trench filled in quickly, but different sections separated by the foundations could have been infilled at different stages and with different materials, accounting for variations along the ditch.

The evidence from within the building for the heating system. floors, and so forth, is fragmentary and best discussed on a room by room basis. Working from North to South within the West Range the evidence revealed for each room was as follows:

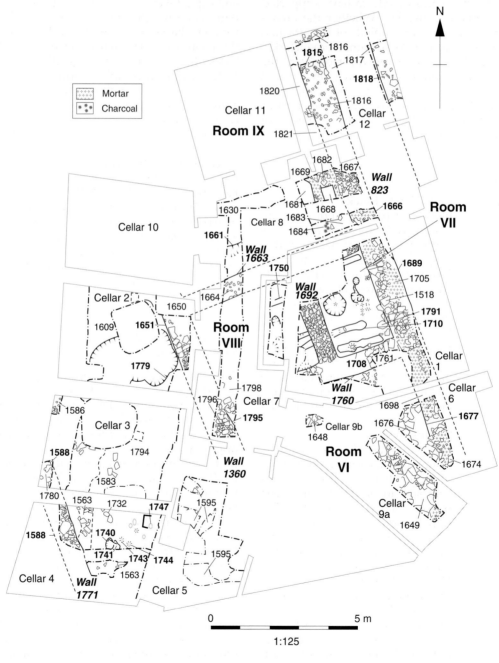

Figure 4.9   Bath Street excavations: Plan of Period 3.1: Building D.

Room IX (Fig 4.9)

The north wall of Building D was explored in a test pit in 1989 (Davenport 1999, fig. I.3). It was interpreted as an apsidal chamber. Excavations in 7–7a Bath Street revealed more of this room. It was defined on the east side by wall 823 and would have been defined on the west side by wall 1796=1360 although the wall fell outside the area of investigation. Within the room traces of two hypocaust chambers (1661 & 1788) were located. On the south side the room was divided from Rooms VIII and VII by wall 1663 (Fig. 4.9). The room measures a little over 6 m east to west internally. North to south it was at least 15 m into the apse.

Rooms VIII and VII (Fig. 4.9)

These two small rooms were defined on the south side by wall 1760 and were divided by the NNW-SSE wall footing 1692. Room VII was the smaller of the two rooms and lay to the east. The garden features assigned to Period 2 (Chapter 3, Fig. 3.6) lay under these rooms. Room VIII measured approximately 3 m x 3.5 m internally; Room VII approximately 3 m x 2 m.

Rooms VI and V (Figs 4.2 & 4.9)

Between Rooms VII and VIII to the north located in the Bath Street excavations and Rooms III and IV located in the Spa excavations, there was a substantial space most of which lay outside the areas of investigation. It is likely that this space, which lies at the centre of the range, was sub-divided (see discussion by Davenport below). To the north the space was divided from rooms VII and VIII by the cross wall 1760. The area adjacent to and south of wall 1760 has been labelled Room VI for convenience.

To the south, the the Spa excavation, the space was divided from Rooms III and IV by cross wall 1366. The area immediately north of wall 1366 is labelled Room V. It fell almost totally outside the area of the Spa excavations (Fig. 4.2). Overall Rooms VI and V measured about 16 m north to south and a little over 6 m east to west internally.

It was noted in Room VI, and also in Room I to the south (see below), that one of the wall foundations (1676) was continuous with the foundation of the floor in the room. A distinct hard layer of cream mortar (1555) was laid across the top of 1676 marking out the line of the wall, which followed the underlying trench precisely, even though the trench edge had been obscured by the rubble foundation layer. This feature was not found throughout the building.

Rooms III and IV (Fig. 4.2)

Rooms III and IV lay between wall 1366 to the north and wall 1380 to the south. The rooms were divided by wall 1368. Within Room III there was evidence for

a probable stokehole [1204] and a tile *pila* (1191) from a hypocaust system. The *pila* was built on the mortar surface 1187, which suggests that the actual floor level was perhaps 0.75m to 1m higher than the mortar surface. An ashlar block [1188] found in Room II outside Room III may have been a facing block associated with the stokehole to Room III. Remnants of the brick lining were preserved along the north edge of the stokehole where it cut through wall 1360. A complete bessalis brick, together with part of a lydion or pedalis brick (Betts below), was used in either the wall or floor of the stoke hole (context 1201) of the hypocaust. Underlying the mortar surface were various layers of limestone rubble and mortar (including context 1110–1112) (Fig. 4.4). No internal features were recovered from Room IV. Both rooms measured about 3.5 m internally north-south, and internally east-west Room III measured 3.5 m, and Room IV about 2 m.

Room I (Fig. 4.2)

The final room in the west wing Room I, was defined by wall 1379 to the south (Fig. 4.10). At their east end the foundation trench of this wall (804) did not connect with the foundations (803) of wall 823, and at the west end the extant wall footing (2307) butted up to the west wall (2313=1360). A feature of wall foundations in this room, and Room VI above, was that where the footing rose above the foundation cut trench, it formed a continuous layer with adjacent floor foundation rubble. Foundation 1036, for wall 1360 was continuous with floor layer 1102.

Within Room I there was evidence for a flue [1087] and a duct (769/863) for a hypocaust system, and for a mortar surface (1051). Underlying the mortar floor were various make up layers of limestone rubble and mortar (including 1099–1101 and 1106) (Fig. 4.4). The linear feature 1087 is the best preserved length of hypocaust flue. It comprised a shallow trench about 0.9 m wide cut across the surface of the foundation make-up (1051) and survived for about 3 m. Its base was lined with roughly shaped rectangular limestone slabs set in mortar, which had all been intensely burnt. It also cut wall 1360 and survived for about 3 m before being truncated by later features. A single large squared limestone block [1189] survived from the basal course of wall 1360 and possibly formed the edge of the hypocaust flue [1087] which cut through the wall. A single rectangular ashlar block [1189] appears to be the lowest course of the facing for the flue where it cut through 1360. The east end of the flue joined hypocaust duct 769/863 at a right angle. The latter features had been completely robbed out. Layer 723 within the robbed feature contained a large quantity of Roman brick and tile, which included *tegulae*, *imbrices*, flue and voussoir (Figs 3.16–3.19). This is similar to the linear feature [60] excavated in BS89 Tr II, which was robbed [23] and backfilled with layers of broken tile, brick, mortar and broken wall plaster. The latter was originally interpreted as a robbed wall

Figure 4.10 Bath Spa excavations: Photograph of floor deposits Room III, Building D, viewed from NNE. In the foreground is pila *base 1191 with wall 1360 (context 1073) to the right, with the remains of the flue from the* praefurnium. *The cuts of medieval pits and other later disturbances are clearly visible.*

trench (Davenport 1999, 18–19), but in view of the recent evidence seems more likely to have been a hypocaust duct. Feature 769/863 appeared to turn at either end to run alongside the north [889=1380] and south walls [996=1379] of the room (Fig. 4.2) and a patch of burning was found on the base of 769 at the north end. The location of flues alongside the walls presumably to conduct hot air up the walls through flue tiles may explain the shallow features noted running alongside some other wall foundations (1661 along the north side of 1663; 1788 alongside wall 1666 [=823] (Fig. 4.9); BS89 Tr I (43)).

The room measured about 6 m east-west, and about 5 m north-south internally.

Room II (Service range or corridor) (Figs 4.2 & 4.9)

In the Spa excavations there was evidence for a corridor or service area on the west side of the west range. A short length of wall footing [1164] aligned WSW-ENE was located on the outside of the range on the same alignment as cross wall 1379. Two small blocks (1371) of oolitic limestone and Pennant sandstone formed facing blocks for the lowest course of wall 1164.

To the north of the wall there was evidence for mortar surfaces (1204, 1037 and 1040) within the proposed corridor (Room II), but no west wall was found. In the Bath Street investigations (Fig. 4.9) the probable west wall [1588] of the corridor was found. The corridor or room was 5.5 m wide internally. It may have served as a service wing since the stokeholes in rooms III and I (contexts 1204 and

1087 respectively) both opened onto this area from the west range.

Rooms X and XV (Fig. 4.2)

On the east of the range was a narrower corridor comprising rooms X and XV. These two areas were defined by two walls – wall 7 to the east of Room X, and further south wall 22=624 (Fig. 4.2). Between areas X and XV there was a short wall 523 which lay between wall 7 and wall 823 and was aligned with walls 115=2175 and 1366. This may have blocked access from area X to area XV, or it may have served simply as a threshold between the two areas. Room X was about 2.5 m wide internally, whereas Room XV was only 2 m.

Walls 7 and 22 were discovered in 1989 and interpreted as parts of two separate buildings E and F (Davenport 1999, fig. I, 34). In 1989 wall 7 was traced to a point just south of its junction with wall 115=2175. On the interpretation offered here walls 7 and 115=2175 formed the corner of a courtyard at the centre of the building and lay in the angle between the West and the South Ranges. It is probable that wall 22 is a later addition to the building (see Davenport below). Its foundations were cut into the fill of trench 1280 from a higher level than those of other walls, and it is slightly out of alignment with wall 7.

South Range

The evidence for the South range was more limited than that for the West range. The north wall was formed by wall 46 and the south wall by wall 326. The internal measurement between these walls was a little over 4 m, which is significantly narrower than the West range.

Room XI

It is possible that a room was defined by wall 22 to the west, wall 326=626 to the south and wall to the east 46=327. There was no evidence for a north wall although truncation by later structures could account for its absence. However, as already noted, the west wall [22] seems to have been of later construction, which suggests that Room XI was a later creation within the south range. It would then have been the westernmost room in the range. No internal features were recovered. The room measured approximately 4 m x 3.5 m internally.

Room XII

To the east of wall 46=327 was a second room (XII) defined on the north by wall 46 and on the south by wall 326. Little of the room was exposed and no internal features were recovered from room XII. The room measured a little over 4 m north to south internally and was at least 4 m wide east to west.

Room XIII (North corridor, South range)

Between the parallel ENE-SSW walls 115=2175 and 46=2149 was a corridor on the north side of the South range. This measured about 2.5 m wide internally. No internal features were found.

Room XIV (South corridor)

To the south of wall 626=326 was a parallel wall 997/653= 623. Its west end appears to align on the south end of wall 1360 of the West range. The corridor is approximately 2.5 m wide between the wall faces. Again no internal features were found.

Dating of Building D

The more easterly of the walls [823] in this range had been exposed in the edge of the 1989 excavation [as 225, 226] and had been assigned an early-mid 2nd-century date. However, Building D was assigned a 4th-century date on the basis of the 1989 excavations under Bath Street. A 2nd-century date for construction for all of Building D is accepted here in view of the relationship of the wall foundations of Building D to the culvert trench [F1280] and the dating evidence from it discussed above. The 4th-century date was assigned on the basis of a single coin, which, in the light of this later evidence, is most easily explained as intrusive. However the possibility that alterations were made in the 4th century, or that the apsidal room is an addition to the north end of the west wing, are other options. The possibility of the wing being extended might allow the garden

features (Chapter 3 above) below rooms VII and VIII, currently assigned to Period 2, to be reassigned to an early phase of Period 3, but this seems unlikely.

The walls identified as buildings E and F in the 1989 excavation, are clearly contemporary and constructed in the same manner. The N-S wall [7] of Building E is now interpreted as the east wall of a corridor running along the east side of the west wing of Building D (Fig. 4.2 and Davenport 1989, fig. I.34). The walls of the South range [46/2149, 327, 326 and 22] produced a small quantity of pottery including samian ware, of late 1st to 2nd-century date, which is consistent with the dating from the earlier excavations, where joining sherds from walls 46 and 115 indicated that they were contemporary (Davenport 1999, 31). All the walls forming Buildings E and F appear to be integral with Building D and continue to the east and north for an unknown distance.

Floor levels and heating within Building D

The very hard flat mortar (1037, 1040) or gravel and mortar (1051, 1187) surfaces within the west range and service range were laid over a series of horizontally laid make-up deposits of limestone rubble and mortar (1050–3, 1099–1103, 1105–7, 1109–14, 1171, 1216, 1220, 1225, 1229–30, 1375) (see Fig. 4.4). Below these and associated with the wall footings were further construction or foundation levels over the culvert trench [1280/888]. The latter comprised dumps of occupation debris (2305–6, 2308–9, 2311, 2315, 2323–8, 2351–2) in a soil matrix with variable quantities of building materials (lumps of mortar, clay tile, Pennant slabs, plaster, opus signinum, tufa) and limestone rubble, and formed a continuum with the overlying layers.

The mortar surfaces do not seem to have been the level on which actual floors were laid. Evidence from Room III indicates that the basal remnants of hypocaust *pilae* [1191] were built off this mortar layer, and this is confirmed by the associated stokehole [F1204] (Fig. 4.11). There is some evidence to suggest that hypocausts were general used within the building: in Room I there was evidence for a stokehole [1087] and hypocaust flues [769/863]; at the north end of the range there is evidence from flues [1661 and 1788] from Room IX (Fig. 4.9). Robber trench 23 in BS89 Tr II (Davenport 1999, 18–19) and the foundation trench [17] with stone lining (16) in BS89 Tr I can be included in this group.

Form and function of Building D
by Peter Davenport

General

The walls, footings, hypocausts and building materials of this building almost all seem to belong to one phase of construction (allowing for minor repairs and maintenance). It is clear, therefore, that these are the remains of a large and ambitious structure of high status, built in one phase for a defined purpose.

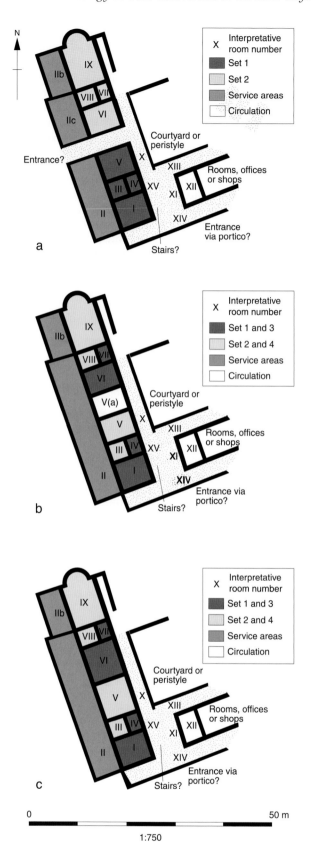

Figure 4.11 Building D: possible reconstructions of plan of West wing and part of South wing, showing possible alternative layouts.

Unfortunately, there is little evidence for its use. Nor is there evidence to suggest that it was later converted other uses, which contrasts with the house at the Bellott's Hospital site which was converted into an iron-working workshop (Lewcun and Davenport, this volume), and with the Antonine house at 132–134, Walcot Street, which had its floors raised and a kiln inserted (Beaton, forthcoming). It is fortunate, nonetheless, that so much of the plan survives or can confidently be assumed. In effect, walls and footings, hypocaust basements and channels and their makeup, external surfaces and make up survive to varying degrees allowing a reasonable level of confidence in their interpretation.

One complication is the presence of much building debris from an earlier building of high status, whose site is unknown but whose materials were used in the footings and makeup of Building D (the possible source for this material is discussed under Period 2 above). Indeed, while this material is extremely informative about the function and status of this earlier building, hardly any of it can be ascribed to Building D. While some breakages from the stock of brick and tile on site from early on might be expected in the footings and makeup, it seems unlikely that much would have been lost this way, and very unlikely that any tiles from heating, vaulting or roofing would have been present at this point to become incorporated in the foundations and lower walls. Even material from the layers post-dating the construction and use of Building D is mostly redeposited from the digging out of the makeup and footings of Building D in the middle ages and, therefore, most probably comes from the earlier, unlocated building. Indeed, some of this material is tentatively datable (Betts, above Chapter 3; Zienkiewicz, report in site archive), and belongs to the late 1st to early 2nd century. One exception to this is the roofing tile of fabrics 1 and 5 (Betts below) found in later deposits. This does not occur in the early levels and seems to date to the 3rd century. The existence of this material means that some of the other associated building material, including a section of cornice (Chapter 3 above, Architectural stone No. 13), in post Roman contexts, could well belong to Building D.

Construction

The building was a substantial masonry structure with carefully laid mortared rubble footings. The survival of a very few blocks above foundation level and the carefully built footings over the ditch, suggest that the wall proper was faced with *petit appareil*, with ashlar detailing. A very high quality wall in this technique, and approximately contemporary, was uncovered in Walcot Street in 1999 (Beaton forthcoming), but is almost ubiquitous in the main Roman Baths, for example. The wall may have incorporated bonding courses of tile, but did not survive high enough to show this. This construction technique is known from the King's Bath (Cunliffe and Davenport 1985, 49) but not elsewhere in Roman Bath, so is perhaps not likely to have been employed here. There is no surviving evidence of extensive use of ashlar masonry, except for the few large blocks associated with the hypocaust flues, one displaced from the wall (1186, 1188–9) (Fig. 4.2).

The footings were cut down into the natural clay and were carefully laid in mortar with flat tabular stone at the base followed by pitched stones and a top levelling mortar bed for the wall proper. This makes an interesting comparison with the footings for the baths recorded by Irvine south of Beau Street. They were described as "laid in clay, in which large pebbles are embedded; upon these a bed of concrete, then a course of tiles, then masonry with joints inclined, somewhat resembling herringbone, upon which stones are laid in regular courses" (Scarth 1864, 136). This may strengthen the case for the two buildings being broadly contemporary. A series of deposits of gravel, mortar and building material was laid within the building footprint to make up the level of the hypocaust floors. This basement level was finished with a good mortar floor. Though fragmentary, its level seems to be constant over the whole of the west range and implies heating in all these rooms, although direct evidence of underfloor heating only occurs in rooms I, III and IX. The discovery of two *pilae* bases and the presence of ducts for channel hypocausts suggest that both construction techniques were employed. The evidence for wall flues, though slight, is persuasive. The southern wing was more poorly preserved, but was essentially similar in structure.

In the north east corner of the site, the make up layers, where they survived truncation by the modern pool, were less hard, of a looser consistency and density, but were otherwise not dissimilar. These are interpreted as the make up for a courtyard area.

The considerable width of the walls, up to 0.75 m, might suggest that an upper floor was envisaged, but instead, it may be that they were necessary to take the thrust of vaulting, which is likely to have existed over some of the heated rooms at least. That the width of the footings is related to structural requirements is supported by the distinct difference in width between the main walls of rooms I-VIII and the "service wing" and corridor or portico footings, which are noticeably narrower. Voussoir box tiles, residual in later contexts, indicate the probable existence of vaults over some at least of these rooms. In this case, an upper floor is still possible but cannot be proved.

The building, or some part of it, seems to have been roofed with *tegulae* and *imbrices*, datable to post AD 160, and repaired or replaced with stone tiles (Betts below). There is next to no evidence of the internal fittings, assuming that the evidence for these which does survive all belongs to the earlier, unlocated, building. However, the wood fragments found in the back fill of the culvert ditch (contemporary with the construction phase) may provide evidence of the use and disposition of timber in the building (see the detailed report by Gale in the site archive). The oak fragments were from large mature trees and presumably reflect the working of structural timbers. These are likely to have been roof timbers as well as elements such as door frames or internal stud walls. The presence of elm might suggest boarding, either for ceilings, panelling or floors in those parts of the building not fitted with underfloor heating. The identification of maple and ash suggests the possibility of the decorative use of timber for doors, built-in cupboards, partitions etc.

Plan (Figs 4.11 & 4.12)

The plan appears to be sophisticated. It is of at least two wings around a courtyard with a corridor or portico along the known sides. The western range or range is symmetrical, over 43 m long and *c*.10.9 m wide without the service range (*c*.16.5 m wide including this range). The southern range is at least 17 m long (but could be considerably more) and is *c*.13.9 m wide. The main rooms are very nearly the same width in each wing. It is a large building on any measure. Evidence for a Roman street is available for both the west and south sides of the building, suggesting that it sat on a street corner or junction.

The western wing is reminiscent of the triclinium range of a large villa with a central room, or rooms (V/VI) symmetrically flanked by smaller rooms (I, III and IV to the south and VII, VIII and IX to the north) and probably opening onto the courtyard via a corridor. The smaller rooms all seem to have been heated and the position of the flues into rooms I, III and probably IX strongly suggest a service wing or range, room II, against the west side of the main range. The existence of a road immediately west of the building would allow the easy delivery of materials to this range.

Room IX has an apsidal north end and is clearly the end of the range. Room I is at the junction of the west and south ranges. These two rooms seem to make sets with the two small rooms adjacent to them (III/IV and VII/VIII respectively). The central room V/VI is very long and may have been subdivided: symmetry would suggest that it was divided into three. If this were the case, then it is possible that Room VI belonged to the north set of rooms (IX/VII/VII) and Room V to the south set, and that there was an entrance passage between the two sets (Fig. 4.11 a).

There are alternative reconstructions. There may have been three rooms of similar size in the centre of the range, namely VI, VIa and V (Fig. 4.11 b). Or, it may be that Rooms V and VI were not separated by lobby (Fig. 4.11 c), and that there were four sets each comprising one large room and one small room: for example Rooms IX and VII, VII and VI, V and II, etc. Again we could then see the range as divided up into four sets of rooms each consisting of one large and one small room, interlocking on plan, either side of the central room. Whatever the actual layout, the range was fronted by and probably linked to a corridor (X), which also served the courtyard as a portico.

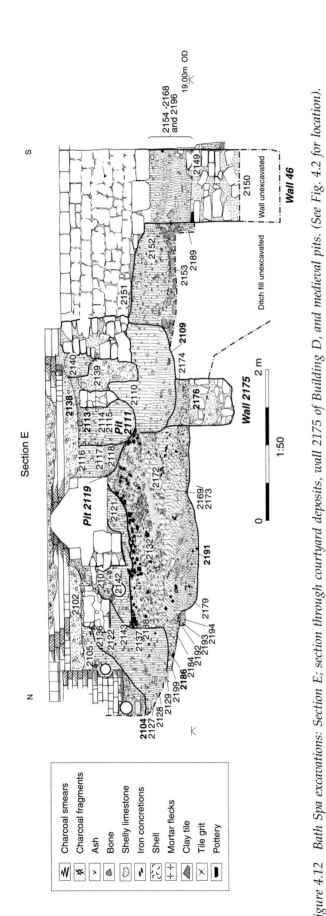

Figure 4.12 Bath Spa excavations: Section E; section through courtyard deposits, wall 2175 of Building D, and medieval pits. (See Fig. 4.2 for location).

The southern range has a corridor on each side. The northern corridor (XIII) is presumably integral with corridor X and together they seem likely to have run around the courtyard postulated in the angle of the two ranges. A small section of wall footing [] suggests that corridor X was blocked off at its southern end. However, when, and indeed if, is uncertain, as the blocking wall was represented by a small piece of mortared rubble, truncated on all sides, which may not have been a wall at all. The southern corridor (XIV) probably fronted on to the street and could have been treated as a covered loggia or walkway. There is only slight evidence of the internal plan of the wing, but it might have been divided into a row of rectangular rooms, if XII is typical. Room XI/XV seems best interpreted as a sort of lobby providing access from corridor XIV and the street to the inner courtyard and corridors/porticoes. The wall [22] subdividing them is difficult to interpret, but appears to have been a later subdivision, as its foundations were cut from a higher level. Furthermore the foundation trench which cut into the fill of the culvert trench [1280] and the footings contained no recycled stonework and set in a different mortar. The alignment of the wall differs from other walls. It is possible that Room XV was built to house a stair to an upper storey; it is of the right shape, and is in a typical position. There is not enough evidence to ascertain whether room XII and its presumed neighbours opened north onto corridor XIII or south onto XIV. If the former, then they might be accommodation; if the latter, then more probably shops or offices.

The identification of two wings and a possible open corridor on the central courtyard raises the question of whether there were further wings. The excavation of the north end of the western wing leaves this question open. The trenches under 7 and 7a Bath Street were not in the right place to show whether there were any walls running off to the east. A northern wing could just have been squeezed in south of the cellars along the north side of Bath Street, but it would have to have been less than 17 m long. Any longer and it would have appeared in the trenches on the north side of Bath Street (Davenport 1999, fig I.3). The existence of a (short) northern wing would all but rule out the possibility of a connected eastern wing, however, as it would be impossibly cramped. Should an eastern wing have existed instead of a northern one, it would have to be considerably shorter than the western wing as it would otherwise impinge on the southern portico of the outer temple precinct, which is broadly contemporary.

It is perhaps more likely that the southern wing continued some distance towards the south-west corner of the baths, whose alignment this building shares. It is still possible that a short northern wing existed, but this remains unproven. The West and South wings could have defined the west and south sides of a metalled or paved open space, perhaps open to the north or perhaps partially defined by a short north wing. The baths and temple precinct walls could have defined the other sides of the open space. However, only further excavation in the relevant areas will advance the discussion.

Superstructure

Little can be said about the upper parts of the building but some possibilities can be discussed. If the rooms were vaulted and had no upper floor then the central range of the western wing (rooms I, III-IX), is likely to have risen higher than the corridors and service rooms to either side. This would permit lighting from small openings in the haunches of the vaults and the roofing of the lateral spaces with lean-to roofs. The latter could account for the roofing tiles found, but the central range was probably also roofed above the vaults. Both *tegulae* and *imbrices* and Pennant sandstone tiles were used.

There is little evidence for the appearance of the outside of the building. Some buildings in the baths were rendered externally, notably the reservoir enclosure building, but there is no evidence for that here and it is likely the building was just plain stone. Decorative or architectural stone work related to this building did not survive on the site, but colonnettes are common in Bath and it would not be surprising if they were employed in the building along the proposed porticos or courtyard loggia, standing on a dwarf wall, and similarly used on the street frontage. Alternatively, full size columns could have been used. Some classical architectural detailing is suggested by the small scale plain cornice block found in a medieval pit, which could have come from this building.

The interior was presumably plastered and painted and the use of decorative woodwork has been suggested above.

Function

Given the state of the remains, it is difficult to find useful comparanda to throw light on the function of this building. It shares the common features of large or high status buildings in Roman Britain of connecting corridors along the outer sides of the building, apsidal rooms and varied room size, and a winged or courtyard plan, found in both rural and urban sites. It certainly shares the attribute of size with superficially similar buildings. At Silchester, for example, Building XIX/2 is slightly smaller and is probably a large house (St John Hope and Fox 1899, pl xi). Building XIV/1 is probably a smaller house behind a range of shops (St John Hope and Fox 1896, pls x-xiv). The *mansio* at Silchester has close parallels but is even bigger (Fox and St John Hope 1894, pl xvii). Building 123 at Culver Street, Colchester shares a plan form, but is probably a house separated from the shops on the street front by the courtyard and is also smaller (Crummy 1992, 96–108 and figs 3.53–3.55). While it cannot be completely discounted that this is a particularly grand house, it is unlikely, especially given the fact that the entire west range

was probably heated and in part vaulted. Clearly the western wing at least is not a range of shops.

It is only in this part of the building that we can see a plan that might suggest sets of rooms as in a *mansio*, but the extensive heating systems might at first glance, make that interpretation, of this wing at least, fairly improbable. On the other hand, we may be looking at different levels of comfort or status in each wing for different social levels of user (cf Black 1995, 9). Baths would not be necessary, as Irvine's baths across the road would serve this function. An interesting parallel, suggested by Prof. Barry Cunliffe, is the east wing at Fishbourne, in the earliest phase of the palace, of later 1st-century date (Cunliffe 1971, 150 *inter alia*). Here small sets of rooms are grouped with colonnaded courtyards and interpreted as guest suites.

A beguiling possibility is that this building was indeed designed for visitor accommodation, but, rather than the official post, was intended for those who had come to benefit from the goddess's healing powers. The parallel would be the Asklepaieon at Pergamon where supplicants would sleep within the temple's sacred precincts hoping for a cure or dream visit from the divinity while being soothed by music, scents and the sound of water. Closer to home, we might consider the "guest block" at Lydney as a possible parallel (Wheeler and Wheeler 1932). Martin Henig, to whom I am indebted for the ideas in this paragraph, has suggested a similar function for Building VII at Nettleton Shrub (Wedlake 1982, 16); and even Chedworth, where Webster (1983) has suggested the whole complex might be an adjunct to a temple. Both these sites potentially offered healing as part, at least, of the pilgrimage experience. Evidence to support the view that this did happen in *Aquae Sulis*, even if not in the present building, was found in 1825 when the lower part of a stone block with an inscription "Novanti fil[ius] pro se et suis ex visu possuit" was excavated under the site of the present Gainsborough Building in Beau Street, only a few metres south of Building D (RIB 153; Scarth 1864, 300). The inscription translates as "... son of Novantius set this up for himself and his family as the result of a vision (or dream)".

If the interpretation of the building as a *mansio* or accommodation for temple visitors is not viable, another possibility is that the building formed part of the extensive leisure facilities around the baths, analogous to the "libraries" and related public rooms formalised in the outer wings and annexes of the imperial baths at Rome. Heated rooms in a northern climate would be an obvious benefit for such public rooms, where meeting and greeting, business and politics, networking and negotiation took place in a quieter, less enervating atmosphere than the baths themselves. In addition, and perhaps running alongside this interpretation, we might consider that the building also contained the offices and work places of the officials and staff running the baths and temple complex.

The possibility that there were shops on the southern side emphasises the remarkable similarity in this case to forum buildings in a larger town. While there is no reason to suspect the former existence of a forum in *Aquae Sulis*, it is not unlikely that there was some sort of administrative centre for the *fanum* of the goddess. The suggestion that this building superseded an earlier administrative building might strengthen this idea.

If any of these interpretations of the function of the building proves to be true, then this will support the view that at least before the 4th century the central area of *Aquae Sulis* around the Baths was largely, if not entirely, devoted to spa and temple related activities, and included shops, but contained few if any houses.

Period 3.2: Later Roman – late 2nd century–4th century

No floor or occupation layers survived within Building D and there was very little evidence for later alterations to the building. The only deposits contemporary with the use of the building are those lying outside the south-west corner. The sequence of these road surfaces is summarised below and a more detailed description can be found in the site archive.

Late Roman activity and Building D

It is likely that alterations or repairs were made to the building in the course of its life, especially if this lasted up to two hundred years. The only possible evidence of this was a wall foundation [22] set in a foundation trench cut into the fill of the culvert trench 808/200 (eastern section of trench 1280). This was s quite clearly different in character from the other walls built across the culvert trench. It was also cut from a high level into the fills of the culvert trench, unlike the other walls. One possibility is that it was constructed in 1829 as a foundation for the central stone drain of the tepid pool, which directly overlies it, but the foundation trench was not lined with the grey puddling clay typical of all other 1829 features and the mortar used was not consistent with that used elsewhere by Manners. The excavators are categorical that the mortar and construction of the foundation is Roman in character. The interpretation that fits best with the available evidence is that this was a later Roman construction and that it either served to divide Room IX off from area XV and to create a narrow passageway to the courtyard, or that it created a space for stair to the upper floor. It is the only evidence for alterations or additions to Building D. However there is no dating evidence for this event.

Southern road

The south-western section of road (Figs 4.4 and 4.13)

The only stratigraphy demonstrably contemporary with the use of the building was found in the area to the south-west of Building D. It comprised a series of road surfaces. Furthermore the road surfaces located in the south east corner of the excavation are thought to belong to same sequence (see below).

The south-west deposits provided a long sequence of surfaces within which were layers containing pottery dating to the 2nd-3rd centuries, with one of the few certain 3rd- to 4th-century sherds in the uppermost layer (1013) over the infilled culvert trench [1280]. The layers here were rather different in character from those inside Building D and, although they too formed a succession of thin layers, they can more convincingly be interpreted as a series of road or yard surfaces, rather than just make-up, as appears to be the case with layers inside Building D at the same level. The road surfaces comprised successive layers of thin spreads of river gravels cemented very hard in mortar and sand, some having the addition of chert pebbles, broken clay tile, Pennant slab fragments or fragments of *opus signinum* alternating with thicker deposits of large stone rubble (oolitic and carboniferous limestone) in a sand and mortar matrix. Some of these harder surfaces were interleaved with softer finer layers of mortary sand often mixed with high densities of red tile dust or grit.

The first of these surfaces (2080) lay at a lower level (19.3 m OD) than the top of the make-up (19.8 m OD) inside Building D. The uppermost surviving layer of rubble (2017), apparently a foundation for a truncated surface, was at 20.12 m OD (Fig. 4.4, see also Fig. 6.6). The original exterior ground surface was considerably lower than the floor inside Building D, which may have been artificially raised by as much as a metre by the construction of the hypocaust system. However by the time the building fell into disuse the exterior ground surface was possibly approaching the same level as the internal floors.

The lowest levels containing pottery of 2nd-century date and likely to be contemporary with the construction and early use of Building D began with a Pennant slab surface with gravel repairs succeeded by two sequences of coarse limestone rubble surfaced with pebbles to form a cobbled road or path. At this level a posthole [2062] was cut at the very corner of Building D and a post 0.4 m in diameter inserted (Fig. 4.2). This makes no structural sense in terms of building construction but may have been placed as a bollard to protect the corner of the building from turning traffic or, alternatively, as a gate post indicating an entrance into a yard to the south or west of Building D.

In the northernmost portion of the road over the infilled trench 1280, the deposits had been slowly subsiding and the layers which were dumped in the top (frequently sandy-mortary sediments with much clay tile dust and grit) contained pottery of 2nd to 3rd-century date (Fig. 4.13). The sequence here included rubble with *opus signinum* surfacing, broken clay tile, tesserae or broken Pennant slabs set in mortar and remnants of a paved Pennant surface. These deposits underwent several repairs

Figure 4.13   Bath Spa excavations: Photograph of Roman street surfaces in the south-west corner of the site, cut by a medieval pit and a post-medieval stone lined well. The masonry in the foreground under the bucket is 19th-century in date.

and resurfacings with similar materials as layers subsided over the culvert trench.

The upper part of the road sequence showed a succession of fairly thin lenses composed predominantly of small gravel, pebbles or crushed limestone in sandy mortar that had often set hard like concrete, and mortar mixed with broken and crushed tile or gravel over limestone rubble in a sequence of alternating surfaces. The uppermost layers in the sequence were only seen in section so no dating evidence could be obtained for the latest layers. However the 3rd to 4th-century sherd in layer 1013 comes roughly half way through the sequence.

Figure 4.14   Bath Spa excavations: Photograph of Roman roadway south of Building D in south-east corner of trench with section of footings of wall 611 (context of the South range clearly visible (cf Section E Fig. 3.4).

All these layers were sloping and undulating, distorted to the north by subsidence into the culvert trench resulting in a distinct hollow which needed to be constantly infilled, then rising over the old bank of the early ditch to slope down again to the south, but with an additional subsidence hollow formed over the decaying tree stump (2341) left in the bank (Fig. 3.3). The layers sloped to the south: while this follows the natural slope of the ground, it obviously made sure that surface water drained away from the building (Fig. 4.4). These surfaces had been kept very clean and no occupation debris accumulated apart from a few thin lenses of charcoal caught in the subsidence over the culvert trench. The soil analysis has also confirmed that there is little evidence of intensive occupation. The camber of the surfaces and their character are compatible with their interpretation as a road running along the south side of the building (Fig. 4.14; see also Fig. 7.2 7). Such an interpretation would fit with the known pattern of roads in the area, which suggests that one ran down the west side of Building D, which could either turn at the corner of the building to run along the south side or form an intersection with a road skirting the south side, which could in turn join with a narrow lane running between buildings to the south of Building D, identified in the Bellott's Hospital excavations (Chapter 10 below and Fig. 4.1).

The only features cutting these layers, apart from the posthole at the corner of Building D, were two trenches. They could be interpreted as robber trenches, but the fills do not support this. The larger, 2021, ran east-west parallel with and *c* 3 m to the south of the south wall of Building D. It appears to have been cut from high in the surviving sequence, certainly in the 3rd century or later, after the deposition of layer 2361. It measured 0.5 m deep and had a flat base 0.5 m wide and sloping sides increasing to 0.7 m wide at the top. If this was the robber trench of a late wall, it had been left open to silt up naturally. The fill had the appearance of natural accumulations of silt and sand, which could have formed in a drainage ditch, possibly originally covered with paving slabs: a shallow ledge which ran along its north edge may have supported something of this sort. The lowest clay and sand lenses (2046) may have accumulated during late Roman use, as might also the stony layer above, which appears to have eroded from the Roman layers cut by the feature. However, in the fill above this were a few potsherds dated to the early 11th century AD. The second smaller trench [2050] measured 0.35 m wide by 0.2 m deep and appears to have formed a subsidiary drainage gully, set at right angles to 2021 and draining into it from the south. The limestone rubble and Pennant slabs filling it may indicate that this smaller channel was also originally covered. It may have become necessary to create drainage channels late in the sequence during the 3rd century or later, when the ground surface had risen considerably and the camber of the street layers was not as pronounced.

The eastern section of road (Fig. 4.14, see also Fig. 3.4)

An area of metalling which could support this view was recorded at the south end of the south-eastern strip. The main element was an area of rubble and gravel layers at first thought to be a segment of an early Roman metalled road or track [317]. The sequence of layers (Fig.3.4) does bear a striking similarity to the road found in the Bath Street excavations (Davenport 1999 fig. I.5). Indeed the road was at first thought to run parallel to that road, ie north-east to south-west, but it is clear that this was an effect created by a modern feature cutting diagonally across its north edge and the narrowness of the exposed section. The road consisted of a primary dump of large limestone rubble up to 500 mm in size (318, 627) laid directly on the Period 1 soils and covered by several surfacings of flint and limestone gravel, cobbles and sand (628–30, 603, 316). Later surfaces of flint and limestone gravel, grit, sand and silt (314–5, 322–3, 588, 639) extended to north and south, widening the road.

The assignment of the road to a period is difficult because the truncation by 19th and 20th-century structures means the relationship to the wall foundations of Building D has been lost. In addition the artefacts found in Building D contexts cannot be differentiated from those in Period 2 contexts. There are no artefacts from the lower layers so it is possible that the earliest levels are of Period 2. The upper layers contained a low density of pottery, which dated layer 316 to the 2nd century, but from the overlying layers none of the pottery could be identified more closely than as of Roman date, apart from some Flavian samian ware from the uppermost layers of the sequence. An *as* or *dupondius* of 1st –2nd century AD came from layer 588, one of the highest deposits. Both the coin and the samian ware could of course have been in circulation well into the 3rd century. However, the roofing and wall tiles incorporated into road contexts were very similar to those in the foundations and makeup layers of Building D and this supports the assignment of the road to same period as the construction of Building D.

The road would have measured *c* 4.0 m wide as first built, increasing to over 5.0 m with additional surfacings. It had a distinct camber, especially noticeable on the south. It survived to a maximum thickness of 0.5 m (19.25 m OD), which suggests that a considerable thickness had been truncated by the Taylor pool in 1925 when compared with the uppermost road surfaces in the south-west area.

Late Occupation

A small quantity of residual 3rd to 4th-century pottery and 4th-century coins in deposits of later periods indicate that Building D may have continued in use through to the 4th century. Pottery was very sparse, suggesting that little waste ceramic material was generated during the life of the building, though this picture may be misleading, created by the severe truncation of pre-19th -century deposits by the construction of the Tepid Bath. Within the cellars of 7–7a Bath Street, material that could date to either the 2nd or 3rd centuries occurred in layers in the west corridor of Building D. However a 3rd-century date would conflict with the evidence of wall and make-up relationships and so a 2nd-century date contemporary with building construction is pre-ferred. Two 4th-century coins were found in the 1989 excavations: one residually in a post-medieval context and the other stratified in a Roman layer (BS89 TrI 18) within the apsidal room at the north end. In this area the ground surface was higher and make-up layers contemporary with the construction appear to be much thinner. It is therefore feasible that layer 18 represents a late re-surfacing or internal alteration at the north end of the wing. The apsidal room may even have been a late addition to the end of the west wing.

Period 3.3: Late-sub Roman – 4th–5th century

There is some evidence to suggest that in the late or sub-Roman period the building may have been subjected to robbing activities predating the clear phase of 11th-century robbing contemporary with the pits and discussed with them below (Chapter 5). This earlier robbing, perhaps occurring as the building first fell into disuse, is hinted at by the remnants of layers representing destruction debris overlying the hypocaust in room III (1058, 1141, 1162, 1182, 1186), layers of tile and brick in the robbed hypocaust channel 769/863 and similar deposits in BS89 Tr II (24, 31, 34), apparently also debris from the robbing of a hypocaust flue. An alternative interpretation is that these deposits may represent a change of use as the building fell into decline and the maintenance of the heating system became impractical or redundant. However, the presence of roofing tile in 769 suggests that the whole building was being demolished, not just specific structures within it.

Three bulk samples were taken from deposits of this period, two (1058, 1141) from the hypocaust. All contained occasional charcoal, but only one (1141) contained a low density of seeds, which included wheat (*Triticum* sp.). These plant remains could relate to the use of the hypocaust as much as to demolition activity.

At the top of the sequence of surfaces in the area south-west of Building D there were the truncated remnants of two layers, which may represent the start of accumulation of soils over the latest road surface alongside the abandoned building (Fig.4.4). The lower (2016) was a silty-sandy grey clay soil, containing flecks of charcoal, clay tile and mortar grit and a scatter of worn oolitic limestone and Pennant stones up to 80 mm. Above was a similar soil but containing in addition to the other constituents larger sub-angular blocks of Oolitic limestone up to 240 mm (2015). These could both be remnants of pit fills truncated on all sides by 19th-century features,

but the alternative is that they are in fact post-Roman soil development with fallen building debris from the collapsing structure. It is known from exca-vations elsewhere in the city that in the post-Roman period thick dark organic soils accumulated (Cunliffe and Davenport 1985; Davenport 1999) and the evidence of pollen (Dimbleby 1969) suggests that some sort of cultivation was being practised. The soil evidence from medieval pits discussed in Chapter 6 below also indicates such activity. These layers may represent the beginning of this process, all evidence of which has otherwise been destroyed on this site.

ENVIRONMENTAL EVIDENCE

Plant Remains from the Culvert

The sample from the sediment accumulated within the stone culvert was processed to recover water-logged plant remains. The material was analysed by Ruth Pelling and the full report can be found in site archive. The material includes a mix of environ-mental and economic indicators. The culvert was constructed *c* AD 150–160 and presumably sediment and debris started to accumulate within it soon after its construction. What are not known are the rate and duration of accumulation, as no independent dating material was found in the sediment. Nor is the source of the water draining into it known, though the character of the sediments suggests that it was not spring water. The sediment was largely derived from the Lias clay, into which the culvert had been cut and which had been packed over the stone structure. The lack of dark soily sediments of the sort that started to accumulate over the Temple Precinct in the 4th century and later suggests that debris was not washing into the culvert by this stage. There is a similar mix of seeds in this sediment as noted for samples from the fill of the culvert trench and this may imply that material was being derived from much the same source over a relatively short period, perhaps until the full length of the ditch was culverted. The indeterminate seeds, stalks, leaf buds and leaf fragments identified are the type of material one would expect to be washed into a storm-water drain. Thereafter it may have served to drain surplus cold water from the Baths.

Indicators of the contemporary environment are provided by tree and wild herbaceous species. The large amounts of seeds/buds from trees, particularly *Acer campestre* (maple), suggest the presence of trees close to the site; *Alnus glutinosa* (alder) is a tree species of damp ground and may have been growing in the lower, wetter parts of the site. The scrubby species, *Sambucus nigra* (elder) and *Rubus fruticosus* (blackberry) are common in urban areas, while *Crataegus monogyna* (hawthorn) is a common scrub-land species. These species suggest that an area of scrubland and trees similar to that described at the end of Period 2, remained in the vicinity after construction of Building D was underway.

While the majority of the ruderal species may have derived from arable fields, it is perhaps more likely in the circumstances that they were growing in disturbed soils in the source area. Some provide a more specific indication of conditions. *Eleocharis palustris* is a damp grassland species, which requires its roots to be in water for at least part of the year. *Carex* sp. (sedges), *Juncus* sp. (rush), *Ranunculus acris/repens/bulbosus*, and *Apium graveolens* are all likely to have been growing on damp ground suggesting quite muddy, marshy conditions. However the cutting of the culvert is likely to have improved drainage generally (Jordan above Chapter 3) and this would imply such damp conditions as implied by the seeds would not have lasted long after the Antonine developments in this part of *Aquae Sulis* and therefore that the sediment accumulated in the culvert represents a relatively short time scale, perhaps confined within the latter half of the 2nd century.

Amongst the economic material Pelling has identified limited cereal remains of a hulled wheat (*Triticum spelta/dicoccum* – spelt/emmer wheat) and *Hordeum vulgare* (hulled barley), represented entirely by chaff. *Vicia/Pisum* sp. (bean/pea) pod fragments also are suggestive of processing waste. Although this is clearly waste from crop processing, it is unlikely that this was going on in the centre of Bath at this stage from what is known of the character of the city and an alternate explanation perhaps should be sought. Chaff could have been used as tinder for starting fires and this could imply contemporaneity with the construction work when bonfires were in evidence as waste ground was cleared of scrub. Some weeds of arable or ruderal habitats are likely to have entered the site with arable crops, but only two species can be regarded as exclusively arable weeds: *Adonis* sp. and *Valerianella dentata*. The latter is characteristics of light soils.

The only certain fruit species identified was *Ficus carica* (fig), Mediterranean in origin, and a common Roman find but only in urban contexts. Fruit and nuts of British species may also have derived from food debris. *Corylus avellana* (hazel nut) represented by broken fragments of nut shell suggesting the extraction of the nut and *Rubus fruticosus* (blackberry) may have been deliberately collected and consumed although they could have been growing in the local conditions outlined above.

Three possible condiments are represented. *Linum usitatissimum* (flax) has been cultivated in Britain since the Neolithic and is used for oil, as flavouring or for fibre. The presence of seeds suggests its culinary use in this instance. *Coriandrum sativum* (coriander) is a Roman introduction, and originally of Mediterranean or Near Eastern origin. *Papaver somniferum* (opium poppy), the seed of which is widely used for culinary purposes has been recorded from the Iron Age onwards, but more commonly from the Roman period. It also occurs as an arable weed. *Papaver somniferum* was found in the latrine deposits at Bearsden (Dickson and Dickson 2000, 274) providing testament to its culinary usage.

Coriandrum sativum was probably initially imported as seed for consumption by the Roman army, although it may have been locally cultivated by the end of the 1st century AD. It has been found in other early Roman sites including Colchester from a shop burnt during the Boudiccan revolt in AD 61 (Murphy 1984), Bearsden (Dickson and Dickson 2000, 243) and more recently from the Roman military site of Alchester in Oxfordshire (Robinson 2000).

MATERIAL EVIDENCE

A very high proportion of the finds from Period 3 was found in the culvert trench 1280 and wall foundations of Building D. This material was not related in any way to the superstructure or use of Building D but is thought to have derived from an unplaced building of 1st to 2nd-century date; it has been described and discussed in the previous section. Material from Periods 3.2 and 3.3 was sparse. A summary of residual Roman material from medieval and later periods has also been included, when this material could have been derived originally from layers contemporary with Building D and therefore may have some bearing on the interpretation of the building.

Roman Pottery
by Lisa Brown

Period 3.2 (Table 4.1)

Pottery recovered from Period 3.2 deposits was associated for the most part with contexts relating to Building D. This accounted for 82% by count and 84% by weight of the total assemblage of 442 sherds (3824 g). The condition of this assemblage was generally poorer and more fragmentary than the Period 3.1 group, with an overall mean sherd weight of only 8.7 g.

The character of this assemblage (Table 4.1) was in stark contrast to the Period 3.1 pottery (see Table 3.5). It was dominated by coarse, utilitarian wares, including BB1, CRW, SAVGT and GRANRW, which together accounted for 70% of the total by count and 77% by weight. BB1 accounted for one quarter of the assemblage, as would be expected for a mid to late 2nd-century domestic collection within the Bath region. Within the Period 3.2 BB1 assemblage, cooking pots were slightly more common than bowls and dishes, in contrast to the culvert trench 1280 assemblage. The unsourced CRW category is likely to include a proportion of Alice Holt and possibly New Forest grey wares. This group represented 40% of the total and the most common form was a copy of the BB1 flat-rimmed bowl, but a bead-rim jar and necked jar were also identified.

The only continental import in the Period 3.2 assemblage was a mortarium sherd of *Gallia Belgica* type, and only two flagons were identified, both ring-neck varieties, one each in Bath fabric FLA and Exeter fabric FLWW. Table wares included a

Table 4.1 Summary quantification of Period 3.2 Roman pottery assemblage.

Fabric	No.	Wt	Forms
BB1SED	98	978	Lid; cooking pot 1, cooking pot 2, cooking pot 3, bead-rim jar, bead-rim bowl, flat-rimmed bowl, straight-sided dish
BB1SW	14	130	Cooking pot 2, flat-rimmed bowl, flanged bowl 2
CRW	178	1609	Necked jar, flat-rimmed bowl, lid
SAVGT	8	75	
GRANRW	8	130	
SMICRW	65	407	Necked bowl, cordoned cup, beaker
SANDRW	2	10	
FMICRW	15	117	Necked bowl, necked jar, lid
MEOR	4	36	
FIOR	12	69	
GRWW	1	5	
FIWW	3	25	
FLA	14	108	Multiple ring-necked flagon
FLB	1	6	
FLC	16	112	
FLWW	1	5	Multiple ring-necked flagon
Mortarium	2	103	*Gallia Belgica*
Total	**442**	**3824**	Mean sherd weight 8.7 g

cordoned cup from 2094 and a beaker sherd from 987 in SMICRW, but these may be residual as the fabric is a generally early Roman type.

Late Roman pottery

A small number of late Roman sherds were identified, all recovered from post-Roman deposits and, therefore, not quantified precisely. This group includes products of the Oxford kilns dating from the mid 3rd century onwards. Four sherds of Oxford red-slipped ware (OXFRS), three of Oxford white-slipped wares (OXFWS) and a similar number of Oxford white ware (OXF WH) were noted. Two mortarium sherds in Oxford white-slipped ware (OXFWS) date to the mid 3rd century or later. Although Oxford white ware was produced from the 2nd century in the Oxford area, distribution of vessels other than mortaria in this ware to the Bath region may have only begun once the importation of the red-slipped wares began in the second half of the 3rd century AD. A single New Forest red colour-coated (NFOCC) mortarium sherd dating to the mid 3rd century or later was also identified. A Trier Moselkeramik sherd, dating from the late 2nd to 3rd century, but from a Period 5 context, is the only example of this ware from the site.

Amongst the BB1 assemblage, three late cavetto-rim cooking pots and two dropped-flange bowls were present, all dating to the 3rd or 4th centuries. The latest sherd identified from the site was a fragment of a triangular rim jar in Late Roman shell-tempered ware (HARSH/LRSH), from the south

Midlands, probably Harrold in Bedfordshire. The type was distributed in the south-west from the mid 4th century (Tyers 1996, 193; Brown 1994).

Clearly, the Spa site had suffered severe truncation, as was the case at the Tramsheds (Brown, forthcoming) and the late Roman sherds were redeposited within post-Roman deposits. The quantities of redeposited late wares were, however, significantly higher at the Tramsheds site. For example, 57 sherds of OXFRS, 24 sherds of OXFWS and 41 sherds of NFOCC from periods 6–15 at Tramsheds contrast with under a dozen sherds altogether of these wares from periods 4–6 at the Spa. This contrast suggests, although it cannot prove, that there was no significant late Roman activity at the Spa site, or at least none that required pottery.

Ceramic Building Materials
by Ian Betts

Period 3.1

Very little building material can be related directly to Building D. Only the bricks used in the hypocaust (1191) and the stoke holes (1142, 1197, 1198, 1201) are primary constructions for Building D. A complete example of a *bessalis* brick, together with part of a lydion or pedalis brick, was used in either the wall or floor of the stoke hole (context 1201) of the hypocaust. The hypocaust itself (context 1191) comprised two tile bases of pilae made from pedalis bricks. Where the hypocaust flue cut through the wall 1360 it was lined with large clay bricks 400 mm wide of which three courses survived, but none were removed during excavation. These are the only bricks found in a primary context relating to the construction of Building D.

The occurrence of overfired roofing tile fragments was discussed in relation to Period 2 (above). It is possible that these derived from a temporary kiln constructed specifically to supply Building D, but they could also have related to the unlocated earlier building.

Period 3.2

Initially it appeared that only a limited number of contexts were contemporary with the use of Building D and therefore little building material was assigned to this period. However more detailed analysis of the stratified levels to the south-west of Building D in conjunction with the ceramic phasing has resulted in the attribution of a more substantial quantity of tile and brick to Period 3.2. This had accumulated reused as paving in road or yard surfaces and includes roofing tile, bricks some with clear wear from their reuse as paving, box flue tiles with both combed and roller-stamped keying and a small number of wall tiles with both combed and scored keying. The fragments of relief-patterned box-flue tile are keyed with West Country die types 25 (context 1184) and 54 (context 1185). Pennant slabs both for roofing and flooring were present. The roller stamped tiles suggest this was also derived from the same demolished building as the material from the preceding period. A further overfired tile (either fabric 2 or 16) was found in context 2076.

Period 3.3

A small number of contexts (1009, 1141, 1182) have been assigned to the final stages of Building D, and may represent robbing or demolition debris from the hypocausts of this building. The material comprises roofing tile, combed box flue tiles and brick.

Late Roman ceramic building material found in Periods 4–5

Although this Roman building material is residual it is of importance as it may derive from Building D. It is significant that the residual material contains roofing tile in fabric 5, which does not occur in earlier periods at the Spa and is known to be associated with 3rd to early 4th-century buildings at the suburban villa sites at Lower Common and Oldfield Boys School (Betts 1999a; 1999b). A similar situation exists for the roofing tiles in fabric 1, which occur in numerous contexts in Periods 4 and 5, but are entirely absent from all earlier periods. A number of the Spa tiles in fabric 5 are slightly different to those on the suburban villa sites in having red rather than black iron oxide inclusions, but there is no reason to think they are not from the same kiln source. The fabric evidence suggests that the Roman building material in Periods 4 and 5 (or at least a major part of it) does not derive from the remains of the 1st to 2nd-century building brought in from elsewhere, as was the case in Periods 2–3, but from Building D itself.

This Roman building material comprises large amounts of roofing tile together with occasional fragments of red and grey coloured Pennant sandstone, suggesting that Building D may have had separate areas of ceramic and stone roofing. A few *tegulae* have nail holes added before firing. These holes, which are round (6 to 9 mm diameter, fabrics 2, 3) and possibly square (? x 8 mm, fabric 7), were situated near the top edge midway between the flanges. In London nail holes do not seem to have been added to tiles prior to firing until around AD 160 (Betts 1991; Pringle in prep). They are also largely absent from the early legionary tiles used in York (Betts 1985, 163). Also present are combed box-flue and a number of partially complete voussoir tiles, indicating that Building D had a vaulted ceiling, which could be interpreted as evidence of an attached bath suite. A more unusual item from Period 5 context 941 appears to be a fragment of brick with a combed surface which may have been used as flooring.

Late Roman Small Finds
by John Clarke

Very few finds of 3rd to 4th-century date were found, but almost all occurred residually in later periods. The majority are coins and included in the list are those from the 1989 excavations in the Bath Street cellars, which produced the only late coin in a layer contemporary with Building D. The late Roman coins from the Spa excavation were all found in residual contexts of a robber trench and medieval pits, as was the glass bead in a feature associated with the Tepid Pool construction. The coin of the house of Constantine occurs in the primary robbing debris from one of the hypocausts of Building D. Of the two coins from the 1989 excavations in the Bath Street cellars (also listed below), one occurred in an 18th-century context and one in a Roman layer, apparently contemporary with Building D.

Brief details are recorded here of residual Roman material found in the Medieval and post-medieval deposits on the basis that material dating from the second half of the 2nd century onwards may be derived from the use of Building D and provide some clues to the interpretation of that building.

Illustrated finds (Fig. 3.13, 9)

9. **Glass Bead**: Half an opaque blue disc bead, possibly late 4th century AD. Diameter 7 mm; thickness 2 mm. SF6032 Context 348 Period 7.2

Not Illustrated

Coin: AE1 of the House of Constantine, 317–64. Obv: [---]STANTI[---]. SF6054. Context 723 (feature 769/863). Period 4/5

Coin: AE4, 4th century, illegible. SF6044. Context 1170 (pit 910). Period 5

Coin: AE4, 4th century, illegible. SF6010. Context 914 (pit 909). Period 5

Coin: CuA, 4th century, BS89 SF7 TrI Context 18. Period 3

Coin: CuA, 4th century, very corroded BS89 SF4 TrII Context 13 (feature 12). Period 7.1

Table 4.2 Mammal and bird bones in period 3.2 and 3.3. Number of specimens identified to species (or NISP). Figures in parenthesis are 'non-countable' bones after Davis (1992).

Taxon	3.2	3.3
Cattle	5	
Sheep/Goat	4	
Sheep	2	
Pig	14	3
Hare	1	
Chicken	2	2
Goose	1	
Pigeon cf. wood/rock pigeon		1
Corvid cf. crow/raven	1	
Cattle/Horse sized	(2)	
Sheep/pig sized	(1)	(1)
Total	**30**	**6**

Mammal and Bird Bone
by Lorrain Higbee

The main analysis of the Roman animal bone has been reported in the previous section, since although the bone was found in Period 3.1 contexts, it is clearly associated with the debris of the demolished Period 2 building. Only 39 bones were found in Period 3.2 contexts and 6 from Period 3.3 (Table 4.2). The quantity of bone is very small and little can be deduced, other than to note that most is derived from the three main livestock species of cattle, sheep and pig. Most but not all of the less common species probably represent food items, but the presence of corvids is not considered to be related to anthropogenic action.

Chapter 5: Spa Period 4: Early medieval (5th-early 11th century AD)

OVERVIEW

Evidence for Period 4, filling the void between the Roman and medieval sequences, is relatively intangible. However, finds and a small number of contexts may be assigned to this period, although the meagre dating evidence clusters at the end of the period. Stratigraphic evidence for this period is almost entirely confined to the western half of the excavation, while dateable artefacts indicate activity during the 10th-early 11th century. A few features in the Bath Street cellars and the north-eastern area of the site have also been attributed to this period. Very few contexts can be assigned to this period on stratigraphic grounds. Most contexts – the majority of them pits – have been assigned on the basis of pottery dating. During the excavations, A number of features were thought to belong to this period when excavated, but subsequent analysis indicated that most of these were Roman in origin. These included three stone blocks (1186, 1188–9) tentatively identified as post pads for a timber building. Similarly, other features have been recognised as part of the hypocaust system of Building D. However, these features may have suffered secondary robbing during this period.

STRATIGRAPHIC AND STRUCTURAL EVIDENCE (Fig. 5.1)

Recognisable and datable activities begin in the late Saxon period. A secondary phase of robbing of the channel [769/863] forming part of the hypocaust system of Building D appears to have taken place during the first half of the 11th century AD. A probable drainage trench [2021] in the road to the south of Building D also contained an early 11th century sherd in its upper layers and may indicate that capping stones were robbed out at this stage, followed by a more rapid accumulation of silts.

Several features were assigned to this period on the basis of their pottery content, where it was exclusively Bath B ware, which suggests they were early 11th century in date (pre-Conquest). They are the robber pit 2197 of Roman wall 2175, the robbing debris over the hypocaust flue 1087 and the pits 1131, 1134, and 1544 (Fig. 6.4). However if the tiles found in pits 1134 and 1544 are medieval, rather than Roman, then these pits would not be earlier than 12th century. In addition, pits 1150 and 1159 must be of this period on stratigraphic grounds, whilst 1125 (Fig. 6.1), though only containing early pottery, must be stratigraphically later. Alan Vince states that the

group of 24 mid 11th century pits assigned to Period 5 could, on pottery grounds, be placed in Period 4, as they contain no certainly post-Conquest types. Of these, at least two are later as they cut post-Conquest pits. A post hole [1066] may be the only feature other than pits belonging to this period.

The pits assigned to Period 4 were all grouped closely together towards the north end of the western area of the excavations, apart from the one further north in the Bath Street cellars. However, they would be much more widespread if the 24 later pits were included. In character, they were no different to the Period 5 pits and the discussion of the pits in the later period applies equally to these earlier ones. The structure and fill of these pits is summarised in Table 5.1. At both the Citizen House site (Greene 1979) and Bath Street excavations (Davenport 1999) there appears to have been a similar pattern with only a handful of pits of 9th-mid 11th century date. The numbers of pits are too few to perceive any meaningful pattern, although clusters of pits may represent ends of tenement yards or gardens.

ENVIRONMENTAL EVIDENCE

Summary of the plant remains
based on the assessment by Ruth Pelling

Fourteen samples (seven from four pits and the remainder debris in robber trenches of the Roman hypocausts) taken for recovery of plant macrofossils may be assigned to this period. Of these, ten can be dated to the first half of the 11th century. The other four lack independent dating evidence so they could belong anywhere within Period 4. However, the characteristics of the contexts, the seed and residue assemblages indicate a close similarity to the 11th century features and they are taken to be contemporaneous. Charred grain was present in all but one of the samples, generally in low to moderate quantities, but one sample contained over 100 grains from one context. The seeds were generally moderately-well preserved.

The seeds recovered appear to represent food sources and included wheat and barley (free threshing *Triticum* sp. and *Hordeum vulgare*). No chaff was observed in any samples, which suggests that crop processing was taking place elsewhere. Occasional weed seeds were observed in five samples and included common arable weeds, fat hen (*Chenopodium album*), brome grass (*Bromus* sp.) and corncockle (*Agrostemma githago*). Two samples contained

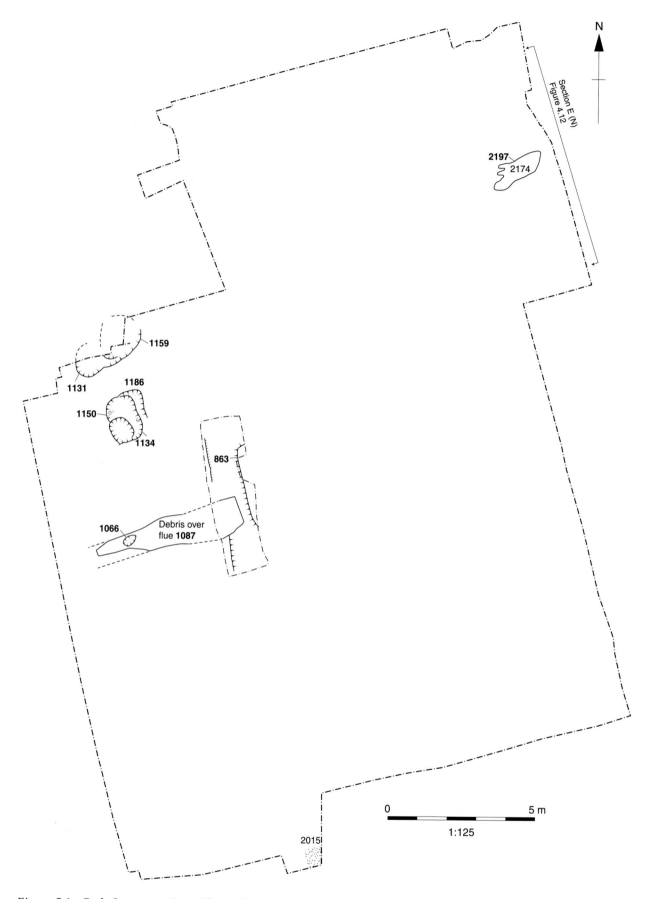

Figure 5.1   Bath Spa excavations: Plan of Period 4: Early Medieval features.

Table 5.1 Summary of pre-Conquest pits assigned to Period 4.

Pit No.	Date	Form	Function	Fill layers of pit	Finds/environmental
1131	Early 11 C	Sub-circular/oval		1145: mortar, grit & small stones, 1090: dark soil + charcoal lens, 1117 (pit cut), 1057=901: dark soil, 1151: gritty soil + charcoal lenses, 1153: gritty soil	Pottery Bath B (+Ro); (CBM), SF6009 CuA frag; Seeds: wheat, barley, pea/bean, hazel nut, brome grass, fat hen; animal bone: cattle, sheep/goat, pig
1134	Early 11th C	Sub-rectangular		1146: limestone rubble + tile, 1059: stony soil + bldg debris, 1147:limestone rubble, 1121:soil + bldg debris, charcoal 1133: gritty soil + limestone & tile, 1148: limestone rubble & op.sig.	Pottery Bath B & EMFL; SF6040 bone pin beater; SF6047 bone ?comb plate; CBM ?flat roof & ?ridge tile (+Ro), (op sig, flint), Fe, Seeds: wheat, barley, charcoal; Animal bone: cattle, sheep/goat, pig, dog, red deer, vole, amph.; Shell: oyster, limpet
1150	Early 11th C	Oval		1149: gritty soil & limestone rubble	(Pot), CBM, flint), Seeds: wheat, barley; weeds; Animal bone: pig
1159	Early 11th C	Circular/oval		1157: gritty soil + charcoal, 1160: gritty clay soil & charcoal	No artefacts; Seeds: wheat, barley, weeds; Oyster & limpet shell
1544	Early 11th C	Sub-square/circular		1543: soil + charcoal, 1655: gritty soil, 1656: clay soil, stone & bldg debris	Pottery: Bath B (+Ro); CBM 2 ?roof tiles (+Ro), Oyster shell; Animal bone: cattle, sheep/goat, pig, dog
2197	Early 11th C	? linear	Robber trench	2174: black soil & occupation debris, 2198: gravel, pebbles, sand & limestone	Pottery: Bath B (+ Ro), (CBM), (pennant – Ro roofing), Fe, slag, oyster shell

mineralised grains, including *Bromus*. Other crop plants represented were the pulses *Pisum/Vicia*. Fragments of hazelnut shell (*Corylus avellana*) are likely to be food waste.

MATERIAL EVIDENCE

Early Medieval Pottery
by Alan Vince

Early to Mid-Anglo-Saxon

There were no sherds of early to mid Anglo-Saxon pottery from the excavations. One would not expect to find pottery of the 5th to 6th centuries in Bath since the area was probably under British control but sherds of chaff-tempered handmade pottery of late 6th to late 9th century date have been found at other sites in the city (Vince 1991, 72) and on rural settlements to the north and west of Bath. In Hampshire and probably parts of Wiltshire chaff-tempering was being replaced by coarse mineral tempers (such as chalk and flint gravel) during the later 7th and early 8th centuries. Finds in north Wiltshire, however, suggest that it continued in use into the 9th century, and may have been in use at the time of construction of the first defences at Cricklade (Radford 1972).

Late Saxon wares

The earliest post-Roman pottery type recognised was Bath fabric E, of which three sherds from jars were

tentatively identified. This ware was widely distributed in Avon, Wiltshire and Somerset (Vince 1985b, fig. 160–161) and from its stratigraphic context at Cheddar Palace (where it was termed Cheddar E ware; Rahtz 1979) it appears to date to a period from the mid 10th to early 11th centuries. Unfortunately, none of the Spa finds was stratified in a late Saxon context, nor is it certain without thin-section analysis that they are in fact Bath E ware. A jar sherd from an early 19th century context (556) was visually similar to Stafford-type ware but given the similarity in appearance of this ware to many Romano-British sand-tempered wares this too is a tentative identification, and is well outside the normal distribution of this ware (the closest finds come from Gloucester and Worcester).

Nevertheless, these wares hint at a period of late Saxon activity, but since the sherds are redeposited they may in any case have been originally deposited elsewhere in the city and brought to the site later.

Bath fabric B

The earliest post-Roman pottery which was undoubtedly used on the site was Bath fabric B/D ware (the distinction made in 1979 between sherds with oolitic limestone and those without is not now thought to be significant). There is no stratigraphic proof that this ware pre-dates the major coarse ware used in Bath in the 11th and 12th centuries, Bath A; but in sequences of 11th/12th century pottery, both at this site and elsewhere, Bath A ware is most common in the earliest levels. At Spa, Bath B jar sherds were present without Bath A sherds in three of the earliest pits (1131, 1134 and 1544) as well as in two other Period 4 features (769/F863 and F2197). The majority of the 100 sherds found were probably contemporary with Bath A, however. They occur in deposits alongside definite late 11th century (or later), and early 12th century (or later) sherds but in the latter association form less than 4% of the sherds found.

Most of the vessels were undecorated cooking pots or jars with everted rims, but four sherds come from decorated spouted pitchers (Fig. 6.8, 2–4), stamped in each case with a ring and dot pattern.

Discussion

Fourteen sherds of pottery were recovered from Period 4 deposits. Of these, one, from 765, is of 19th century date and must be intrusive. The remainder all have a *terminus post quem* of early to mid 11th century, apart from three pits and feature 2197 which contains a sherd of Bath fabric B, which may have a slightly earlier starting date (Table 5.2).

The three pits, features 1131, 1134 and 1544 (in cellar 2), contained sherds of Bath fabric B without Bath fabric A. These may therefore have a slightly earlier ceramic *terminus post quem* than those containing Bath fabric A. In the first two cases there appears to be no stratigraphic objection to an early date, which would make these pits contemporary with feature 2197. One unusual sherd in pit 1134 is tempered with coarse flint gravel in a silty groundmass (EMFL). The form of the vessel is unusual, having a pronounced lid seating (Fig. 6.6, 10).

The sherd of Derbyshire stoneware in feature 769/863 is assumed to be intrusive from the period of 1829 construction work. The sherd of Winchester-type ware from this latter feature has a distinctive raised curved band with finger-nicked decoration, similar but not identical to several vessels published by Barclay and Biddle, some of which were found in

late 10th century deposits. However, the ware is thought to have been produced throughout the 11th and into the early 12th century (Biddle and Barclay 1974).

Saxon artefacts of the 9th–10th century
by John Clarke

A total of six small finds, four bone and two stone, may be dated to the Saxon period.

The two bone pin beaters (SF6004, context 552 and SF6040, pit 1134, context 1059) (Fig. 5.2, 1 & 2) are a class of object often found in late Saxon contexts. In London these artefacts generally date from before *c* 1000 (Pritchard 1984, 46-76) and in Winchester they first occur in the 9th and 10th centuries (Brown 1990, 227–8). In Bath, examples have been found at the Bath Street excavations of 1986 in a layer consistent with the above dates (Bircher 1999, 96–97, no. 117), from Citizen House, thought to be not later than the 11th century (Ambrose and Henig 1979, 56–57) and at Seven Dials (Clarke forthcoming, no. 33).

The identification of two bone strips is more tentative. One (SF6029), found in context 705 dated to the mid 11th century at the beginning of Period 5, has a hole drilled near one end and is broken through a second (Fig. 5.2, 3). It may be a connecting plate of a composite double–sided comb or comb case. The example from Bath Street (Bircher 1999, 96–97, no. 116) was interpreted as a case from the wide spacing of the holes. On these grounds, the Spa example, with closer-set holes, would be a comb connecting plate, as more rivets are needed to keep the toothed plates in position. It may date from the 10th–11th centuries (Mann 1982, 7–8; Rogerson and Dallas 1984, 167). The other strip (SF6047, context 1133 – not illustrated) may be an unfinished example. It was found with the pin beater SF6040 (Fig. 5.2, 1) in the fill of pit 1134.

A whetstone of Norwegian schist (SF6051, context 546, not illustrated) dates from the 9th century onwards (Fiona Roe, pers. comm.). The roughly polygonal Oolitic limestone lamp (SF6063, U/S) has part of the side missing down to the thick base and traces of burning around the surviving inner rim (Fig. 5.3). It is likely to date from the late Saxon period. Part of a smaller example was found at Citizen House (Ambrose and Henig 1979, 56–57) and dated from the Saxo-Norman period. Examples from Cheddar were found in contexts varying in date but essentially late Saxon to early 12th century (Anderson 1979, 228, fig. 78).

One pin beater (SF6040) and the other possible comb plate (SF6047) are from fills of the same early medieval pit (1134), while the bone comb plate (SF6029) is from a slightly later layer in robber trench 863. The remainder are from disturbed and redeposited layers or make-up associated with the tepid pool construction of 1829. This had completely removed all deposits (except Roman foundations), though it is clear that some post-Roman layers were redeposited as make-up and it is from these layers

Table 5.2 Medieval pottery in Period 4 features (TPQ early 11th century).

Context group	BATHA	BATHB	DERBS	EMFL	WINC	Total sherds
F1087	2	0	0	0	0	2
F2021	1	0	0	0	0	1
F2197	0	1	0	0	0	1
F769/F863	2	1	1	0	1	5
P1131	0	1	0	0	0	1
P1134	0	2	0	1	0	3
P1544 (cellar 2)	0	1	0	0	0	1
Total no. of sherds	5	6	1	1	1	14

that the finds derive. However, the mere presence of these artefacts, along with those from Citizen House and Seven Dials, is an important addition to the archaeological evidence for this period in Bath.

Illustrated finds (Figs 5.2–5.3)

1 **Pin beater**, pointed at one end. Bone. Context 552, Sf 6004.
2 **Pin Beater**, flat in cross-section and pointed at each end. Pit 1134, context 1059, Sf 6040.
3 **Bone pierced strip or plate**. Possibly a comb plate. Has two drilled nail or rivet holes, one broken. Bone Context 705, Sf 6029.
4 **Stone lamp**, Oolitic limestone. U/S, Sf 6063

Human Bone

Two pieces of human skull were found in the fills of mid 11th and mid 13th century pits (732 and 1098 respectively). The mid 13th century specimen has cut marks across its surface which cannot be easily explained. Two further fragments of human bone (pelvis and femur) were found in Period 6 and 7.2 contexts. None was part of an *in situ* burial.

Animal Bone
by Lorrain Higbee

The bone for this period was sparse and the quantity and list of species is shown in Table 6.9. It is dominated by domestic species, identified as cattle, sheep (or sheep/goat), pig, dog, chicken, plus non-domestic species including red deer and fish, probably representing food sources and non-economic species vole and frog/toad. Butchery marks were noted on slightly less than a third of the bone. The patterns are broadly those observed for the bone of Period 5.

GENERAL DISCUSSION

There is very little evidence of any intrusive or structural activity on the site in the centuries following the end of the Roman period until the 10th–11th centuries, when pit digging commenced.

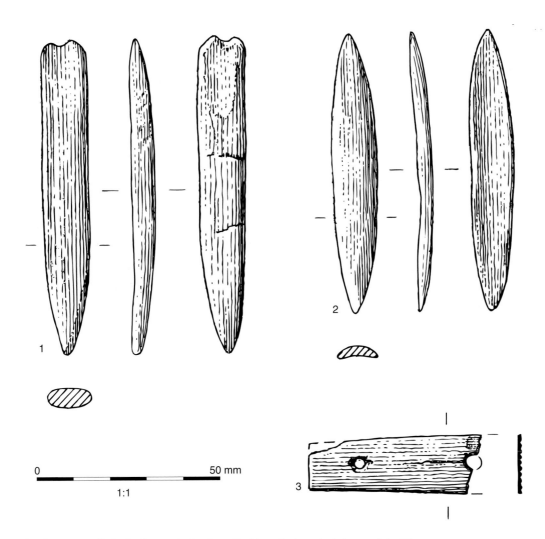

0   50 mm

1:1

Figure 5.2 Saxon small finds: bone pin beaters (1–2) and pierced strip or plate (3).

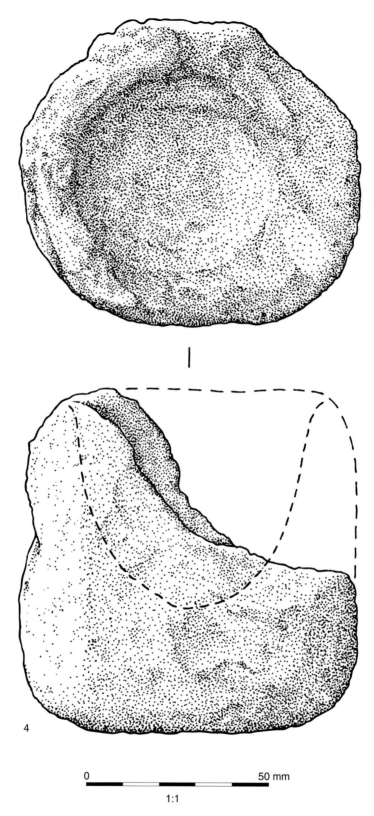

Figure 5.3   Saxon small finds: stone lamp (4).

This lack is due to the destruction of deposits by the work of George Manners in 1829. In addition, while the gap in structural activity may be quite genuine, David Jordan suggests in his study of the soil micromorphology (Chapter 6 below) that there may have been a long period of soil accumulation and development between Periods 3 and 5. Possible evidence of this has already been highlighted in the previous section, describing Period 3.3. The uniform nature of the soils in the pit fills, which are not contaminated with any quantity of Roman deposits, indicate that they were derived from a relatively homogenous soil, itself implying processes of large scale as well as small scale mixing. This could be interpreted as post-Roman agriculture taking place within the former city boundary and there is ample evidence from other sites within the city of thick dark soils starting to accumulate from the 5th century (Greene 1979, 9–10; Davenport 1991, 47; Davenport 1999, 48–49). The magnetic susceptibility of the soil also showed the addition of considerable quantities of domestic waste and burnt debris, which were probably being added to the soil as part of a manuring process. Clearly the domestic waste had to be generated by someone. The evidence on site is insufficient to allow us to say whether there was domestic habitation locally, with rubbish being added to small cultivated garden plots; or whether there were fields within the city boundaries to which the domestic debris was brought as manure from outside. It has been suggested (Davenport 2002) that this area of the city may have formed the core of a lay settlement growing outside the ecclesiastical foundation after 675 (Sims-Williams 1975), in which case small scale cultivation within garden plots would be the more likely.

Alan Vince comments that the post-Roman pottery from these excavations throws some light on the history of activity on the site, which, in the main, parallels that provided by the stratigraphy. Pottery also provides useful dating evidence. At first, it seems to imply that there is no activity on the site between the end of the use of Romano-British pottery (whenever that might have been in Bath) and the late Saxon period. It also confirms that there was indeed occupation on the site before the Norman Conquest, albeit probably only from the late 10th or early 11th century onwards. However, we should be wary of interpreting this lack of pottery as an absence of all activity. There was an abbey within a hundred metres by 757 and traditionally from 675. The *burh* was founded *c* 900 (Hill 1969) and there was, after all, a mint in Bath from the early 10th century, while the late Saxon abbey flourished from about the same time. There is obviously not a simple relationship between occupation and use of ceramics on or near this site. The soils evidence shows considerable activity, even if only horticulture or agriculture.

The pottery from this period amounts to only 13 sherds, the majority, Bath types A and B of the early-mid 11th century. Three sherds have been tentatively identified as the earlier fabric Bath type E (mid-10th–early 11th century), but all of these occurred residually in Period 5 contexts, suggesting

that they may have entered the soil fills during the cultivation phase of activity.

The pottery assemblage, as with other medieval assemblages in Bath (Vince 1979; 1991; 1999), is made up of local fabrics and those centred on west Wiltshire, suggesting that Bath tended to look south and east in its contacts, possibly reflecting the existence of this hinterland as a source of wool for the textile industry. Trade with more distant areas may be reflected in the presence of the whetstone of Norwegian schist, possibly coming to Bath via the port of Bristol, but also a reminder of the presence of Norse armies here in the late 10th and early 11th centuries.

Nearly all the pits contained various building materials, almost all of which was residual Roman. Two pits contained what may have been flat roof tiles and a ridge tile of medieval type. They could not be certainly distinguished from Roman forms, but if they are genuine medieval roof tiles, it would imply that these pits were 12th century or later in date. A small number of bone and stone objects of 9th–11th century date (p.00) confirms that there was some Anglo-Saxon activity on or close to the site. One of the bone objects occurred in the trench 769/863 and another in pit 1134. The remainder occurred residually in later medieval pits or in redeposited medieval soils used as make-up below Manners' Tepid Pool. Tools associated with weaving or textile production (pin beaters) complement those found in the Bath Street excavations (Bircher 1999) and Citizen House (Ambrose and Henig 1979), which are also dated to the 9th–10th centuries. The wool and cloth trade was an important element of Bath's wealth during the middle ages and the scatter of artefacts found in the south-west quadrant of the city may hint at its origins in the Anglo-Saxon period. By the 14th century a single tailor is the only worker connected with these trades recorded in this area of the city originally known as Binbury, clothworkers mostly having moved to the suburbs by this time (Davenport, 2002, 106).

The isolated human bones found in Periods 5–7.2 were all redeposited. There is no evidence that a graveyard ever existed in the immediate vicinity of the site at this time, although the cemetery at St John's Hospital was founded just to the west in the 14th century. However those found in Period 5 were deposited earlier than this. The most likely explanation is that the bone derived from burials taking place in the immediate post-Roman centuries before graveyards became formalised. Alternatively the bones came in from elsewhere, being added to the cultivation soil and redistributed during subsequent pit digging. A similar occurrence of a "stray" human femur was also recorded in pre-Conquest levels at Bath Street in 1986 (Bath Street site archive, Roman Baths Museum, Bath, unpublished).

Chapter 6: Spa Period 5: The medieval pits, 11th–16th centuries

OVERVIEW

No structural remains of medieval occupation were present, but evidence of intense pit digging was found. Pits survived in the western and central areas (Figs 6.1 & 6.3), which were less severely truncated, together with a few pit bases in the cellars of 7–7a Bath Street (Figs 6.2 & 6.4). Several pits were exposed in section in the north-east area, but could not be excavated. The latter area, together with evidence from the adjacent Bilbury Lane cellar, suggests that preservation to the east of the Taylor buildings was better, with pits apparently cut through dark soil deposits (Fig. 4.12). However, the development plans were modified and no further work was undertaken in the Bilbury Lane cellar.

A total of 60 pits was identified, 52 within the main excavation area, seven within the cellars of 7–7a Bath Street and one in the Bilbury Lane cellar. Of these, all but six were excavated, most in their entirety, including a dense complex of over a dozen intercutting pits at the north end of the western area. It would have been very easy to regard this latter group as an area of homogeneous garden soil. However, careful (and time consuming) excavation and recording allowed each individual feature to be identified and excavated. This detailed sequence of activity has allowed a body of data of artefactual and environmental evidence to be recovered. Environmental sampling of pits was undertaken for plant macrofossils, animal bone, pollen and soil micromorphology. Pollen proved to be poorly preserved and no further work on this was done following the assessment. No environmental samples were taken from the pits in the cellars of 7–7a Bath Street. Palaeo-environmental analysis included the work on soil micromorphology and the animal bone, but following the post-excavation assessment of the plant macrofossils no further analysis was undertaken on the plant remains, though the material is available for future research.

GEOARCHAEOLOGY OF THE MEDIEVAL DEPOSITS
by David Jordan

The medieval deposits contrast with the Roman strata and consist entirely of pit fills. As a result the evidence is in the form of redeposited strata, limiting the inferences that can be drawn and the range of observations that can be made on the processes of deposition. What can be done is to infer details about the medieval occupation of the site from those characteristics of the deposits, which they have inherited from the contexts in which they were originally formed.

The depositional structure of most of the fills suggests that they may not be the result of natural silting and may, instead, represent deliberate filling. There is little evidence of fine-lens sorting typical of natural erosion silting and the coarse inclusions are not very clearly orientated with the strata boundaries, which suggests that they were deposited in individual episodes rather than as part of a gradual process of accumulation.

The form of some pits suggests that they were dug, at least in part, as quarry pits. It is interesting, therefore, that most of the fills are very different from the Roman strata through which they are partly cut, implying that the pits were filled quickly with material derived from other medieval strata above and not left open to fill with unconsolidated Roman strata collapsed from the pit walls.

Samples from 103 medieval pit fill contexts were analysed. Most are dark, granular, finer and much less stony than the earlier deposits and of very high magnetic susceptibility. They are almost all calcareous, although the calcium carbonate is well dispersed within them. The strong granular structure includes a high proportion of faunal excrement indicating that it has been repeatedly reworked by an active soil biota, although much of this structure could be seen, in thin section, to be 'aged' and thus perhaps to have been inherited from an earlier soil. Indeed the general "garden soil" character of many of the medieval deposits is similar to that found in urban medieval surface soils, sometimes under small-scale cultivation as, for example, at sites outside the medieval city at Walcot Street, Bath.

The dark colours reflect the abundance of finely divided organic matter, most of which appears to be uncarbonised very humified organic matter, a consequence of the strong biological activity. Any colour variations usually results from the addition of earlier deposits, especially Roman building debris.

The magnetic susceptibility is much higher than that of the earlier deposits and the presence of charcoal suggests that much of the additional susceptibility is due to the addition of burnt domestic debris and, perhaps, the formation of biogenic magnetic minerals during the decomposition of domestic waste. The strength of the susceptibility suggests, moreover, that the volume of such debris and waste within the medieval strata must be very considerable – perhaps one of the main contributions to the additional depth of medieval deposits over the Roman surfaces.

The relatively fine soil texture results partly from the gradual weathering and physical decay of the Roman building materials as evidenced by common fragments of Oolitic limestone and mortar and partly from the addition of finer occupation debris, perhaps including daub.

Pits fills, not strongly contaminated by the debris of pit-side collapse are relatively uniform both internally and in comparison to each other. The variations, which do occur, are within a relatively narrow range of properties and values, suggesting that they derived from relatively homogeneous deposits, which imply processes of large as well as small scale mixing. Cultivation is the most obvious explanation. There are few other processes which are likely to have brought about such a large-scale remixing of the surface soil and allowed the soil biota to flourish to the extent which these well-formed soil structures imply. At the very least there was sufficient, persistently open ground for a dense soil biological community to develop and remain active over a long period. The variations in magnetic susceptibility in these otherwise homogenous deposits suggest, on the other hand, that this homogenisation was not complete and it is possible that dumps of occupation debris, containing differing concentrations of susceptible contaminants, may have remained as patches of variation within the soil.

The conclusion is that the occupation/cultivation soils had been accumulating for some time before the pit digging episodes, which must have extended back at least into the period of the foundation of the Alfredian *Burh c* 900, if not earlier.

STRATIGRAPHIC AND STRUCTURAL EVIDENCE

Introduction

The pits which survived to the highest level date to the mid 11th century, which implies that the ground surface had generally reached the level of about 20.7–20.8 m by that date. At Bath Street the equivalent ground surface was 22.3 m OD. This difference in level can be partly accounted for by the natural slope, but not wholly, as the original drop in level of the pre-Roman ground surface from Bath Street to the western area of the spa site was about 0.75 m. This in itself could argue that occupation north of Bath Street was more intense (if that is what increased deposition means).

The only area where actual remnants of medieval/post-medieval garden soil may have survived was in a small isolated section at the northernmost limit of the central strip of excavation. Here an earlier pit (443) appeared to be sealed by a fairly horizontal layer of garden soil (430) (Fig. 6.1). In view of the presence of the complex of intercutting pits only a few metres to the south it could be argued that this overlying layer was in fact pit fill truncated on all sides by later walls. However, the presence of clay pipe fragments suggested that this deposit was later than the pit fill and may have been a more general soil layer of late medieval to post-medieval date. Pottery within it includes both medieval wares and later 16th century material. It is also at a higher level, the surface being at 21.12 m OD compared to the top of the 11th and 12th century pits at *c* 20.7 m. A slightly higher level of preservation to 20.85–20.9 m OD was observed in the north-east corner of the site in the section exposed following demolition of the Taylor pool walls. Here some fills of a series of intercutting pits survived to just below the modern floor foundations, but no *in situ* soil survived here. These deposits may be continuous with those exposed in the Bilbury Lane cellar, where garden soils (1901) appear to survive together with one pit (1917) cut through them at *c* 20.3 m OD.

Pit Structure and Function

The pits encompassed a variety of shapes and sizes. Bearing in mind that most have been truncated by later activity it is impossible to know their full depth, though an indication of this is provided by those surviving to a higher level in the north-east and north-west areas. It is also apparent that shallow pits comparable to 701 would not have survived in the heavily truncated areas and that the sample is, therefore, incomplete.

Pit depths ranged from 0.45 m [701] (Fig. 6.5) to 1.45 m [950] in the NW area and up to 1.65 m [2109] in the north-east area (Fig. 6.1). However, if some of the adjacent truncated pits were cut from the same levels, depths could have been as much as 1.85 m. Pit widths/lengths also vary considerably, from 0.9 to 3.0 m.

Pit shape shows considerable variation. In plan, they range from circular through oval, kidney shaped, subrectangular to rectangular. In profile, they cover bowl or basin shaped, cylindrical, conical, straight-sided, barrel and undercutting. The bases may be irregular, with shallow rounded scoops cut to different levels [1096–7, 935, 2022–4], and in the base of some, which had been cut into the natural palaeosol, circular or semi-circular scoops from spades could be seen cutting into the clay base [909, 960].

The variation in shape and size may reflect differences in their primary function, which is an aspect of medieval pits that has not been specifically addressed, other than to accept the traditional view that they were dug for the disposal of rubbish or as cesspits, which may in fact represent their secondary function. An obvious pattern among the pits was the preference to chase the tops of the main Roman walls as reflected in pits 998, 954, 1010, 935, 1096 and 1097. In the more truncated levels below 7–7a Bath Street small pockets of material (1612, 1652, 1807) akin to pit fill occurred intermittently along the tops of the two main walls of Building D. Only occasionally

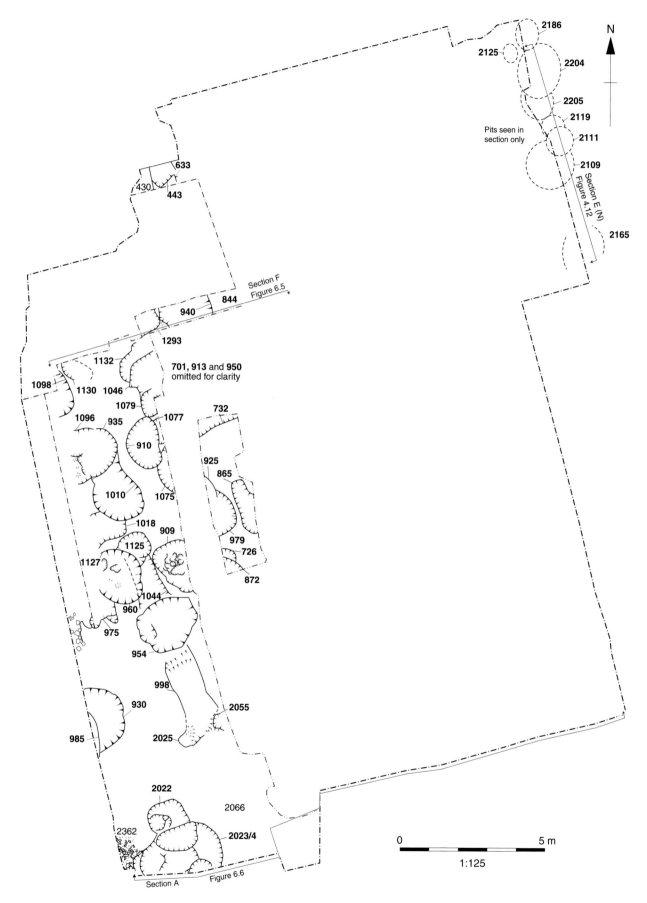

Figure 6.1   Bath Spa excavations: Plan of Period 5 features.

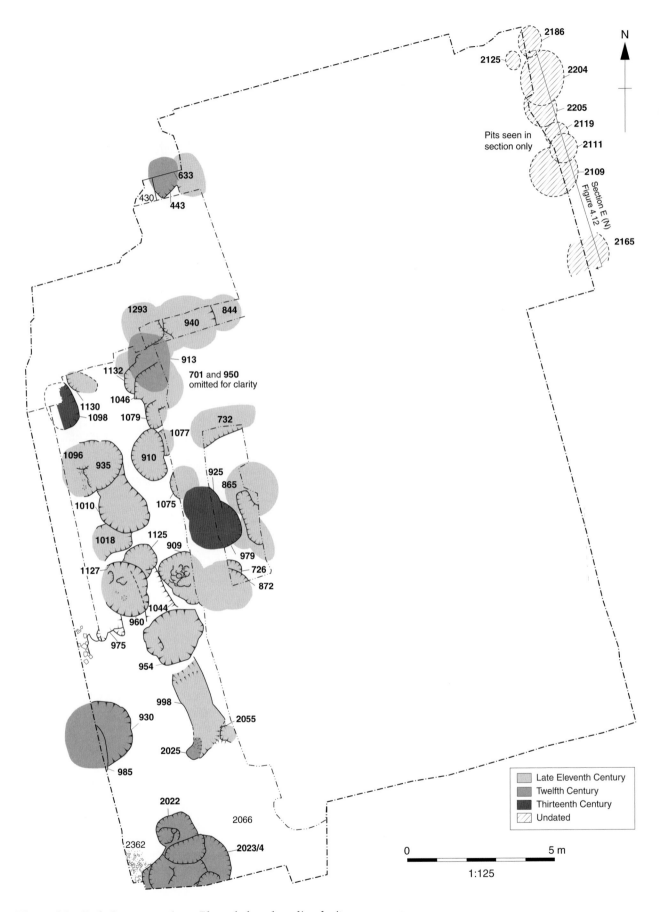

Figure 6.2 Bath Spa excavations: Plan of phased medieval pits.

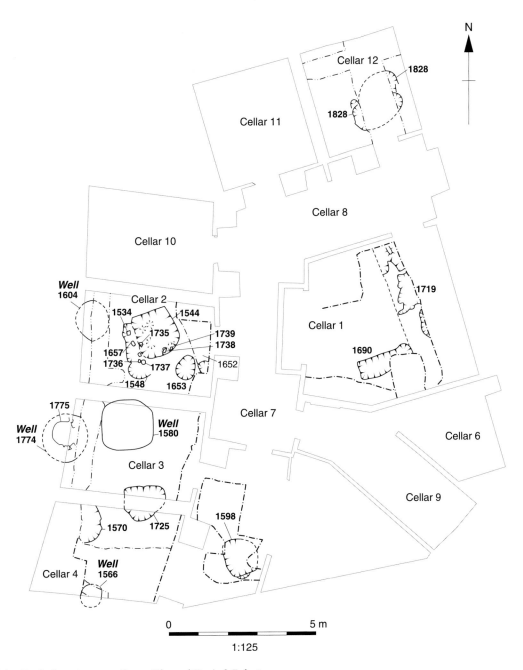

Figure 6.3   Bath Street excavations: Plan of Period 5 features.

was a feature (such as 1719), specifically designated a robber trench (Fig. 6.3). This observation
implies that many of the pits were dug primarily
as quarries for Roman building material. The fills
of all these features, whether regarded as pits or robber trenches, were similar, suggesting there was
little material difference between their subsequent
treatments.

These activities represent a phase of deliberate
reclamation of stone or mortar from the Roman
foundations. This is best illustrated along the line of
the western wall [1360] of Building D, which had
clearly been robbed out along much of its length by
the digging of a series of pits chasing the wall during
the mid 11th century [pits 935, 954, 998, 1010, 1130].

Only one pit cutting into the wall was dated to the
16th century and its position is probably coinciden-
tal [1097] (Fig. 7.1). These features represent a series
of individually dug features and so can be regarded
as robber pits, rather than robber trenches. Medieval
robbing was observed along several other Roman
walls, including pit 732 over wall 1380, dated to the
mid 11th century, and pit 2195 over wall 2149 [=46].
The robbing over wall 2149 was only observed in
section and no dating evidence could be obtained,
however layer 2174 over wall 2175 produced a
single early 11th century pot (see Fig. 5.1 for
location). The fills of all these incidents of robbing
are very similar to those in many of the other
medieval pits.

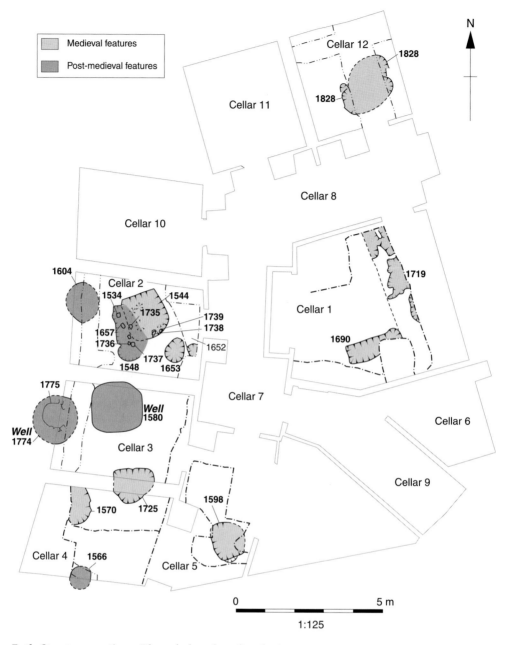

Figure 6.4   Bath Street excavations: Plan of phased medieval pits.

Three pits have the appearance of small scale quarrying activity relating to Roman make-up deposits. These pits usually have distinct undercutting of the pit walls or appear to be a series of interconnecting hollows. The latter was clearly the case for pit 2023–4, which was initially thought to represent two or more intercutting pits (Figs 6.1 & 6.6). However no evidence could be found in the fill to indicate more than one feature and in general character it resembles a series of interconnecting scoops, expanding out from a central core, probably representing a large area of quarrying into the adjacent Roman deposits, which consisted of very hard gravel, sand and mortar. In pit 1075 (Fig. 6.1; see Fig. 4.4), the surviving west wall had been quarried to create an extreme overhang of 0.55 m

suggesting that one particular seam within the Roman floor make-up layers was especially desirable. Something similar may have been done in pit 909, where a large solid block of Roman floor make-up deposits 0.5 m long had slumped into its base, suggesting deep undercutting on the south side of this pit also. A mid 11th century date is attributed to these pits, although a single sherd of mid 12th century date in the upper fill of pit 2023/4 may indicate later activity also (Fig. 6.6). It is reasonably clear, then, that a substantial group of the pits on this site are robber or quarry pits

The other pits appear to have had a different primary purpose, though any Roman material encountered could have been used to create or repair gravelled surfaces or yards, as little of this material returned in the pit fills. Most of the deeper pits [1098, 1046] (for Pit 1046 see Fig. 4.4), which cut through the Roman levels stopped close to the surface of the palaeosol. In these cases the intention may have been to create better drainage within the soil, as iron-panning within the Roman layers may have caused waterlogging in places. If so, it was successful, as there was no evidence of waterlogging here, in contrast to the Bath Street pits. Later disturbances, such as the creation of the Tepid Bath, are also likely to have drained the site in recent centuries. A few pits dug more deeply into the palaeosol may have been continued to obtain clay for daub or other purposes [909, 960, 1544]. However, some pits were cut only into the surface of the surviving Roman deposits [930, 940, 1018, 1079, 1096, 1131, 1303] and in some areas pits were cut entirely within other pit fills [eg. 701, 913, 950 cut within or into pit 940] and these may have been intended purely for waste disposal.

Pit Fills

The immediate impression of virtually all the soil fills of the pits was that they consisted of homogeneous dark organic or humic rich, sandy-clay soils. Detailed observation of the pit sections generally revealed considerably more variation than this. It became clear that most pit fills were made up of a series of deliberate tips, in which the basic matrix was rich organic soil, but contained in addition a variety of other materials. These included limestone rubble, river gravel and pebbles, clay tile, mortar, carbonised material, both charcoal and seeds, and bone. In some cases fills were dominated by fine, soily material, and noticeably lacking in the coarser components.

The apparent absence of eroded layers from the pit sides or natural soil accumulation suggests that the pits were refilled fairly rapidly or were protected in some way from an excess of weathering. However, where pits were cut through soil layers (within other pits) very similar to the material they were filled with, it may be difficult to distinguish between dumped and eroded soil material. Nonetheless, the profile of many of the pits is not consistent with erosion of the pit walls. The micromorphology analysis confirms that pits were rapidly infilled with a typical urban medieval "garden soil" subject to small scale cultivation. Similarity of deposits and inclusions, such as the tips of grain in pit 443 or pit 913, sometimes suggests that material filling the pits was coming from the same source and being deposited in rapid succession.

The pits produced relatively prolific quantities of finds, predominantly pottery and animal bone, together with ceramic building material (though most is residual Roman tile), slag and infrequent metal, stone, glass or other artefacts. A low density of residual Roman material was present in the form of samian ware and other pottery, tile, brick, *opus signinum*, wall plaster, tesserae and some coins.

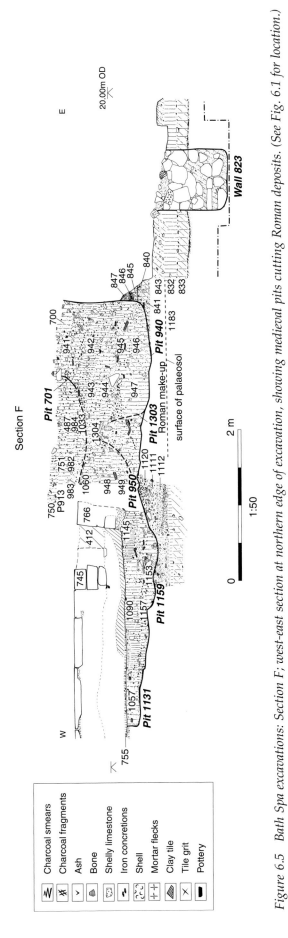

Figure 6.5 Bath Spa excavations: Section F; west-east section at northern edge of excavation, showing medieval pits cutting Roman deposits. (See Fig. 6.1 for location.)

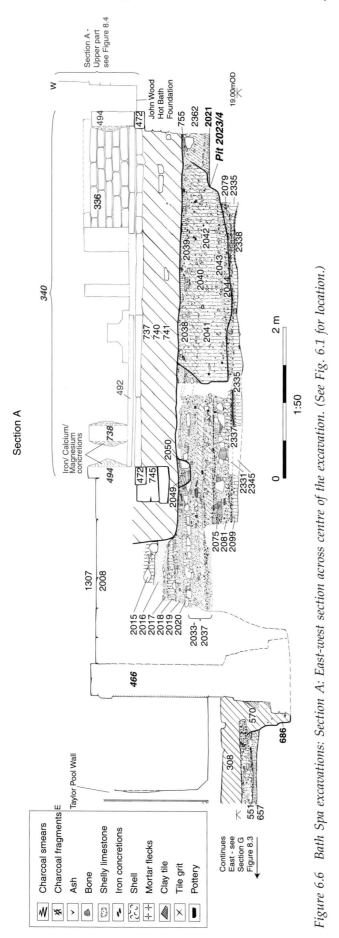

Figure 6.6 Bath Spa excavations: Section A: East-west section across centre of the excavation. (See Fig. 6.1 for location.)

A certain amount of residual worked flint was also recovered. This residual Roman material appears to have derived both from the foundations of Building D (ultimately from the early Roman unplaced building) and from the superstructure of Building D itself. A large proportion of the Roman pottery from post-Roman levels is moderately or very abraded, suggesting it had been incorporated in a cultivation soil that had accumulated over the building, entering the pit fills as a constituent of this soil.

Two pits (960, 1152 the latter not seen in plan) contained solid tips of bone, which probably represent dumps of butchery waste. In the case of 960 the soil matrix in which the bone occurred was very clayey and greasy, suggestive of cess or, perhaps in this case, the discarded soft tissue of the animals, such as skin and offal, that was not utilised. In most cases the organic material within the pit fills did not have the appearance of cess type waste, but rather that of rotted humic material. A few pits (including 443, 940) contained large dumps of carbonized grain (1000+ grains per sample), whilst more moderate quantities of 50–100 grains were common throughout the pits.

Dating (Tables 6.1–6.3)

The majority of the pits date to the 11th century. Nothing intrinsic in their characteristics distinguish early 11th century from later pits. Thirty-three are assigned to the mid 11th century on ceramic evidence or stratigraphical relationships. Two thirds of the latter group could, in fact, be pre-Conquest and technically of Period 4, as they contain no certain post-Conquest pottery types. Clearly the subdivision of the pits into pre- and post-Conquest is artificial but as far as it goes, it does suggest that the practice of pit digging started to diminish after the Norman Conquest. After the 11th century the digging of pits was sporadic: 5 or 6 are assigned to the 12th century, three to the 13th century, two to 16th century and one to the 17th century. Two contained 18th century ceramics, but the one in cellar 5 [1598] was probably earlier in date: it contained a single 18th century sherd, which was almost certainly intrusive from service trenches cutting it (Fig. 6.3). There were six undated pits seen only in section in the north-east area, some or all of which are likely to have been 11th century in date. Clearly the frequency of pit digging was not great: even in the 11th century the numbers represent an average of only one pit every three years. In the subsequent centuries it was a rare event: it is summed up in Figure 6.7.

Spatial distribution

The spatial distribution of the pits is also uneven with intense pit digging in the north-west corner of the excavation resulting in much intercutting with more dispersed and isolated pits beyond this core area (Fig. 6.1). The impression in the cellars in Bath

Table 6.1 *Period 5: Summary of 11th century pits (Finds in brackets are residual prehistoric-Roman).*

Pit No.	Date	Form	Function	Fill layers of pit	Finds/environmental
701 section F	Mid 11th C	Sub-conical		751 sandy gravelly silt, 487 stony soil & occupation, 982 stony soil with sparse occupation, 983 gritty soil charcoal & little occupation, 984 charcoal & ash, 1033 stony soil with freq. charcoal & mortar lenses	Pottery (+Ro), (CBM, Tesserae), daub, glass, Fe, slag, CuA dribble, (Ro coin), oyster shell, bone, seeds
726	Mid 11th C	Cylindrical		727 Dark gritty clay soil with freq. charcoal & occupation	Pottery (+ Ro), (CBM), slag, bone, soil micro
732	Mid 11th C	Sub-oval/ linear	Robbing	733 Brown loam with Lst., charcoal & occ., 753 dark soil with flint gravel, Lst. mortar, charcoal & occ., 754 dark soil with Lst. + charcoal, 756 sandy loam, flint gravel, Lst. frq. occ. & charcoal, 735 dark soil on base	Pottery (+Ro), CBM:Med/P-M flat peg/nib tile (+Ro), (Op.sig, tesserae, flint) slag, Pb disc & frag (?Ro), bone, seeds
844 section D & F	Mid 11th C	Base only		848, 847, 846, 849, 845	(CBM), bone, wood
872	Mid 11th C	Circular, basin		871 soft dk loam, charcoal & occupation	Pottery (+Ro), (CBM), bone, seeds
909	Mid 11th C	Sub-circular/oval	Quarrying?	912, 914, 916–8, 924, 928, 994	Pottery (+Ro), (CBM), pennant, (flint), Fe, (Ro coin), oyster shell, bone, seeds
910	Mid 11th C	Sub-oval		911, 919–20, 932, 939, 967–8, 1170	Pottery (+Ro), (CBM), slag, (Ro coin) bone, seeds
925	Mid 11–13th C	Circular		926	(CBM), bone; seeds
934	Mid 11th C	Circular/oval		771–778, 937, 951, 957, 964, 966, 971	Pottery (+Ro), (CBM), mortar, (pennant roof tile), (flint), Fe, slag, bone, seeds
935	Mid 11th C	Circular/oval	Robbing	936, 972, 1027, 993	Pottery (+Ro), (CBM), daub, (flint), slag, crucible, oyster shell, bone, charcoal, seeds
940 section F & D	Mid 11th C	Sub-circular/oval		700, 941–7, 1207, 1221	Pottery (+Ro), (CBM), wall plaster ?Ro, (pennant roof tile), glass, Fe, slag, oyster shell, bone, seeds
950 section C, F	Mid 11th C	Oval/conical	Robbing	948, 949, 1060, 1093, 1122	Pottery (+Ro), (CBM), slag, oyster shell, bone, seeds
954	Mid 11th C	Sub-oval		955, 1005, 976	Pottery (+Ro), (CBM), glass, bone, seeds
960	Mid 11th C	Oval, basin		958, 959, 1034, 1026	Pottery (+Ro), (CBM), spindle whorl, (flint), stone rubber, glass, crucible, slag, Fe, SF6028 Fe sheet, SF6056 Pb; SF6020 metal strip; oyster, egg shell, bone, wood, seeds
998	Mid 11th C	Rectangular	Robbing	1000, 933, 1004, 999, 1055	Pottery (+Ro), (CBM, Op.sig, pennant roof tile), SF6061 whetstone, (flint), glass, crucible, slag, SF6019 AE strip, oyster shell, bone, seeds, soil micro

Table 6.1 (Continued)

Pit No.	Date	Form	Fill layers of pit	Function	Finds/environmental
1010	Mid 11th C	Circular bowl	1011 Brown clay soil, charcoal, few stones, 1022 Lst. rubble & building debris, 1023 brown gritty clay, small stones & charcoal, 1024 clean Lias clay with oyster shell & CBM flecks, 1025 gritty Lias clay & flint gravel, +shell & CBM	Robbing	Pottery (+Ro), (CBM), (Op.sig, wall plaster, mortar, flint) glass, Fe, slag, SF6023 AE sheet frag, oyster shell, bone
1018	Mid 11th C	Sub-rectangular	1019 Lst. grit, sand & gravel with ash, charcoal & CBM		Pottery (+Ro), (CBM, flint), bone, seeds, pollen, soil micro
1044	Mid 11th C	Rectangular	1038–40, 1043, 1055, 1119–20	Robbing	Pottery (+Ro), (CBM, pennant roof tile, flint), slag, oyster shell, bone, seeds
1046 section C	Mid 11th C	Oval, cylindrical	1085–6, 1092, 1179–80		Pottery (+Ro), (CBM), slag, oyster shell, bone, seeds
1075 section C	Mid 11th C	Circular, beehive	1076, 1363, 1104	Quarrying	Pottery (+Ro), (CBM), bone, seeds
1077 section C	Mid 11th C	Circular, bowl	1078		Pottery (+Ro), (CBM), slag, bone, seeds
1079 section C	Mid 11th C	Sub-rectangular	1080–2		Pottery (+Ro), (CBM, pennant roof tile), slag, bone, seeds
1125/7 section F	Mid 11th C	Oval, bowl	1124, 1095, 1118, 1126, 1030		Pottery (+Ro), (CBM), (flint), oyster shell, bone
1130	Mid 11th C	Oval	1089, 1129	Robbing	None
1132 section C	Mid 11th C	Oval, cylindrical	1123, 1135–6, 1140		Pottery (+Ro), (CBM), Fe, slag, bone, seeds
1152 section C	Mid 11th C	Circular, conical	1045, 1070–2, 1083–4		Pottery (+Ro), (CBM), Fe, crucible, slag, oyster shell, bone, seeds
1226	Mid 11th C	Truncated base	1219		Pottery (+Ro), (CBM), slag, bone, seeds
1263 section F	Mid 11th C	Oval/sub-rectangular	1262, 1281–3	Robbing	Pottery, (CBM), slag, bone
1293	Mid 11th C	Sub-circular/sub-rectangular	1290–2, 1301–2, 1350–4		Pottery (+Ro), (CBM), wall plaster, (flint), oyster shell, bone, organic
1303 section F	Mid 11th C	Truncated base	1304–6, 1308–9		None
1570	Mid 11th C	Circular	1571, 1733	Robber trench	Pottery (+Ro), (CBM), mortar, bone
1719	Mid 11th C	Irregular linear base	1612, 1688		Bone
1725	Mid 11th C	Cylindrical	1726–8		Pottery, stone shingle, slag, oyster shell, bone
2025	Mid 11th C	Oval, beehive	2051–4		Pottery (+Ro), (CBM), mortar, (flint), glass, bone, seeds
2055 section C	Mid 11th C	Circular/oval	2056–7		Pottery (+Ro), (CBM), wall plaster, bone, seeds

Section A: Fig. 6.6; Section C: Fig. 4.4; Section D: Fig. 42; Section E north: Fig. 4.12; Section F: Fig. 6.5.

114

Table 6.2 Period 5: Summary of 12th–13th century pits.

Pit No.	Date	Form	Function	Fill layers of pit	Finds/environmental
633	pre- Mid 12th C	?Sub-oval		488, 489	None
443 section D	Mid 12th C	Sub-rectangular		434–9, 444, 703	Pottery (+Ro), clay pipe (intrusive), (CBM), daub furnace lining; wall plaster, (pennant roof tile), (flint), slag, Fe, bone, seeds
913 section C	Mid 12th C	Conical		748, 759, 749, 760, 921, 923, 922, 761, 750, 915, 929	Pottery (+Ro), (CBM, op.sig, flint), Fe dividers, nail, arrow/spear head, slag, bone, seeds
930	Mid 12th C	Circular		931	Pottery (+Ro), clay pipe (intrusive), (CBM, flint) Fe, slag, bone, seeds
2022	Mid 12th C	Sub-rectangular		2029	Pottery, (CBM), Fe, slag, bone, seeds
2023/4 section A	Mid 12th C	Sub-oval, undercut	Quarrying	2038–44	Pottery (+Ro), (CBM, Op.sig, flint), glass, Fe, slag, oyster shell, SF6084 drilled scapula, bone, seeds
794	Mid 13th C	Circular		793, 795, 798, 900, 903–5	Pottery (+Ro), (CBM, Op.sig, mortar, pennant roof tile, flint), daub furnace lining, glass, Fe, slag, bone, seeds
1098	Mid 13th C	Sub-rectangular		1029, 1166–8	Pottery (+Ro), (CBM), oyster shell, bone, charcoal, seeds

Section A: Fig. 6.6; Section C: Fig. 4.4; Section D: Fig. 42; Section E north: Fig. 4.12; Section F: Fig. 6.5.

Table 6.3 Summary of undated pits.

Pit No.	Form	Function	Fill layers of pit	Comments
1653	Dished base		1654	
1828	Base		1819	(residual Roman sherd)
2109	?Cylindrical		2110	Seen in section only (Section E –N)
2111	?Cylindrical		2112–5, 2147	Seen in section only (Section E –N)
2119	Truncated base		2116–8	Seen in section only (Section E –N)
2125	Truncated base		2124	Seen in section only (Section E –N)
2165	Rectangular	Robber trench	2154–64	Seen in section only (Section E –N)
2186	Barrel		2136, 2122, 2143, 2187–8	Seen in section only (Section E –N)
2204	?Cylindrical, oval		2142	Seen in section only (Section E –N)
2205	Not visible		2121	Seen in section only (Section E –N)

Section E north: Fig. 4.12.

Street is of a more dispersed pattern of pits (Fig. 6.3), as would appear to have been the case also in the 1989 excavation. This could be deceptive in view of the severe truncation both areas have suffered. Another dense group was present in the north-east area as exposed in section E (Fig. 4.12). The pattern may suggest that some areas were preferred for pit digging and/or, as one might expect, that the areas available for this were limited by adjacent occupation and land use.

Patterns in spatial distribution of pits have not been easy to perceive in Bath. It is reasonable to hypothesise that distributions may reflect property boundaries or the layout of tenements. It was suggested in the Bath Street report that pits occupied open spaces at the backs of tenements, but in that excavation no clusters or patterns could be discerned and there was little intercutting of pits (Davenport 1999, 62). In contrast, at the Citizen

House site there is a much greater concentration of pits with a greater amount of intercutting, more closely comparable with the pattern in the Spa excavations. It is significant that the medieval stratigraphy at that site was much less truncated and presumably more representative. It is now possible to suggest that there are areas in the town with and without clusters of pits, but it will only be possible to refine such patterns when further areas of medieval deposits become available for study.

ENVIRONMENTAL EVIDENCE

The pits were extensively sampled to recover plant and animal remains for environmental and economic data. Assessments only were carried out on the plant material, though the seed from the pits has good potential for further study. The pollen assessment by Heather Tinsley and the assessments on plant macrofossils by Julie Jones and Ruth Pelling can be found in the site archives. The comments below are based on the assessment reports.

As part of the pollen assessment, six samples were selected for analysis from the fills of six medieval pits. Four of these were of mid 11th century date, one of early 11th and one of early 12th century date. Reasonable preservation was found in some samples, but it was noted that generally the assemblage was biased towards *taxa* more resistant to decay, in particular dandelion type and cabbage family. The pollen assemblages are all similar and are typical of pits on urban sites (Greig 1982), which have a small pollen catchment area. However, interpretation of the assemblages can be very difficult as, while grass and weed pollen could be derived from plants growing within the city, some *taxa* could be brought in from outside the urban area, for example as hay for animal feed. It was this uncertainty in determining the source of material found together with poor preservation that led to the decision not to proceed with full analysis. The pollen identified is summarised in Table 6.4.

One hundred and two samples were taken from 33 pits for recovery of plant macrofossils. The dating of samples reflects the date distribution of pits as a whole with the majority (25) dated to the mid 11th century and smaller numbers from 12th, mid 13th and 16th century. Charred remains were widespread throughout the samples and only two samples (from the same pit) contained no seed (Table 6.5). Six samples contained well in excess of 1000 grains (three of these from P443), whilst a further 29 contained over 100 grains. There are no obvious differences between the assemblages of different dates, though a more detailed analysis could throw up some variations.

Cereals were dominated by free-threshing Triticum sp. (wheat), while *Hordeum vulgare* (barley), *Avena* sp. (oats) and occasional *Secale cereale* (rye) were also noted. Grain from a small number of samples (mostly from pit 913) was 'clinkered' (distorted by excessive heat). Chaff was rare, occurring in low quantities in nine samples, mostly

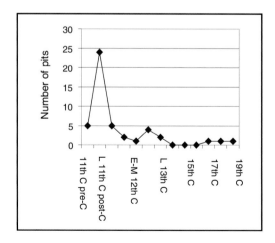

Figure 6.7 Graph showing chronological distribution of pits by number in Periods 4–6.

116

Table 6.4 *Quantification of pollen and spore types from the medieval pits.*

Context	P1134 (1133)	P1077 (1078)	P1044 (1039)	P998 (933)	P701 (487)	P??? (???)
Sample No.	5778	5757	5759	5737	5719	?
Date	E 11th C	E-M 11th C	M 11th C	M 11th C	E 12th C	?
Pinus		1				
Quercus		1	1			
Fraxinus			1			
Alnus		1				
Corylus	1					
Poaceae	4	5	3		+	1
Cereal	4	8			1	
Lactuceae	39	21	32	10	8	18
Chenopodiaceae			1			
P. lanceolata	1					
Cirsium	1					
Centaurea	1		1			
Apiaceae		1				
Brassicaceae	7	3	9		1	4
Solidago virgaurea		2	1			
Cyperaceae			1			
Pteridium	7		8	1		
Filicales	3		2	1		2
Sphagnum moss			1			
Unidentified		++		+		+
Total	68	43	61	12	10	25
Charcoal	+++	+++	++	++	+++	
Trichuris egg case		1	1			

in the form of culm nodes, plus some rachis segments of *T. aestivum* type (bread wheat) and *H. vulgare* (barley). The evidence suggests that grain was reaching the site in a fully processed state.

In all samples weed seeds were few in relation to grain. About twenty different types were noted and species included common arable weeds such as *Agrostemma githago, Bromus* and *Anthemis cotula*, all

Table 6.5 *Summary of plant macrofossils identified from the medieval pits.*

Cereals	Weeds	Other crops	Fruit	Other
Triticum sp.	*Agrostemma*	*Vicia sativa*	*Malus*	Bracken
T. aestivum	*Bromus*	*Pisum*	*Pyrus*	Fly puparia
Hordeum vulgare	*Anthemis cotula*	*Linum usitatissimum*	*Prunus*	Dung?
Avena	*Centaurea*	*Brassica*	*Rubus*	Egg shell
Secale cereale	*Chenopodium album*	*Corylus avellana*		*Chara* oospore
	Atriplex			
	Fallopia			
	Polygonum			
	Rumex			
	Lithospermum			
	Euphorbia			
	Vicia/Lathyrus			Charcoal
	Ranunculus			*Quercus* sp.
	Grass			*Prunus* sp.
	Medicago/Trifolium			Pomoideae
	Papaver			
	Odontites			
	Umbelliferae			
	Silene			
	Galium			
	Malva			
	Carex			

of which may remain with the grain through the various stages of processing. Additional crop plants were also present including *Vicia sativa* (fodder vetch) and *Linum usitatissimum* (flax). Fragments of hazelnut shell are likely to have derived from food waste and amongst the mineralised seed were *Malus/Pyrus* sp. (apple/pear) and *Prunus* sp. (sloe, cherry etc.). Mineralised fly puparia including some of faecal origin frequently occurred in association with mineralised seed, suggesting some pit fills included a cess element.

Non-charred seeds of *Sambucus nigra* (elder) were present in about 60% of the samples and in very large quantities in some. These seeds are particularly robust and can be found when all other non-charred material has decayed. Occasional non-charred *Papaver* sp. (poppy) was also observed.

MATERIAL EVIDENCE

Medieval Pottery
Summary of the report by Alan Vince

The full report may be found in the site archive.

Mid-11th to mid-13th century

The majority of the early medieval pottery from the site is of Bath fabric A, and accounts for 87% of the material (by sherd count) from both the 11th century pit groups and the later ones in this period (Tables 6.6–6.7). It is ascribed to a so-far-unidentified west Wiltshire source. Some sherds have calcareous inclusions (but are distinguishable from Bath B fabric) and it is suggested that these may be a marker for an 11th to early 12th century date. Over 96% of the sherds are from jar forms: sooting suggests use predominantly in cooking. Bowls, spouted or otherwise and spouted and tripod pitchers are correspondingly rare. Glazed tripod pitchers are late in this period and residual in later periods.

Only 6.5% of the pottery was Bath fabric B, a similar fabric to A, but with fossiliferous and oolitic limestone tempering. Although Bath A and B wares account for the vast majority of the pottery used in the late 11th to early 13th centuries there are other wares present. These consist of a few sherds of coarse wares from surrounding regions and a range of non-local glazed wares. Specifically these were: single examples of Box B ware, Newbury B ware,

Table 6.6   Period 5 pottery from mid 11th-century pits (sherd count) (sp indicates revised dating based on stratigraphic phasing).

Context Group	SPOUT	Bath B	Bath A	Winchester	Stamford	Total
P726	0	2	12	0	0	14
P732	0	1	13	0	0	14
P872	0	0	1	0	0	1
P909	0	0	2	0	0	2
P930	SP	1	1	0	0	2
P934	SP	0	4	0	0	4
P940	0	3	11	0	0	14
P950 (sp L11th C)	0	4	26	0	0	30
P954	0	0	4	0	0	4
P1044	0	1	14	0	1	16
P1075	SP	2	6	0	0	8
P1077	0	0	2	0	0	2
P1079	0	0	3	0	0	3
P1125	0	0	4	0	0	4
P1132	0	2	10	0	0	12
P1226	0	0	1	0	0	1
P1263	0	0	1	0	0	1
P1293	0	1	3	0	0	4
P1570 (cellar 4)	0	0	1	0	0	1
F1719 (cellar 1)	0	0	1	0	0	1
P1725 (cellar 4)	0	0	2	0	0	2
P2025	0	0	3	1	0	4
P2055	0	0	1	0	0	1
TOTAL		17	128	1	1	147

Table 6.7   Period 5: pottery from late 11th-century and later pits (sherd count).

Context Group	Date		Bath A	Bath B	Bath E	Ham Grn	Minety	Newbury B	SE Wilts	SW Cht	Warm coarse	Stamford	Winchester	Total
P910	L11th	SP	7	0	1	0	0	0	1	0	0	0	0	9
P935	L11th	SP	15	2	0	0	0	0	1	0	0	0	0	18
P960	L11th	SP	123	5	1	0	0	0	7	0	0	0	1	137
P1046	L11th	~	6	4	0	0	0	0	1	0	0	0	0	11
P1152	L11th	SP	32	5	0	0	0	0	6	0	0	0	1	44
P701	E12th	~	68	6	0	0	1	0	3	0	0	0	1	79
P2022	E12th	SP	16	2	0	0	1	0	0	0	0	0	0	19
P1044	E-M 12th	~	14	1	0	0	0	0	0	0	0	1	0	16
P443	L12th	~	74	5	0	7	6	0	2	0	0	0	0	94
P913	L12th	SP	152	6	0	1	3	0	2	1	1	0	0	166
P930	L12th	~	0	1	0	1	0	0	0	0	0	0	0	2
P2023 /2024	L12th	SP	102	4	0	0	0	1	0	0	0	0	0	107
Total			595	37	2	9	11	1	23	1	1	1	3	684

chert-tempered ware and Warminster coarse ware from central Wiltshire. The glazed wares are more common. They consist of Ham Green ware, Minety ware, South East Wiltshire glazed ware, Stamford ware and Winchester ware.

Late 13th to early 16th century (Table 6.8)

The later medieval pottery supply in Bath is poorly known and almost every assemblage dated to this period contains only a few sherds of types of this date together with numerous sherds of earlier types. The condition of the entire assemblage suggests that it has been mixed through redeposition and does not allow it to be separated into a 'contemporary' and 'residual' component. There are hints with the Spa assemblage that some of the Bath A vessels are contemporary with the later contexts.

Of the wares first produced in the late 13th century (continuing to the 15th century where an end date is known) the most common was Nash Hill ware, all the identified sherds being from jugs. The remaining wares were from Bristol, Laverstock and an unknown source. The lack of jars suggests that either handmade Bath A vessels were used alongside glazed wheelthrown jugs or metal vessels had supplanted ceramic for cooking.

Later medieval material of late 14th to mid 16th century date consisted of Tudor Green ware and

Table 6.8   Period 5: pits containing late Medieval pottery.

Pits	Date	Bath A	Bath B	Nash Hill	N H?	Winchester
P794	L13th	40	5		1	2
P1098	L13th	3		1		

Malvern Chase glazed ware. All occurred residually in post-medieval contexts, as did two sherds of black glazed Cistercian ware, which is likely to be of mid-16th century or later date in Bath, though known elsewhere from the later 15th century.

Discussion

Pottery was recovered from 40 pits assigned to Period 5. Bath fabrics A and B dominated the assemblage throughout the period. Twenty-two of the pits contained no certainly post-Conquest types and may therefore be contemporary with the pits of Period 4. The dating of some of the later pits was based on a single sherd.

The forms produced in Bath fabrics A and B were predominantly jars and spouted pitchers. During the late 11th and early 12th century tripod pitchers were coming from South East Wiltshire and Minety, whilst later, during the early-mid 12th century, some pitchers were arriving from Stamford. During the late 12th century jugs were obtained from Ham Green and a single sherd from a jar of Newbury type B ware was present. During the late 11th–12th centuries examples of Winchester type ware, nearly all pitchers, occurred including some with incised and roller-stamped decoration.

The pottery indicates that few of the surviving pits were dug after the middle of the 13th century, and the rarity of contexts from later periods, and therefore pottery from them, means that there is only a small amount of evidence present for activity in the area during the late medieval period. Many of the wares which could date to the late medieval period are probably to be interpreted as either late 13th/early 14th century, or as early to mid 16th century finds.

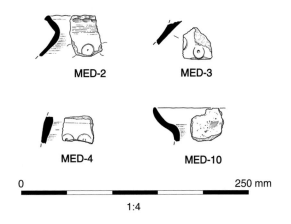

MED-2   MED-3

MED-4   MED-10

0   250 mm

1:4

Figure 6.8   Medieval Pottery, Nos 2–4, 10.

Stratified groups of pottery for the late 11th, 12th and early 13th centuries confirm that Bath was supplied mainly from sources to the east, in central Wiltshire, but including vessels from sites on the Gloucestershire/Wiltshire border (Minety) and a number of vessels from south-east Wiltshire. The very small quantity of pottery from the Bristol area in this sequence is a feature first noted in the 1970s (Vince 1979). A few Ham Green vessels, all jugs, were present together, later on, with a few Bristol vessels, also all jugs.

Ceramic Building Materials
by Ian M Betts

The vast majority of building material in Period 5 is of Roman date, although there are a few fragments of medieval flat tile, probably either nib or peg roofing tile (contexts 733, 986, fabric 15). Similar tiles were found in medieval contexts on the Tramshed site (Betts in prep). These tiles are 11–13 mm in thickness.

The crest of medieval ceramic tiled roofs would have been covered by curved ridge tiles, a probable example of which was found in context 1133 (fabric 28). There are further possible examples from contexts 1543 and 1571, but as they lack glaze and decoration (common features of medieval ridge tiles found elsewhere in Britain) they are extremely difficult to distinguish from Roman *imbrices*. Two fragments of medieval ridge tiles from the Nash Hill kilns (contexts 755, 1029), which date to the late 13th–15th century, were identified amongst the medieval pottery by Alan Vince.

Small Finds
by John Clark

Copper alloy dribble. 30 × 12 × 11 mm. Context 487 SF 6031.

Irregular lead disc, possibly an off-cut. *c* 55 mm diam. Context 733 SF6058.

Iron nail-like object with a circular flat head the same thickness as the shank. 33 × 16 × 5 mm. Context 750 SF6053.

Iron Arrow head; 75 × 40 × 9 mm. Triangular head with shoulders sloping towards the socketed shaft. Possibly the spear point type of arrow head, dated as early medieval. (Saunders and Saunders 1991). Context 750 SF6017.

Iron object. Y-shaped object with one arm partly missing and the other broken off, but present. The stem is curled into a loop. 70 × 28 × 5 mm. Context 750 SF6024.

Two **irregular lead fragments**. Context 959 SF6056.

Whetstone fragment. Devonshire Bats (Upper Greensand). One sharpening surface worn concave. 49 × 45 × 35 mm. Context 1000 SF6061.

Mammal and Bird Bone
by Lorrain Higbee

Introduction

The medieval and later assemblage comprises 1160 countable bones. The vast majority of the assemblage was recovered by hand during the normal course of excavation and smaller quantities were retrieved from the residues of bulk soil samples processed by wet sieving. The bone has been quantified in Table 6.9. An initial assessment (Higbee 2004) highlighted the potential of the relatively large medieval (Period 5) assemblage to elucidate aspects of animal husbandry, dietary provisioning, butchery, animal health and the size/shape conformation of live stock species.

Occurrence and relative importance of species

A complete list of the species identified is given in Table 6.9. In common with most archaeologically recovered animal bone assemblages from Britain the majority of identified fragments from Bath Spa belong to the three main livestock species. Cattle, sheep and pig together account for *c* 84% of the total number of specimens identified to species (or NISP) from all medieval and later periods. A relatively large number of other mammalian species have also been identified, together they account for only *c* 5% of the total NISP and include horse, dog, cat, red deer, fallow deer, rabbit, mole, field vole, house mouse and wood/yellow-necked mouse. Bird bones are more common, accounting for *c* 11% of the total NISP although this is largely due to the large number of chicken bones which alone account for 8% of NISP. Less common bird species include pheasant, duck, goose, pigeon, crow/raven, curlew, passerines and a small species of wader. In addition a very small number of amphibian bones (frog/toad) was also recovered. Most but not all of these less common species probably represent food items whilst the presence of others, such as mole, crow, mice, vole and amphibian, is not considered to result from anthropogenic activity.

Looking more specifically at the relative importance of the three main livestock species by NISP and minimum number of individuals (or MNI) for

Table 6.9 Quantification of Mammal, Bird and Amphibian bone for medieval and post-medieval periods. Number of specimens identified to species (or NISP) for Periods 4–9 for Bath Spa assemblage. Figures in parenthesis are 'non-countable' bones after Davis (1992). * denotes figure includes 16 bones from partial skeleton from P960.

	Period				
Taxon	4	5	6–6.1	7–7.2	9
Human		2	1	(1)	
Cattle	21 (2)	280 (60)	17 (3)	63 (9)	7
Sheep/Goat	23 (3)	501 (52)	26 (2)	87 (13)	9 (2)
Sheep	2	36 (15)	2	2 (2)	(1)
Goat				1 (2)	
Pig	16	143 (25)	11	29 (8)	5
Horse		11 (6)		3	
Dog	2	6 (2)	1	1	
Dog/Fox		1			
Cat		20* (7)		1 (1)	1
Red deer	1	4 (1)		(1)	
Fallow deer			1	1	
Rabbit		8 (2)	1	2 (1)	1
Mole		1			
Vole cf field	1	1			
Mouse cf house		3			
Mouse cf wood/ yellow-necked			1		
Small mammal		(24)			
Chicken	1	108 (1)	3	14	1
Chicken/ Pheasant		2			
Pheasant		4			
Duck		4	1		
Goose		7	2	1	
Pigeon cf wood /rock pigeon		3		2	
Corvid cf crow /raven		4			
Curlew		1			
Passerine		7			
small wader		1			
Frog	1	2			
Cattle/Horse sized	(1)	(99)	(2)	(16)	(2)
Sheep/pig sized	(5)	(162)	(12)	(19)	
Total	68	1160	67	207	24

the medieval periods, sheep is the most abundant species accounting for 56% NISP and *c* 61% MNI in the medieval assemblage. Cattle are the second most abundant at *c* 29% NISP and *c* 24% MNI, followed by pig at *c* 15% NISP and 14% MNI.

The relative frequency of livestock species in the medieval assemblage, with its high proportion of sheep and low frequency of pig, is similar to the 10th-13th century Citizen House assemblage (Grant 1979). Both assemblages derive almost entirely from

pits, indeed 93% of the medieval Spa assemblage was recovered from pits, the majority of which date to the 11th century. Grant used several methods to quantify the Citizen House assemblage of which the 'epiphyses only' method is considered the most comparable in this instance; by this measure sheep account for 49% of the assemblage, cattle for a further 37% and pig only 14%. However, the relative frequencies of livestock species recorded for a number of other medieval assemblages from Bath show a different trend. The medieval assemblages from Orange Grove, Upper Borough Walls (Bull and Payne 1991) and Tramsheds (Higbee n.d.2) all have higher percentages of cattle (by NISP) and the Swallow Street assemblage (Browne 1991) is unique in having a very high proportion (56%) of pig, but in this instance it reflects the monastic origin of the bone waste. These Bath assemblage with their high frequencies of cattle are more in keeping with general national trends for urban assemblages (Sykes 2001), but a regionally distinct pattern based upon sheep husbandry is beginning to emerge and this is reflected in both rural and urban assemblages. For example at the late Saxon-medieval farmstead of Eckweek, Peasedown St John, 5 miles south west of Bath (Davis 1991), sheep comprise 62% of NISP in the early periods (AD 950–1250) and 65% of NISP in the later periods (AD 1250–1400); at Union Street, Bristol (Higbee n.d.3) sheep account for *c* 44–61% of NISP in the earliest periods (early/mid 12th-late 13th/14th centuries) and similar frequencies have been noted for Ilchester, Somerset (Levitan 1982) and Malmesbury, Wiltshire (Sykes 2002). Furthermore, although the Bath Spa assemblage does not fit with expected national trends for an urban assemblage it does appear to reflect wider national trends that are characterised by an increase in the number of sheep relative to cattle and a decline in the number of pigs (Grant 1988; Albarella and Davis 1996). These changes can generally be linked to the increasing use of horses as plough animals, the growth of the wool industry, which reached its height in the Middle Ages, and the loss of woodland for pannage.

Sheep

Body part distribution

The medieval sheep bone assemblage shows most parts of the mutton carcass were represented, with large numbers of bones of high meat value from both the fore and hind limbs. Mandibles, loose teeth and bones from limb extremities are less common, and although skulls and horn cores are present the numbers are small. The medieval assemblage shows a degree of similarity with the Citizen House assemblage but also a few marked contrasts. All parts of the mutton carcasses are represented in both assemblages, suggesting the presence of whole carcasses, however the Citizen House assemblage includes a greater proportion of skulls, mandibles and horn cores (Grant 1979, 63). Most of the horn cores were chopped at the base and all were recovered from just two 11th/12th century pits, compelling evidence for a horner's industry within Bath at the time. Similar evidenced was recognised at Bath Street (Davenport 1999, 54–55). In view of this it seems reasonable to suggest that the under-representation of waste elements within the medieval Spa assemblage is because most meat was procured as dressed joints, with the waste elements passed on by the butcher to local craftspeople working in a different area of the town. It seems reasonable to conclude that only small quantities of butchery waste were deposited and that the majority of bone waste represented is kitchen/table waste of domestic origin.

Butchery

Butchery marks were recorded on 22% of medieval sheep bones and chop marks made with a cleaver are more common than knife cuts in both periods. The ratio of chop to cut marks suggests extensive use of a meat cleaver to dismember and reduce mutton carcasses. This practise is common for medieval assemblages (Grant 1987) and similar evidence has been recorded at Citizen House, Bath (Grant 1979) and Malmesbury, Wiltshire (Sykes 2002).

Chop marks were most frequently observed on the mid-shaft region of long bones and the neck of the ilium (i.e. pelvis) indicating rough division of the carcass or the reduction of individual joints. By way of contrast most knife cuts occur around joint surfaces suggesting that sheep carcasses were indeed jointed in the usual way and probably by a skilled butcher, hence the relative lack of such evidence. One skull had been cleaved open along the sagittal suture, presumably to gain access to the brain tissue, and the horn cores removed by chopping through the basal section. Nine vertebrae centra had been chopped in half (i.e. dorso-ventrally) indicating that carcasses were divided into left and right sides, and three other vertebrae had their transverse processes removed, another method of splitting the carcass. The former technique is thought to have become more common with the advent of professional butchers (Sykes 2001) and has previously been recorded on sheep vertebrae from Citizen House (Grant 1979), Union Street, Bristol (Higbee n.d.3), Abingdon Court Farm, Cricklade, Wiltshire (Higbee n.d.4) and Malmesbury (Sykes 2002). Cut marks noted on some skull and foot bones (eg three metatarsals and a first phalanx) probably result from skinning.

In addition to chop and cut marks a small number of other butchery marks were noted. These include a hole on the blade of one scapula made by a butchers hook, shallow scoop marks from filleting meat off the bone, and puncture and saw marks. One metatarsal had been modified to form a possible handle, the modifications include: a circular hole through the proximal articular surface, polish to the surface of the proximal shaft, a straight cut section just above the distal fusion point and a corresponding hole through the trabecular bone. A small number of bones were burnt or charred (Archive report, table 4) and it is assumed that this occurred during cooking.

Ageing

The age information available from epiphyseal fusion of the post-cranial skeleton for medieval sheep is informative and suggests that a small percentage were culled as lambs but that most sheep were culled in their second or third years of life. The mandibular wear stage data for medieval sheep confirms this and suggests that only 12% were culled under 1 year (wear stages B–C), 20% were culled as 1–2 year olds but the majority were culled aged 2–3 years, and a proportion of older sheep are represented (wear stages F–H). This general pattern is repeated when the wear data from isolated teeth are amalgamated with the data from mandibles (Archive report, tables 8 and 9). The kill-off pattern for medieval sheep suggests that although sheep from a range of ages were selected for slaughter the prime management strategy was wool production, which is consistent with regional and national trends for urban assemblages.

Pathology and non-metric traits

Abnormal inter-dental attrition was recorded between the fourth premolar (or p4) and first molar (or m1), of one sheep from the medieval period, the result of over-crowding and a reflection of genetic characteristics and/or a susceptibility to environmental stress (eg malnutrition). Five cases of penning elbow were noted on sheep humeri and a radius from the medieval assemblage, the condition is generally thought to be caused by trauma suffered in cramped conditions, such as being confined to a pen.

Biometry

Twelve medieval sheep bones were used to calculate withers height; these gave a range of 464–694 mm with a mean value of 560 mm. The mean values compare well with those previously recorded from medieval Bath. However, the upper size range for medieval sheep is considerably greater than any previously recorded from Bath, and this could suggest the presence of a different breed or simply a large male.

Cattle

Body part distribution

In the medieval assemblage the most common skeletal element of cattle is the femur, which provided a good deal of meat, and other long bones of high meat value are also relatively common. Bones from the ankle (e.g. astragalus and calcaneus) are also present in reasonable numbers as are cranial elements, including loose teeth, but all other foot bones are under-represented, indicating that the foot was detached at the ankle. This suggests that most of the bone waste is from dressed joints.

Butchery

Butchery marks were common on cattle bones; they were recorded on 49% from the medieval period. Once again chop marks are more abundant than cut marks. These were generally observed at major joints and in the mid-shaft region of long bones, and relate to dismemberment and reduction of the carcass.

Beef carcasses appear to have been divided in a similar way to mutton carcasses; that is through the mid-line of the vertebral column. A small number of long bones, most typically metapodials, were split axially, presumably to gain access to marrow-fat, and cut marks were frequently observed on the shafts of long bones. Most of these probably relate to filleting meat off the bone, but the location of some suggests that they were caused during skinning.

Ageing

Epiphyseal fusion data suggest that the majority of cattle were culled at the optimum age for prime beef, although a small proportion were calves and older adults. The kill-off pattern established from epiphyseal fusion suggests that most of the cattle culled to satisfy the urban meat markets were animals in their prime. The older animals may have been culled from dairy herds and the calves may have been surplus to requirements or killed to meet a demand for veal from the urban population.

Pathology and non-metric traits

One severely remodelled astragalus was noted; a pathological condition of joint disease that may have been triggered by trauma or stress to the joint. One third molar (out of five) was recorded without its distal cusp (or hypocondylid); this trait is thought to be genetic in origin but its significance at present is little understood.

Biometry

Comparison of medieval astragalus (Gli, Bd and Di) and tibia (Bd) measurements with those from other sites revealed that medieval cattle from Bath Spa are generally less robust than those from other Roman and medieval assemblage from Bath. Withers height estimates (Archive report, Table 12) for medieval cattle suggest a mean value of 942 mm and a range of 898–986 mm. Much larger cattle have previously been recorded from Bath; for example, the cattle from medieval periods at the Tramsheds site gave a mean value of 1050 mm and a range of 1024–1077 mm. This could indicate that different breeds of cattle are represented, or that the difference is due to sexual dimorphism, or it may simply reflect small sample size.

Pig

Body part distribution and butchery

All parts of the pork carcass are represented and the most common skeletal elements in the medieval period are femora. Other common elements include the major meat bearing bones from the fore and hind limb. All other body parts are under-represented suggesting that, like mutton and beef, most pork was procured as dressed joints. Butchery marks were noted on 20% of bones from the medieval period. Chop marks are more common than cut marks on medieval pig bones.

Ageing and sexing

Epiphyseal fusion data show that most pigs survived into their first year but a significant proportion was culled early in their second year of life and only a small proportion survived into their third year of life. The information available from tooth eruption and wear is of limited analytical value. Pigs are primarily meat animals and are usually killed at a relatively young age in most societies.

Of the canines/alveoli that were assessed for sexual differences 78% from the medieval period are from females. Males tend to be aggressive once they reach sexual maturity, so normally high numbers of young males are sold to supply the urban meat market. The high incidence of females with the medieval period is a little surprising but perhaps these individuals were surplus to breeding requirements.

Pathology and biometry

Only one pathological specimen was noted; a ridge of bone was recorded on the lateral shaft of a femur from the medieval assemblage. The precise cause of this abnormality is uncertain. The appearance of the ridge is smooth and regular, and there are no signs of any underlying trauma or infection.

Other less common mammals

A small range of other mammalian species was present which account for only *c* 5% of NISP in the medieval period. The species identified from the medieval period include horse, dog (and possibly fox), cat, red deer, rabbit, mole, field vole and house mouse. The horse bones are scattered across contexts; most are from adult animals but one unfused distal tibia is from a young animal less than 20–24 months of age (Silver 1969, 286). The majority of the dog bones are from pit 998 (933) and include a skull, radius, humerus and pelvis, which could be from the same individual. One of the dog bones from a different feature, pit 960, was complete and gave a shoulder height estimation of 393 mm (Archive report, table 12). It could represent a small breed of dog or possibly a fox. Cat is represented by a few isolated bones and the partial skeleton of a kitten from pit 960. The four red deer bones are from separate features and include two astragali, a humerus and a femur. The long bones bear chop marks on their distal shafts. Rabbit bones are also scattered across a number of features and most of the ageable specimens are from immature animals. The remaining three species, mole, vole and mouse, are incidental finds whose presence does not reflect anthropogenic activity. The rodents in particular are likely to have fallen into open pits. Most were found in the lowest layers of pits or in the layers at the interface of intercutting pits, suggesting they had fallen into the later pit and burrowed into the fill of the earlier feature.

Birds

Bird bones account for *c* 12% of NISP in the medieval period. A relatively wide range of species is represented, but most bird bones are of chicken.

Domestic birds

Of the domestic bird species, chicken is the most common accounting for *c* 78% of all bird bones in the medieval period. Similar high frequencies of chicken have been recorded from a number of other medieval sites in Bath. All parts of the chicken carcass are represented suggesting that whole birds were procured, perhaps still in their plumage. It is of course highly likely that chickens were kept by individual households for their eggs and were slaughtered once they become less productive. Unfortunately it was only possible to establish the sex of a few bones from each period using the methods outlined above and additional analysis of selected measurements that generally show greatest sexual dimorphism (Archive report, fig. 3 and table xxvi). It is clear, however, that the majority of chickens were adult, 68% in the medieval period.

Duck, most probably mallard, and goose account for a very small fraction of the domestic poultry consumed. All of the bones from these two species are from adult birds and cut marks were noted on a goose tarso-metatarsus from the medieval assemblage.

Wild birds

Pheasant, pigeon and crow (or raven) curlew, passerines and a small species of wader are present in the medieval assemblage. All of these species have previously been recorded from other sites in Bath. Some such as pheasant and pigeon probably represent food items whilst the others are considered incidental finds.

Amphibians

Two frog bones were identified from the medieval assemblage. They are from separate pits and probably represent animals that fell into the features whilst they were open.

Summary and Conclusions

Analysis of the Bath Spa assemblage has shown that preservation and recovery are good, and that the assemblage is dominated by domestic livestock species. Sheep is the most abundant species accounting for 56% of NISP and 61% of MNI. Cattle are the second most abundant species followed by pig. This is a reversal of the Roman pattern. The basic trend that emerges is a decline in the proportion of pig and an increase in the proportion of cattle over time, with sheep of prime importance overall. Cattle are usually the most common species from medieval urban assemblages (King 1978; 1984; 1999; Grant 1989) and this general trend has been recorded for a number of sites in Bath (Browne 1991; Bull and Payne 1991; Higbee n.d.1; n.d.2; Lovett n.d.). The medieval assemblage is sufficiently large to give a good indication of what was consumed within the town during this period. Indeed, species frequencies are similar to those from contemporary deposits in the Citizen House assemblage (Grant 1979) and other local (Davis 1991; Higbee n.d.3), and regional sites (Levitan 1982; Sykes 2002) and this has led to the suggestion that there is a regionally distinct pattern based upon sheep husbandry, which generally reflects wider national trends. These trends include an increase in the number of sheep relative to cattle and a decline in the number of pigs, changes which can generally be linked to the increasing use of horses as plough animals, the growth of the wool industry and the loss of woodland for pannage.

Information on the age structure of sheep supports this view and indicates a significant shift in the pastoral economy over time. The kill-off pattern in the medieval period shows that few young sheep were selected for slaughter; the majority were culled between 2–3 years and a proportion of older sheep are represented. This kill-off pattern suggests that although sheep from a range of ages were selected for slaughter, the prime management strategy was wool production. The presence of a small number of young sheep from which one or two clippings might have been collected suggests a degree of compromise between consumer demand for lamb and prime mutton, and market forces for wool production.

The kill-off pattern established for cattle and pig indicates that the majority were slaughtered at the optimum age for the production of prime beef and pork. Some older cattle were also present and these may have been culled from dairy herds. The presence of calves also suggests that there was a demand for veal. Pigs are primarily meat animals and this is reflected in the relatively young age at which the majority were slaughtered.

Butchery techniques include evidence for the division of mutton and beef carcasses in the medieval period. The type of bone waste deposited at the site is very consistent. Very little primary butchery waste was present, indicating that most meat was procured as dressed joints and suggesting that professional butchers were operating within the town.

Not all of the animal based protein consumed within the town was provided by the three main livestock species; chicken formed a significant part of the diet and it would seem that further variety was provided by the occasional bit of venison, hare, rabbit, duck, goose, pheasant, pigeon, and both marine and freshwater fish (see Humphrey and Jones below).

Fish Bone
by Alice Humphrey and Andrew K G Jones

A total of 257 fish remains from forty-four contexts were recovered by bulk sieving of selected soil samples and by hand collection; most of the bone was recovered from residue of sieved samples. The majority of the assemblage was recovered from medieval layers (11th to 16th century) (Table 6.10).

The medieval deposits contain the largest number of bones and greatest diversity of taxa. Large marine fish (thornback ray, conger eel, cod, hake) outnumber exclusively freshwater fish (carp family, pike and perch) although the range of freshwater taxa present is also greater than in the Roman contexts. In addition remains of herring family fishes (Clupeidae) appear for the first time in the archaeological record. The remains were dominated by vertebral centra and it was not possible to ascribe these to species. However, they are judged to be either herring, *Clupea harengus,* or pilchard, *Sardinus pilchardus.*

The widest variety of fish appears to date from the mid 11th century although this may be because only two early 11th century deposits contained fish bone. Barrett *et al.* (2004a and b) surveyed 127 assemblages of fish bones from English archaeological sites and showed that there is an increase in the occurrence of fish bones in deposits dated to 'within a few decades of AD 1000'. The Bath Spa assemblage appears to conform to this pattern, something that had been hinted at by various authors over the last 20 years.

The majority of elements present are vertebrae and aside from conger eel (which is also represented by jaw bones) large marine fish are only represented by vertebrae. While this may be interpreted as evidence that fish preparation took place at some distance from the site, it is important to recognise that the assemblage is small.

Interest in large gadid fish exploitation in the medieval period has been a focus of much scholarly work and there is growing evidence that there was widespread trade in dried fish products (eg Wilkinson 1979; Jones 1991; 1995; Barrett 1997). By far most numerous are herring family and eel. Eel and flatfish are the only taxa present in all periods from Roman to post-medieval.

GENERAL DISCUSSION

The majority of features of this period are 11th century pits together with a scatter of later medieval and post-medieval features. The evidence from the

soils within these indicates that the Roman period was followed by a long phase of soil accumulation and development with evidence for agriculture. Artefactual material suggests that occupation was re-established in the area from the 10th or 11th century. The digging of pits through the 11th century is indicative of more intensive activity, some of which may have been associated with robbing of Roman building materials as well as disposal of rubbish, probably in the back yards of tenements. Pit digging continued sporadically until the 17th century.

The pits and the material within them are the only source of evidence for occupation on the site throughout the medieval period. Pits are normally found on most sites in the centre of Bath, though often only as bases cut into Roman stratigraphy. The pits present at the Bath Street site (Davenport 2000), where it was estimated that all surviving pits must have originally been over 1.5 m deep, had comparable depths to those at the Spa site, but in other respects they exhibited less variation in overall shape and profile, being cylindrical or rectangular and measuring about 1 m in diameter. However, those at Citizen House (Green 1979) bear a much greater similarity to those at the Spa site, being equally varied in size and shape. At Citizen House there was much better preservation of the medieval levels and it is clear that pits were frequently 2–3 m deep. Diameters or widths ranged from 0.8 to 3.0 m across. They also exhibit a similar range of shape and profile to the Spa pits with undercutting of the pit walls in some cases.

The pottery found at the Spa indicates that there was very little pit digging on the site after the middle of the 13th century and that there is very little evidence for activity in the area during the late medieval period generally. The presumption is that the truncation of the medieval stratigraphy has removed all such evidence. The wares which do date to the late medieval period, are interpreted as late 13th/early 14th century, and as early to mid 16th century finds and all were found residually in later deposits. However it is worth considering that the sparsity of late medieval pottery on site may be genuine, and what this implies about occupation on the site. Layer 755 (see Period 7.2 Chapter 7 below), which is interpreted as soil from the medieval and post-medieval deposits removed in 1829 and trampled over the base of the 1829 construction trench, could be a genuine reflection of the quantity of pottery arriving on the site. It contained 64 sherds of Roman pottery in addition to the medieval and post-medieval material shown in Figure 6.9. The proportion of late medieval pottery compared to the much larger quantities of earlier and later material in layer 755 suggests that pottery was just not being incorporated into deposits during the 14th and 15th centuries. A similar rise in quantities of 16th century pottery can be seen in the remnant of soil layer 430 sealing pit 443, but again is preceded by equally small quantities of pottery from the earlier centuries.

Table 6.10 *Quantification of fish bone from medieval and post-medieval periods.*

		Period 4		Period 5				Period 6	Period 7.2	
		11th C	Early 11th C	Mid 11th C	Mid 12th C	Mid 13th C	Late 16th C	1765–76	1829	Total
Elasmobranchii	Rays & sharks			1	2					3
Raja clavata L.	Thornback ray			2						2
Clupeidae	Herring family	1	1	47	11	14	7	3		84
Salmo trutta L.	Trout	1								1
Esox lucius L.	Pike			1		1				2
Cyprinidae	Carp family		3	4	1		1			9
Anguilla anguilla (L.)	Eel			44	2	6		1		53
Conger conger (L.)	Conger eel				3					3
Gadidae	Cod family			1						1
Merlangius merlangus (L.)	Whiting			3						3
Gadus Morhua L.	Cod				1		1			2
Merluccius merlucius (L.)	Hake	1		2	1		2			6
Perca fluviatilis L.	Perch			2						2
Sparidae	Sea bream family				2					2
Scomber scombrus L.	Mackerel			1	2					3
Pleuronectidae	Flatfish	2		2	4			1	1	10
Unidentified				19	25	11	15	1		71
Total		5	4	129	54	32	26	6	1	257
Average number of bones per context		2.5	2	5.8	6	6.4	13	6	1	
No of contexts	+	2	2	22	9	5	2	1	1	

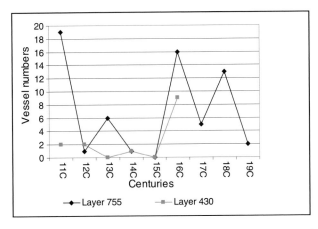

Figure 6.9 Graph showing comparison of quantities of dated pottery in layers 430 and 755.

This suggests that little discarded pottery was being incorporated in 'garden soils' until the 16th century and that in preceding centuries large amounts of pottery only survived where it had been discarded directly into pits. The pattern of pottery occurrence in layer 755 reflects for the 11th-15th centuries that of pit numbers as illustrated in Fig. 66 and overall is a combination of the pit pattern and the soil pattern, as might be expected for this layer.

The primary activity of much of the pit digging has been interpreted as recovery of Roman building materials. This suggests a piecemeal, less organised approach to obtaining Roman building materials than the robber trench system: a private or individual enterprise, rather than a corporate or industrial one.

A small quantity of medieval tile included both flat tiles and ridge tiles. Similar flat tiles were found on the Tramsheds site in medieval (probably 14th century) contexts (Betts in prep). These are presumably roofing tile, although in the absence of peg holes or nibs the type is uncertain. Such tiles probably continued in use until at least the 17th or 18th century, when pantiles were introduced into Bath. The small quantity of medieval building materials found suggests that structures in the area were mainly constructed in timber and thatch as little in the way of demolition or construction debris has been observed in this period. However, the only evidence is material that entered the pit fills and it is possible that building materials were reused rather than discarded. The evidence for opportunistic robbing of buried walls into the post-medieval period both here and at Swallow Street (Davenport

1991, 53), suggests that building materials were not wantonly discarded and may be under-represented in pit fills.

The occupation debris and artefacts that were dumped in the pits provide some insights into the character of the locality. The pottery for the late 11th, 12th and early 13th century confirms that Bath was supplied mainly from sources to the east, in central and south-east Wiltshire, but with some vessels from the Gloucestershire/Wiltshire border (Minety). The very small quantity of pottery from the Bristol area in this sequence, initially Ham Green jugs and later a few Bristol vessels, also jugs, is a feature first noted in the 1970s. Other artefacts were sparse and apart from an arrowhead, most appeared to be waste fragments. Slag was more common, though frequently undiagnostic. Lynne Keys (see Assessment in site archive) has identified smithing hearth bottom, possible smithing slag and hammerscale, which may indicate that smithing had been taking place in the area. A small number of fragments of crucible and possible furnace lining could indicate other industrial activity. In comparison to the Bath Street pits, which produced evidence of craft/industrial activities in the form of working of horn, leather off-cuts, metal working debris and possible evidence of cloth-working, those at the Spa contained little comparable material.

The quantity of carbonised plant remains contrasts with that in the samples analysed from Bath Street (Jones 1999) where waterlogged seeds predominated and carbonised material was relatively sparse, and where no sample produced more than 50 cereal grains. The Spa deposits may indicate that activities associated with the processing of cereals were taking place close by. It is possible that this area was given over to trades associated with food production or processing such as butchers, brewers and bakers. The presence of what has been tentatively identified as dung mixed with the carbonised seeds from pit 443 may indicate an establishment with stables attached, such as an inn. The Bell Inn, situated on Binbury Lane close to the south-east corner of the site, is known to have existed by 1635. Historical records (Manco 1999) of the 14th century show that this was one of the poorest areas of Bath with labourers almost the only category of occupation identified. The archaeological evidence may be reflecting the relative poverty of the site and small scale domestic activity, related to private households or small scale trades serving the immediate locality.

Chapter 7: Period 6: 16th-mid 18th century

OVERVIEW

The very limited evidence of features and stratigraphy for this period is a result of the wholesale destruction of deposits effected by the construction work for the Manners' structures and the cellars of 7–7a Bath Street, rather than any absence of occupation and activity. Historical research (Manco 1999) has shown this area of Bath to be fully developed, though most of the areas excavated appear to have formed the rear gardens or yards of buildings lying beyond the excavated area. A large rectangular trench, a fragmentary stone lined gully or drain, some wells, a small number of pits of 16th-18th century date and a remnant of garden soil are the surviving deposits.

GEOARCHAEOLOGY OF THE POST-MEDIEVAL DEPOSITS
by David Jordan

The analyses of samples from only three, quite different, post-medieval contexts produced limited results. These deposits were very variable and difficult to characterise with the addition of large amounts of building material, including mortar, stone and clay, reflecting the complex post-medieval history of the site. The post-medieval deposits within late pits appear very similar to the medieval fills but have been even more fully reworked and structured before deposition. Thus, it may be concluded that these were secondary and derived from already reworked granular soils.

Post-depositional reworking included hydrochemical alteration, which had resulted in secondary precipitates at significant hydrological boundaries, especially feature cuts, development of secondary blocky structure, and an accumulation of fine mineral-organic soil matter above the pit cuts, which suggests contamination by fine matter derived from the upper strata – including those now lost by truncation. The medieval and post-medieval deposits appear to be largely inactive biologically; a result, almost certainly, of early burial beneath the 17th and 18th century structures.

STRATIGRAPHIC AND STRUCTURAL EVIDENCE (TABLE 7.1)

In the preceding section the medieval pits have been fully described. In terms of overall character, there is nothing to distinguish the later post-medieval pits from the earlier ones in form or fill. Nothing further need be added here. One of the pits [1598] in the Bath Street cellars may well belong to an earlier post-medieval period, as the single 18th-century sherd dating it is likely to derive from the fill of a late sewer trench cutting through it, rather than from the pit itself. Pit 1096, though only producing 11th century pottery, cut pit 1097 and contained a fragment of clay pipe stem. Although if the pipe were intrusive, both these pits could be medieval.

There was one major feature of this period within the main excavation area (Fig. 7.1). This was a large rectangular trench [907, 975] with straight vertical sides and a flat base surviving to a depth of almost 1 m, with a stepped profile on its south side. Only a narrow strip of this feature remained in the northwest corner of the excavation and its full extent is unknown. It continued northwards for an unknown distance measuring in excess of 8.0 m long north-south by more than 1.9 m wide east-west. It may have been as much as 2 m deep originally. Though the trench may relate to constructional activity associated with the John Wood Hot Bath, it is more likely to predate it. A clay pipe from the top of its fill dated to AD 1635–50, although the pottery indicates a date after AD 1765. Moreover, its west edge had probably been destroyed by the Hot Bath. The trench was backfilled with deliberate dumps (Fig. 7.2, section B) of redeposited river gravels (988, 1002, 1006), tips of ashy mortar (1007, 1364) and limestone building rubble (965, 974). The infilling may have been associated with the demolition of nearby buildings prior to the construction of the Wood Hot Bath and the feature may represent part of an infilled cellar, though no evidence of lining walls was present. It is unlikely to have been related to construction work for the Hot Bath, such as a foundation trench, as it did not continue for the full length of the Hot Bath wall. What appeared to be two small postholes [990, 992] (Fig. 7.2) cutting the fill of this trench may have been the remains of temporary structures such as scaffolding relating to the construction of the Hot Bath.

This trench and a short length of drainage gully 973 nearby to the south-east provide the only hints of any structural activity on site. In spite of the absence of any structure, the best explanation for the trench is that it represents the remains of a cellar or basement level of a demolished building and the depth at which the gully was found suggests that it was a service trench also at cellar or basement level. Though not directly related to well 2004 (see below), the gully ran north-westwards a short distance from it and may have held pipes for pumping water from the well to a nearby property, possibly a building represented by 907. Trench 907 contained a high density of occupation and building debris, including building stone, an architectural moulding, clay tile, brick and painted plaster.

Table 7.1   Details of post-medieval pits and features.

Pit No.	Date	Form	Function	Fill layers of features	Finds/Environmental
1096	Late 16th C	Pit: circular, basin		956	Pottery (+Ro), (CBM, Op.sig.), clay pipe, slag, oyster shell, bone, seeds
1097	Late 16th C	Pit: sub-rectangular	Quarrying/Robbing	962, 1028, (1128)	Pottery (+Ro), (CBM, Op.sig., flint), glass, slag, bone, seeds
985	Late 17th C	Pit: oval, cylindrical		986 (Unex below 986)	Pottery (+Ro), CBM: flat roof tile (+Ro), (pennant roof tile), bone
1548	Mid 18th C	Pit: sub-rectangular		1549	Pottery (+Ro), (CBM), wall plaster, oyster shell, bone
1598	Mid 18th C?	Pit: rectangular		1599, 1621	Pottery ?intrusive sherd, (CBM), bone
907	AD1765–1775	Trench: rectangular	?cellar	908, 938, 965, 973–5, 988, 1002, 1006–7, 1364	Pottery (+Ro), clay pipe, CBM: pantile, bricks (+Ro), (Op.sig, flint.), painted wall & ceiling plaster, stone, arch. moulding, glass, Fe, slag, SF6011 AE frags; 6012 ?Ag cuff link early C18; SF6021 Pb offcut, oyster shell, bone, seeds
973	Late 16th C	Gully (stone lined)	Drain, culvert	1032	Pottery, (CBM), slag, bone, seeds
430	Late 16th C	Layer	Garden soil		Pottery (+Ro), clay pipe, (CBM), slate, glass, bone
1566	Unex	Sub-circular shaft	Well	1567 coal dust	–
1580	Mid 18th C	Sub-square shaft	Well	1579, 1721, mixed gritty clay, rubble & charcoal	Pottery (+Ro & Samian), bone, clay pipe, glass, CBM
1604	–	Circular shaft	Well	1605 humic silty soil with charcoal & rubble in top	–
1774	–	Circular shaft	Well	1775 dry stone wall lining; 1784 rubble infill	~
2004	–	Circular shaft	Well	2001–3 stone capping, 2005, 2030 dry stone wall, 2031 rubble in top, 2005, 2047–8 Fill	Clay pipe

Within the cellars of 7–7a Bath Street one stone lined well [1774–5] and three other probable wells [1566, 1580, 1604] were exposed (Fig. 6.4), all of which appeared to have been infilled immediately prior to the construction of the cellars *c* 1791. The only dating evidence was a sherd of cream ware from well 1580 placing the infill after AD 1765. In all cases their fills had subsequently compacted and slumped, resulting in subsidence of the cellar floors or leaving gaps under the cellar walls. A fifth well [2004], also stone lined (2030), was found in the south-west corner of the main excavation area; this had been infilled with soil (2048), clay (2047) and rubble (2031) and capped with large Pennant slabs (2001) in preparation for the construction of the 1829 baths complex.

A group of eight stakeholes [1534, 1657, 1735–9] cut two of the pits [1544, 1548] in cellar 2 of 7–7a Bath Street and could represent a post-medieval structure (Fig. 6.4). They had contained rectangular, trapezoidal and circular stakes with pointed ends measuring between 60 × 80 mm up to 130 mm wide and from 80 mm to 450 mm deep. Their function is unclear, but in view of their depth below the contemporary ground surface, they may represent a temporary structure associated with preliminary activity or the actual construction of the Georgian cellars, unless earlier buildings on the site were also cellared. A late date is also indicated by the relationship of at least some of the stakeholes to the fill of pit 1548, which contained pottery of mid 18th century date.

ENVIRONMENTAL EVIDENCE

The limited number of deposits suitable for environmental sampling in this period resulted in only four features being sampled: two pits [1096, 1097], the gully [973] and the large rectangular trench [907]. All features produced good quantities of seeds, with over fifty cereal grains in three of the samples and *c* 100 from one of the pits. The species present were free-threshing wheat (*Triticum* sp.), barley (*Hordeum vulgare*) and less commonly oats (*Avena* sp.) and Rye (*Secale cereale*). A few weed seeds were observed in the trench and the pits, including arable weeds, stinking mayweed (*Anthemis cotula*) and Brome grass (*Bromus sp.*), which probably stayed with the grain through processing. In addition, lucerne/clover (*Medicago/Trifolium*), buttercup (*Ranunculus* sp.),

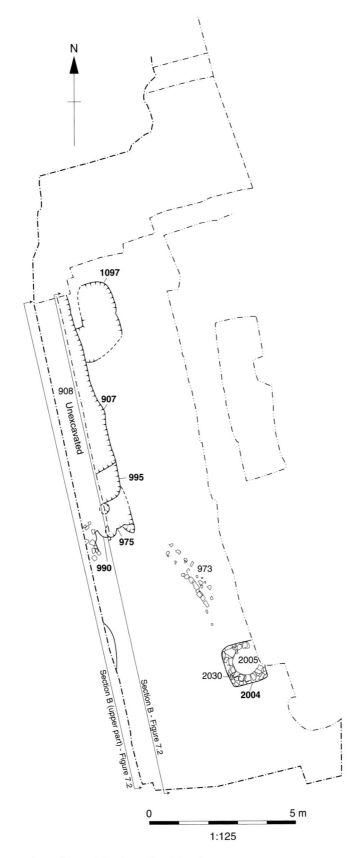

Figure 7.1   Bath Spa excavations: Plan of Post-medieval levels.

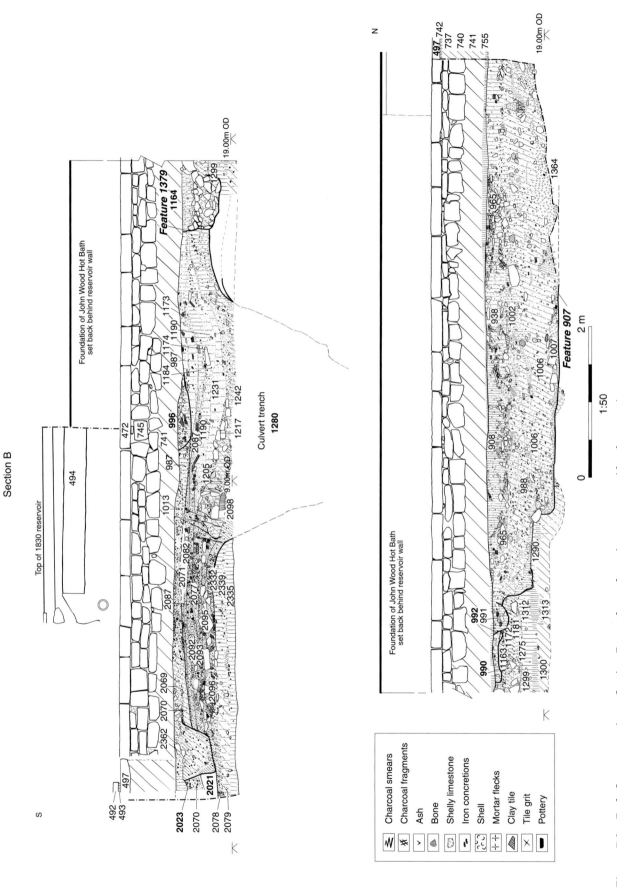

Figure 7.2   Bath Spa excavations: Section B; south–north against western side of excavation.

vetch (Vicia/Lathyrus) and grass tubers, which could derive from pasture or meadow habitats, possibly coming in with hay for animals, were present. Elder seeds were present in half the samples, being particularly abundant in the gully, but otherwise sparse. The essential picture is similar to that produced by the medieval deposits, though the range of species is fewer, reflecting probably the small sample base rather than environmental or economic changes.

THE MATERIAL EVIDENCE

Post-medieval pottery
by Alan Vince

Late 16th to mid 18th centuries

One hundred and forty-nine sherds of pottery were recovered from Period 6 deposits (Table 7.2), of which forty-six were medieval and forty-one from pits (Table 7.3), which have been assigned to this period on the basis of dateable artefacts. Thirty-two of the sherds from pits are medieval. The largest assemblage comes from F907, which contains Creamware and is clearly later than *c*1765 on that basis. It contains no examples of later 18th and 19th century wares, such as transfer printed vessels or Pearlware. F1580 in Cellar 3 contains two sherds of similar date but probably deposited immediately before the construction of the cellar in 1790-95. The remainder contain medieval wares, presumably residual, or South Somerset wares, which are likely to date to the later 16th to 18th centuries. The only coarse ware likely to be contemporary with the 18th century fine wares in F907 is South Somerset ware.

The excavators suggest that the main features in this period were backfilled shortly before the construction of the Hot Bath in the mid 1770s or immediately prior to the 1829 works. Feature 907 must be earlier than the Hot Bath building, but since it contains sherds which cannot be earlier than 1765 this gives a tight date for the assemblage, which therefore repays more detailed study.

Much of the pottery present in feature 907 is clearly residual and of medieval date. There is also definite evidence for a later 16th-early 18th century

component, consisting mainly of small abraded sherds of South Somerset ware, Cistercian ware and a few more closely datable types, such as Frechen stoneware. Some component of the wares could be residual and there is clear evidence for the redeposition of fill from feature 907 in context 755 during the construction of the overlying reservoir 340 in 1829-30.

The feature 907 contemporary assemblage contains approximately equal quantities of English coarse wares and fine wares with a very few imported vessels. This is in contrast to many mid 18th century urban assemblages where Chinese Export Porcelain provides much of the fine ware. Whilst it may be an indication of relative poverty it is more likely in this case to indicate the success of Wedgwood's Creamware production in supplying the English fine ware market.

South Somerset ware is the most common coarse ware and includes a jar or chamber pot with a moulded base, internal glaze and a band of combed decoration on the shoulder (Fig. 7.3, 19) and a complete profile of a shallow pie dish, probably oval (Fig. 7.3, 20). Vessels in a local red earthenware (LPMLOC) probably from a source in the Avon valley at Bath included internally-glazed bowls and unglazed flowerpots.

The most common fine ware in the assemblage is Creamware. Four vessels are represented: a bowl with a small moulded band below the rim externally (Fig. 7.3, 21); a plain shallow dish (Fig. 7.3, 22); a tea pot (Fig. 7.3, 23); a lid, probably from this or a similar vessel (Fig. 7.3, 24) and a tankard, with a complex handle probably formed using a decorated nozzle (Fig. 7.3, 25). English white salt-glazed stoneware is the second most common type with examples of a plain bowl (Fig. 7.3, 27) and two small cups (Fig. 7.3, 26 & 28). A sherd from a tankard handle is slipped in the manner of early 18th-century examples and is either an heirloom or residual. Tin-glazed earthenware is also present. Sherds of plain chamber pots could be residual, but several sherds from a cylindrical ointment pot (Fig. 7.3, 29) decorated with horizontal blue lines and an undecorated bowl with a tall footring base are probably contemporary. Two sherds of a Staffordshire brown stoneware tankard

Table 7.2   Period 6: Pottery types in contexts of Period 6. (Terminus post quem (TPQ) is based on dating of the pottery; Terminus ante quem (TAQ) is the known date for the building, which put the context out of use).

Context Group	TPQ	TAQ	Med (resid)	South Somerset	Cream	Other post-med wares	TOTAL
F1580 (Cellar 3)	1765 +	1790–5	0	0	1	1 (Verw)	2
F907	1765 +	1775–6	36	23	14	52	125
G973	L16th +	1829	6	1	0	0	7
PH990	L16th +	1829	0	1	0	0	1
PH992	L16th +	1829	0	1	0	0	1
430	L16th +	1829	4	8	0	1 (TUDG)	13
TOTAL			46	34	15	54	149

Table 7.3   Pits containing post-medieval pottery.

Context Group	Date	Bath A	BR	FREC/LONS	Laverstock	Nash Hill	S Somerset	STCO	WSM	Pearl	Total
P1096	sp L16th C	2									2
P1097	L16th	26	1	1	1	2	4				35
P985	L17th							1	1		2
P1548	L18th								1		1
P1598	E19th									1	1
Total		28	1	1	1	2	5	1	1	1	41

base are definitely contemporary (Fig. 7.3, 30), but a single sherd from a flanged dish, possibly a pie dish (Fig. 7.3, 31) in Nottingham stoneware may be residual. Finally, several sherds of Andalusian coarse ware jar represent several different vessels and were clearly imported with their contents rather than as souvenirs of an Iberian holiday. Sherds have also recently been recognised in two rural pipeline collections in the area and support the interpretation that these vessels represent a trade in their contents via the port at Bristol.

The pottery does not indicate a large amount of activity on site during the later 16th or early 17th centuries, though the material deposited immediately before the construction of the Hot Bath in the 1770s encapsulates the characteristics of 18th century occupation. The pottery from feature 907 is important for ceramic studies in that its deposition can be dated by internal evidence to *c* 1765 or later and by stratigraphic and historical evidence to no later than the early 1770s.

Discussion

There was a fundamental change in pottery manufacture in the West Country in the middle of the 16th century. This was reflected both by the cessation of production of medieval industries (at Bristol, Laverstock and Nash Hill) and by the emergence of new centres (such as South Somerset and Verwood). The period also saw the importation of Frechen stoneware from the Rhineland. In the mid 17th century tin-glazed vessels made their first appearance in the area.

Towards the end of the 17th century a range of slipware vessels, produced both in Staffordshire and at Bristol, was introduced alongside the earlier earthenwares. Such vessels continued to be produced throughout the early and middle years of the 18th century. Alongside these wares some coarse earthenwares were introduced. Almost all of these wares were actually recovered from late 18th century or early 19th century contexts and there is thus little evidence for the date of the Spa finds. There is a strong suspicion that many of them date to the mid 18th century and could therefore have been still in

use in the late 1760s/early 1770s. However, with the exception of one of the coarse wares (PMLOC) only a handful of vessels were represented by more than a single sherd, in contrast to some of the definitely contemporary late 18th-century vessels. Some, at least, of the coarse earthenware vessels therefore probably dated to the late 17th to mid 18th century.

Clay tobacco pipes
by Marek Lewcun

The pipes from the Spa site comprise a small assemblage of 119 fragments. Most are unmarked stems, to which it has been necessary to apply relatively wide date brackets, but for others it has been possible to narrow them down to the 17th or 18th centuries. The last pipe factory in Bristol closed in 1921, outliving the last Bath factory by four years, and this is the *terminus ante quem* applied to a large number of stems. However, the absence of any decorative bowl fragments or embossed spurs typical of the second quarter of the 19th century onwards suggests that the vast majority of those pipes are unlikely to date after 1835. This nicely matches the construction of the Tepid Bath and associated structures in 1829–30, which is the latest date that fragments could have been incorporated into any deposits.

There are only six complete or nearly complete bowls, two other bowl fragments and three makers' marks present in the assemblage. Of these, two are marked on the stem and the third is on the heel of another. A pipe by Thomas Hunt of Norton St Philip, dating to between 1635 and 1650, bears one of the earlier and rare examples of his bowl form and stamp. A pipe by Richard Greenland, also of Norton St Philip, stamped on the stem, dates to 1700–1710, and has a high quality stroke burnish applied to the bowl. While this is not unusual and appears commonly on his pipes it is not always preserved by ground conditions. The third maker's mark is one by Robert Carpenter of Bath, and is very common in the city. This grouping of makers is quite typical of what is found in Bath on sites of these dates.

Ceramic building materials
by Ian Betts

A small quantity of post-medieval tile and brick was found, some of which was found in Period 6 contexts and some incorporated within the make-up layers and foundations for the 1829 spa complex and for 7–7a Bath Street houses built *c* 1791.

The earliest pantile roofing (fabric 12) from the Spa was found in the infill of the large steep sided trench 907 (Period 6), together with a number of brick fragments (context 988, fabrics 10 and 24). Fabric 12 is similar to the fabric of what are believed to be Dutch imports in London. However, by Period 7 the pantiles were almost certainly from brick and tile works situated in Somerset. Pantiles were still being made at Bridgewater, Somerset, in the 1890s

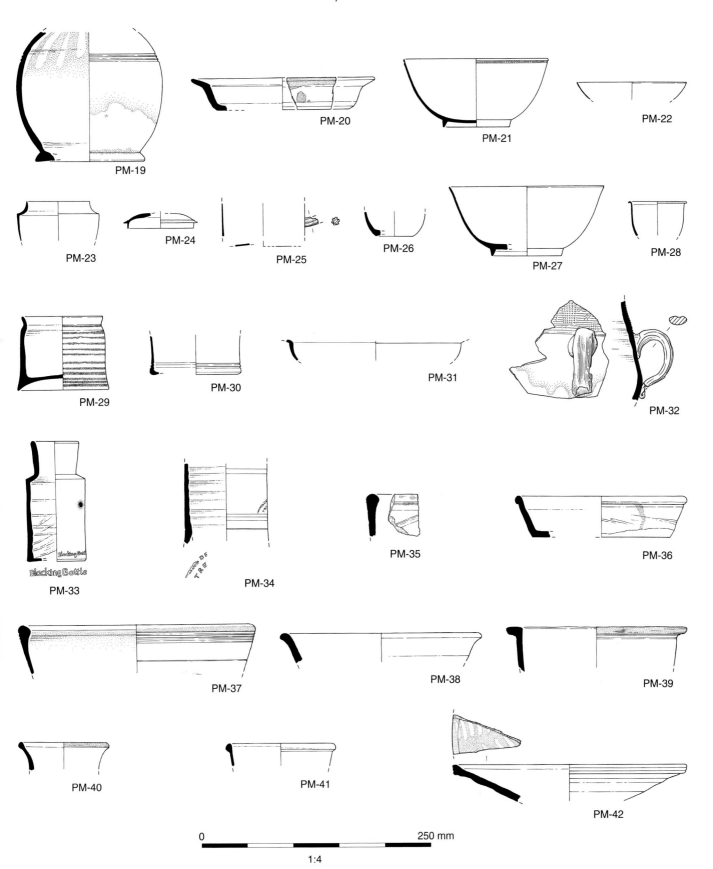

Figure 7.3 Post-Medieval pottery: late 16th-early 18th century (19–32); late 18th-early 19th century (33–41).

(Murless 1991, 9). Found associated with the 19th century baths, although not necessarily derived from them, were numerous fragments of pantile roofing, along with a fragment of ridge tile. Further bricks were found in the Bath Street cellars in contexts 1542 and 1607 (fabric 19) and pantiles in context 1542 (fabric 12). These probably represent the demolished remains of 18th century brick and pantiled roofed buildings located nearby.

Small finds
by John Clarke

Copper alloy cuff links (not illus.) 14 mm diam. Georgian or later. Two discs depicting a horse rider facing left and a barely legible inscription. Each has an attachment loop in the centre of the reverse, one retaining a broken and distorted chain link. Context 907 *SF6012*.

Small finds were very few and the only additional items were some fragments of copper sheet and a lead off-cut, all from feature 907.

Mammal Bone
by Lorrain Higbee

The animal bone is quantified in Table 6.9 and is dominated by domestic species: cattle, sheep/goat and pig plus a few examples of dog, chicken, duck and goose. Approximately a quarter of the bone, mainly cattle and sheep/goat, exhibited signs of butchery in the form of cut or chop marks in roughly equal proportions. Other species present, fallow deer, rabbit, pigeon and fish, are rare and nearly all probably represent food items. The quantity of bone surviving from this period was too small to warrant full analysis.

Fish Bone
by Alice Humphrey and Andrew K G Jones

Small numbers of remains were retrieved from one late post-medieval feature. All come from small to medium sized fish. Exclusively freshwater fish are not present although both eel (*Anguilla anguilla*) and some flatfish (Pleuronectidae) are migratory. Clupeidae (herring family) are also present testifying to the importance of this species in Bath's economy. A summary of the species appears in Table 6.10 above.

GENERAL DISCUSSION

The archaeological evidence for this period is very limited, and the presence of the wells indicates the excavated areas represented rear gardens or yards. One might expect these wells to relate to medieval or post-medieval property boundaries. When comparing their positions to the late 18th century property boundaries and buildings of 1604 published in Davenport (1999, fig. I.47) two appear to lie close to property boundaries, suggesting that some wells served more than one property. The well

[2004] in the south-west of the excavation appears to lie close to the boundary of plots numbered 19 and 20 by Manco (1999, 123) and she notes that a house plan on plot 20 in 1797 shows the positions of wash house, pump and privy at the back. The well and remnant of stone drain may have been part of these structures. The well [1566] in cellar 4 was near the boundary of plots 10, a house and its garden, plot 11. The other three all lie within plot 8, which was the garden leased to plot 7. It would be logical for these three wells to represent a sequence, but the subsidence of cellar floor and walls suggests that all were infilled immediately prior to the construction of Nos. 7–7a Bath Street. However, the property on plot 7 had been divided into two residences by 1717 and this may account for the number of wells.

The large trench 907 may indicate the presence of a cellared building and the building material recovered provides some insight into the type of structure. The brick and pantile fragments suggest that nearby buildings were built or altered in the 18th century. The plaster recovered included fragments with bright white paint, some with lath impressions on the back indicative of ceiling plaster, as well as fragments with black paint. Building materials of the same type occurred dumped in the foundation trenches for 7–7a Bath St, suggesting that similar buildings were replaced on this site also.

The collection of pottery from trench 907 is of interest as a result of the tight dating for this assemblage between 1765 and 1775 and it is likely that it represents the contents of a domestic dwelling demolished to make way for the construction of the Hot Bath. It contained roughly equal quantities of English coarse wares, most commonly South Somerset ware, and fine wares, predominantly Creamware. Alan Vince notes that though this could be an indication of relative poverty contrasting with the prevalence of Chinese Export Porcelain in many urban assemblages, it is possible that the dominance of Creamware in fact results from the successful marketing of Wedgwood's products in the mid 18th century. Wedgwood had a successful outlet in Milsom Street, only a few hundred yards away, at this time. The few imported vessels, in the form of sherds of Frechen stoneware from the Rhineland and Andalusian jars, are likely to result from trade via the port of Bristol.

The range of ceramics reflects the fundamental changes in pottery manufacture in the West Country in the 16th century, with the emergence of new production centres in South Somerset and Verwood. The range of forms is typical of what would be expected in a domestic situation, with vessels mostly associated with cooking and dining such as pie dishes, bowls, a teapot, cups and tankards, together with cosmetic or medicinal items such as an ointment pot and other essentials such as chamber pots. Fragments of Andalusian jars suggest the household could afford occasional imported exotic or luxury goods.

Chapter 8:   Spa Periods 7–9: The Georgian and Modern Structures

OVERVIEW

The Georgian developments began in Period 7 with subsequent alterations occurring in late Victorian times and the 20th century. The earliest buildings to be constructed were 7–7a Bath Street, built c 1791 (Period 7.1), which are still standing, although they have undergone various internal alterations. On the Spa site the plot was used for spa and treatment facilities beginning in Period 7.2 with the construction of the Tepid Pool and associated private baths and hot water reservoir by George Manners in 1829. The major alterations that could be detected archaeologically were those by Major Davis in the 1890s (Period 8) and the more major refurbishment and construction of the Beau Street Baths by A. J. Taylor in 1925–7. All the archaeological deposits and features took the form of construction levels and foundations or demolition debris. Artefacts not surprisingly were few and virtually all those that were not associated with construction activity were residual, derived from earlier deposits.

STRUCTURAL AND STRATIGRAPHIC EVIDENCE

Period 7.1: Georgian

The construction of the John Wood Hot Bath built in 1776–8 and the buildings currently forming 7–7a Bath Street between 1790 and 1795 are assigned to this phase. The east wall of the Hot Bath formed the western limit of the excavation and no evidence of activity contemporary with it survived within the excavation area.

The buildings of 7–7a Bath Street have been examined as part of the excavations, as areas below their cellar floor levels were excavated to reveal the underlying deposits, which inevitably included features and stratigraphy relating to the construction of these buildings (Fig. 8.1). The cellars (assigned numbers 1–12 for ease of reference) divide into two groups: those which lie directly below the building (cellars 1, 5, 6, 7, 8, 9) and those projecting out under the adjacent pavement and road (cellars 2–4, 10–12). Cellars 10 and 11 were excavated in 1989 and contained the same pattern of features as the adjacent cellars.

The features belonging to this period comprise foundation trenches [1547, 1585, 1573, 1825] for the buildings as a whole, the foundations of the walls themselves (1503, 1633), make-up and foundation layers for floors (1504, 1569, 1576, 1584, 1589) and service features, originally stone lined drains [1565, 1600, 1624, 1539, 1638], subsequently replaced in the

19th or 20th centuries (Periods 8–9) by ceramic sewer pipes (1513, 1526, 1564, 1597, 1602–3, 1634). The original floors in the main cellars below the building were Pennant paving slabs (1521) (in places replaced by concrete flooring: 1500, 1522, 1550, 1560, 1590, probably during the 20th century), whilst the floors in the small cellars projecting under the road were of massive slabs of Lias limestone. These latter cellars appear to have been used for coal storage and in cellar 4 a deep void partly below its south wall was filled with over a metre of fine coal dust that had filtered through a gap in the paving into what is presumed to be a settlement void in the top of a well [1566] (see Fig. 6.4 above).

Eight sherds of pottery were recovered from construction trenches in cellars 2 and 3 (Vince below, see also Pottery report in site archive), all Weston-super-Mare type coarse ware apart from three sherds; a South Somerset bowl, an unidentified porcelain jar and a residual late medieval or early post-medieval Crockerton ware. From the deposits in an earlier well [1580], which was filled in as preparation for the construction of these buildings, came a sherd of Creamware plate and a Verwood ware jar. The group is of interest in that it seems to show that by the 1790s South Somerset wares had fallen out of use, their place being taken by Weston-super-Mare type coarsewares.

Period 7.2: The Tepid Bath and associated structures of AD 1829–30 (Figs 8.2–8.5)

In 1829–30 George Manners, the city architect, designed a new spa complex to be built to the east of and to include the John Wood Hot Bath buildings (Bernhardt 2003). Some preliminary designs had been made by Decimus Burton, but it was Manners who in fact designed and oversaw the construction, which comprised the tepid pool, private baths with associated rooms and a reservoir to hold hot spring water. This work had removed evidence of any earlier post-Roman structures.

Large foundation trenches were cut for the main structures. In the eastern area, a deep rectangular trench [635] had been cut to the depth of 18.70 m OD to hold the foundations for the tepid pool [300] (Figs 8.2 &; 8.3), whilst in the western area a shallower trench was excavated to 19.8 m OD for the construction of a reservoir [340] (Fig. 8.4). Further, deeper foundation trenches were cut between these areas where small private baths were to be constructed and even deeper trenches around the perimeter of the pool and along the west side of the suite of private baths,

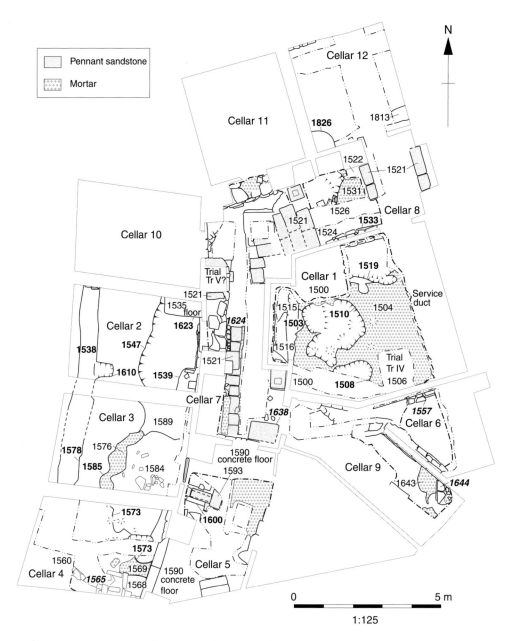

Figure 8.1   Bath Street excavations: Plan of Period 7.1: the Georgian cellars.

to hold their walls. Wall foundations were constructed of large rough blocks of Oolitic limestone set in tough grey ashy mortar, whilst the main walls were constructed of ashlar Bath stone blocks. The blocks for the tepid pool and reservoir had semi-circular grooves along their joints filled with a brown waterproof mortar. The foundations for the private baths were massive, especially below 402, where a platform of huge limestone blocks over 1 m in size was constructed in a trench cut down to 18.2 m OD. The foundations for these small baths were constructed integrally with those of the tepid pool walls.

Following construction of the wall foundations, the interior of the pool was levelled up with dumps of building debris and redeposited Roman and later material. Similar deposits of make-up occurred below the changing rooms for the private baths.

All of these areas were then lined with thick layers of Blue Lias Clay as a form of waterproofing for the structures. Below the tepid pool a herringbone arrangement of stone drains lined with ashlar blocks was set into the clay and these served both the pool and the private baths. The pool itself was oblong with apsidal ends and the wall survived on the east and north. The wall surface had been plastered and a row of glazed tiles set around the top edge.

The three small private baths (Fig 8.4) were each paired with a room with a Pennant-paved floor, taken to be a changing room. The two southern baths [402, 405], constructed back to back in mirror image, were octagonal in form with two slate seats built in at either side. They were lined with white glazed tiles and had steps leading up to the adjacent changing rooms to north [495] and south [1307] respec-

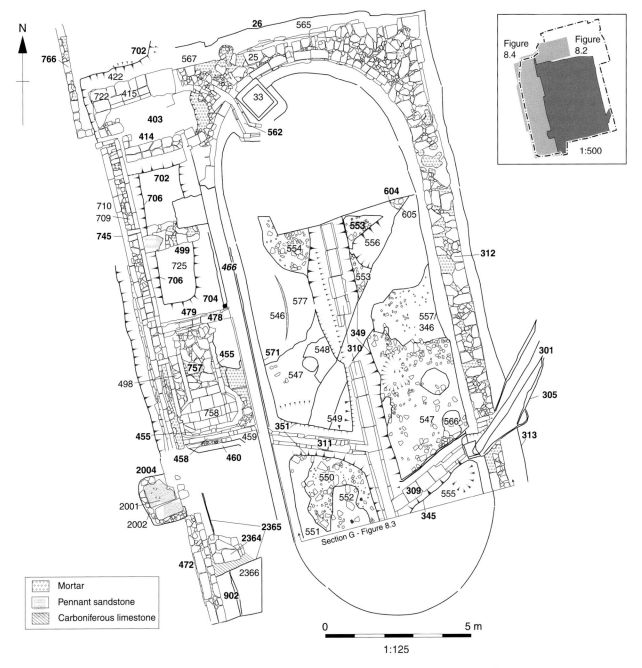

Figure 8.2   Bath Spa excavations: Plan of Period 7.2: George Manners's Tepid pool and adjacent structures.

tively. The southernmost bath had been refurbished with a shallower bath constructed within the earlier one. The northernmost bath [403], was partly destroyed by the construction of the Taylor pool, but from the plan, was semi-circular with steps leading out to the west with a doorway through to the changing room to the south [496].

In the western area the hypocaust-like structure [340] (Figs 8.4–8.5), which documentary evidence has shown to be a reservoir for the hot spring water, had walls constructed of cut ashlar Bath stone blocks, a lower floor surface of two courses of large cut limestone flagstones and resting on these up to seven rows of cut Bath stone pillars. The pillars were

0.58 m high and held an upper floor of large limestone paving slabs. The walls and pillars had a thick encrustation formed of lime, iron and manganese from the spring water and a thick layer of fine brown sediment across the floor.

Constructed under one of the service rooms to the north of the Tepid pool was a cellar [606], measuring 5.2 m by 2.9 m. (Fig. 8.3) It was reached by stone steps leading to an ante-chamber subdivided from the main cellar by a partition of ashlar Bath stone slabs. The floor was paved with limestone and Pennant flagstones and set into it was remains of a small stone lined cistern [663] about 1 m square against the south wall. The central stone drain of the

139

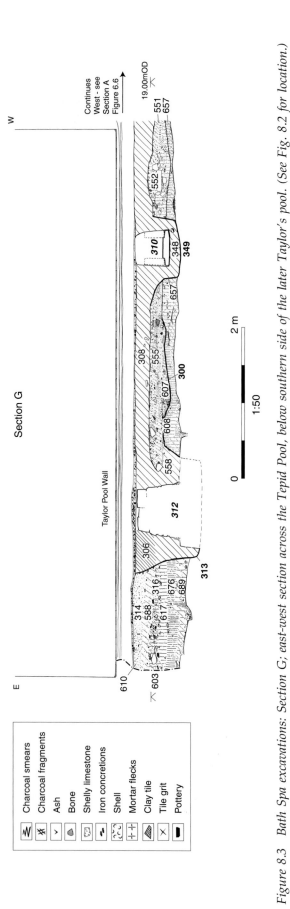

Figure 8.3 Bath Spa excavations: Section G; east-west section across the Tepid Pool, below southern side of the later Taylor's pool. (See Fig. 8.2 for location.)

tepid pool ran from this cistern and it may imply that the cellar housed machinery associated with maintaining or controlling the water supply to or from the tepid pool.

The archaeological evidence for this period was structural, and artefactual material was relatively sparse. Much of it was clearly residual deriving from all preceding periods, incorporated in the make-up and construction layers. Some mention of these has been made in the preceding sections where relevant and details are available on the web site.

Ian Betts notes that associated with the 19th century baths, a variety of plain and decorated wall tiles appear to relate to the construction or refurbishment of the baths, some examples having been found *in situ* in the private baths.

Other building materials derived from the construction of the baths comprised a variety of stone fragments including Pennant sandstone, slate, marble and schist, probably used for fixtures, fittings or flooring, fragments of lead including a pipe junction clearly derived from the plumbing for the baths, and a copper nail.

Period 8: Victorian. Alterations by Major Davis *c* 1882

Evidence for alterations to the bathing complex, which can be attributed to Major Davis in about 1882, was exposed in the western area. Here the private baths and reservoir were demolished and filled in and a new suite of private baths was constructed alongside the east wall of the Wood Hot Bath, together with ducts for drains and services. The wall foundations [336] for these formed seven square cubicles each of which had a cast iron drain leading from it to the main pipe running along the adjacent service duct bounded by wall 410 of reused ashlar stone slabs. The insertion of these foundations into the reservoir indicates that it had already gone out of use or its use was terminated at this stage.

Most of the Davis alterations were demolished in the refurbishment by Taylor. Large quantities of encaustic patterned floor tiles typical of the Davis period of work were found in the demolition debris dumped into the reservoir. The tiles included a variety of geometric shapes, colours (mostly red, black and yellow) and patterns. A large block of flooring gave an indication of the pattern of tiling. Flooring of this type was also seen *in situ* during monitoring of works in the Hot Bath, also refurbished by Davis at this time. This was sandwiched between the stone flag floors of 1776 and the concrete floors of 1925 (see below).

Period 9: The Beau Street Baths of A. J. Taylor, 1925–27, remodelled 1956

The pool and associated buildings constructed by Taylor, as modified in 1956, were standing until the present work commenced, all but the façade being demolished shortly before the excavations began.

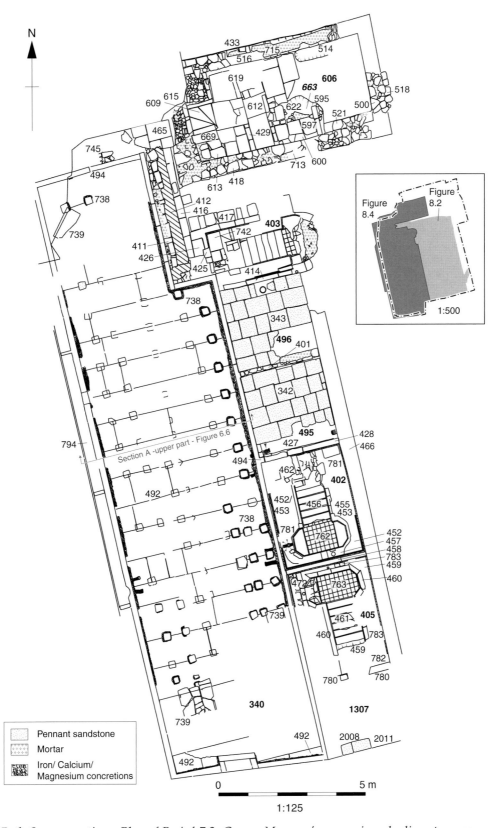

Figure 8.4 Bath Spa excavations: Plan of Period 7.2: George Manners's reservoir and adjacent rooms.

Recording of the 20th century remains was outside the design brief of the excavation (but was undertaken under a separate contract by Archaeological Investigations of Hereford). However, a number of structures and features associated with the Taylor building were identified in the excavation. These included the infilling of the cellar [606], construction of service ducts for pipes, the concrete beam to

Figure 8.5   Bath Spa excavations: Photograph of the Tepid pool and reservoir designed by George Manners.

support the rear wall of the viewing platform and the concrete foundations for the steel stanchions, which supported the west side of the Taylor roof. Clear evidence for the demolition of the 1829 private baths was seen at this stage; for example, much of the wall tile from them was used to backfill the surviving portions of the pool and the reservoir, together with the material from the demolition of Davis' works.

The Taylor building had consisted of a swimming pool with changing cubicles running along the north and east sides of the pool. To the west was tiered seating used as a viewing platform for the pool. Below this were further changing cubicles. However, a number of features impinged on the earlier archaeological deposits, including the remains of the swimming pool itself [610], which partially survived during the first phase of excavation, and drains relating to it [301, 304–5] (Fig. 8.2). In addition, a row of five large concrete stanchions running down the west side of the pool formed the foundations of the roof supports [463, 711]. A concrete beam running north-south and resting on the base of the Manners reservoir was the footing for the rear support of the viewing platform [338]. A service duct [447], which cut across the top of the infilled cellar, also belongs to this period of activity.

MATERIAL EVIDENCE

Pottery of the late 18th to early 19th centuries
by Alan Vince

The excavations produced important collections of late 18th and early 19th century pottery to which deposition dates in the 1760s/70s, 1790s and 1820s can be assigned. However, all of these groups contain definite or probable residual sherds and the exact age of many of the finds is therefore a matter of debate. The wares can be considered as three groups: coarse earthenwares, sometimes at this period known as Country Pottery; English factory products and imports.

The coarse earthenware consists of a single variety, termed here Weston Super Mare type (WSM), which has a plain lead glaze, usually brown with clear demarcation between glazed and unglazed areas. The vessels appear to have been turned to trim away unwanted clay. Of the 45 vessels recovered, 39 were bowls, whilst the remainder comprised two jars and single examples of a dish, a jug, a flowerpot, a sherd from either a jar or a jug and a pipkin. There are no sherds of this ware in either feature 907 or any other deposit earlier than the 1790s and it is therefore likely that the ware was introduced between c 1770 and 1795.

The factory products include refined earthenwares of two types: Creamware (CREA) and Pearlware (PEAR); stonewares of three types: White salt-glazed stoneware (SWSG), London stoneware (LONS) and Bristol stoneware (BRIS) and tin-glazed ware (TGW). Of these, the White salt-glazed stoneware and the tin-glazed ware are types which ceased to be manufactured during the late 18th century. Imports consist of Chinese Export Porcelain (CHPO), European Porcelain (CONP) and Andalusian coarse ware. The Andalusian coarse wares were made in the Malaga region. Finds from Southampton indicate that alongside and later than 13th and 14th century fine ware imports, coarse ware vessels were being imported, probably as containers, in the late medieval and early post-medieval periods. However, it is not until the late 18th century that Andalusian coarse ware vessels are found at other sites in the British Isles (Gerrard and others 1995). The early 19th century saw the introduction of more factory-made refined earthenwares. These were mainly transfer-printed whitewares (TPW, 41 vessels) but include vessels with a porcelain body (ENPO, 1 vessel), wares with a buff body (NCBW, 4 vessels) and Derbyshire stoneware (DERBS, 6 vessels). All of these types occur first in deposits associated with the 1829 rebuilding.

Four hundred and seventy one sherds were recovered from Period 7.2 contexts associated with the construction of the Tepid pool and associated baths in 1829/30. Given the closed nature of the deposit, these are of some interest for the dating of early 19th-century pottery, especially the coarse wares, which are rarely recovered from datable deposits. This assemblage contains the earliest stratified examples on this site of several wares (Table 8.1). In some cases, the ware itself may have been in use at an earlier date but because of the small size of the assemblages was not present in any earlier stratified context. This explanation may apply to Staffordshire/Bristol mottled-glazed ware and North Devon Gravel-Tempered ware (STMO and NDGT). The major group of new wares consists of factory products made in refined bodies. These include transfer-printed vessels (TPW), Pearlware (PEAR), buff wares (NCBW), European porcelains (CONP) and plain white earthenwares (WHITE – without a cobalt tinge to the glaze, as found in Pearlware). Sherds of five Chinese Export Porcelain vessels (CHPO) were present. The assemblage also contained London stoneware vessels, Derbyshire stoneware vessels, all black-leading jars, (Fig. 7.3, 33–34) and a sherd from a Bristol stoneware vessel.

Finally, it seems that Weston-super-Mare-type coarseware had replaced South Somerset and the local red earthenware, (LPMLOC). The earliest documentary reference to pottery production at Weston is dated 1837, and so this deposit predates, but only just, the known starting date of the pottery. Most of the vessels were large internally glazed bowls, (Fig. 7.3, 35, 37 & 39) together with some shallow, internally-glazed dishes (Fig. 7.3, 36 & 38) and jars (Fig. 7.3, 40).

The 1829–30 assemblages, by contrast, conform very much to accepted ceramic dating although in the future it may well be worthwhile studying the wares in more detail since there is increasing interest in the pottery of this period, both from an archaeological and art-historical viewpoint. None of this latter assemblage seems to indicate any unusual activities on the site, although it is presumably mainly derived from domestic refuse from houses demolished to make way for the baths and incorporated in the construction levels of the baths.

Table 8.1   Period 7: Pottery quantification.

Code	Name	No. of Vessels
WSM	Country	34
NDGT	Country	3
TPW	Fine	35
PEAR	Fine	12
NCBW	Fine	3
CONP	Fine	2
WHITE	Fine	1
CHPO	Porcelain	5
STMO	Staffs/Bristol	2
LONS	Stoneware	7
DERBS	Stoneware	6
BRIS	Stoneware	1

Ceramic Building Materials
by Ian M Betts

Various Victorian wall tiles in a variety of different glaze colours, plain white, maroon, green and bluish-white, were found associated with the 19th century baths. There was also a mottled blue and white tile and a cream example decorated with a black line. A fragment of black limestone and unglazed wall tiles in red and cream probably date to the same period.

Brick (fabric 25) and various plain white glazed wall tiles, together with a blue glazed circular example, were recorded in Period 8 contexts. Yet more 19th century wall tiles were recovered in Period 9. These are plain white and pale green or decorated with various designs. Also present are decorated and plain floor tiles of Victorian date.

GENERAL DISCUSSION

While the record of the Manners Tepid Bath was of some interest in clarifying the details of the water management and more practical features of an otherwise quite well known design, and indeed the impact of foundation design for such a building, the main interest of this period is perhaps the light it casts on late 18th to early 19th century pottery production and distribution. Despite its provenance, the pottery assemblage clearly represents typical domestic use in Bath and, therefore, allowing for the small sample, throws light on the sources of supply and patterns of use in the late Georgian and early Victorian city.

The 1830 bath was indicative of the increased interest in swimming in the waters, as swimming itself came into fashion in the early years of the century (as seen in the river-fed Cleveland Baths in Bath built in 1817). Rebuilding of the bath in 1925 and the major remodelling in 1956 reflect the increasing provision for heathful exercise for the masses, with increased facilities for changing and also of seats for observation.

Chapter 9: The Hot Bath Spring

INTRODUCTION

The physical geomorphology of the Hot Bath Spring is assumed to be similar in character to that exposed in the King's Bath Spring (Cunliffe and Davenport 1985), namely a tapering funnel-shaped pipe eroded into the Lower Lias clay filled with sands and gravels and slumped clay. (A similar situation appears to have been found in a borehole drilled by the city council under the direction of Prof. Kellaway north of the Cross Bath in the late 1980s.)

Nothing is known of the original environment immediately surrounding the spring, though it is possible to postulate a very wet, boggy, area with its own microclimate and specialised suite of vegetation. A handful of hazelnut shells recovered could be contemporary with Mesolithic activity. Their incorporation in the sediments may be fortuitous, as all were broken, indicating they were in fact waste products from food consumption and suggesting that the food source was readily available in the area. The study of the soils (Jordan above Chapters 2–4 and 6) in the Spa excavation showed that very little spring water or sediment was reaching that area in the prehistoric, Roman and early historic periods, suggesting that the spring water flowed generally to the south-west towards the river Avon. By the Roman period the spring water was probably being conducted along stone culverts, possibly joining with that from the Cross Bath, which appears to head towards the Roman Hot bath buildings to the south (Davenport 1999).

Between 1774 and 1776 John Wood had excavated the upper part of the spring to a depth of *c* 5 m in order to construct an ashlar-lined reservoir *c* 2 m in diameter to capture the spring water. The presence of fossil shells derived from the Lias clay and the heavy wear on most artefacts suggests that the sediments were subject to constant reworking by the spring water. At the time of Wood's work the discovery of coins was recorded, as well as two altars, one dedicated to Sulis Minerva and the other to Diana (*RIB* 150 and 138 respectively; Cunliffe 1969, 152–3). Although nothing is known of the structure or physical layout around the spring, the finds recovered hint that the site bore similarities in terms of usage to the King's Bath Spring (Cunliffe 1988). As a result of the sieving programme a total of 494 struck flints and about 330 coins were found, plus a small quantity of other artefacts, predominantly very worn ceramic material. The numbers of artefacts may not initially appear large compared to those recovered from the King's Bath Spring; however, the borehole sample implies a density of approximately 1700 flints and 1100 coins per cu m.

In fact, even the mere number of flints is more than twice as many as recorded from the King's Bath Spring. The analysis of the artefacts points to the unusual character of the collection.

PREHISTORIC ASSEMBLAGE

The unexpected recovery of a large quantity of flint from the borehole has shown that the spring had special significance in the earlier prehistoric period. The assemblage is of early Mesolithic date and in character it appears to be wholly atypical, with little to compare from elsewhere either in Britain or Europe. Ian Brooks' report and discussion has been included in its entirety here in recognition of the exceptional nature of the results.

Flints
by Ian Brooks

The flint assemblage recovered from the spring proved to be most remarkable. Four hundred and forty artefacts were flakes or flake fragments, of which a surprising 167 (38%) were blades or broken blades (blades being flakes with a length:width ratio of 5:2, or greater, and generally with parallel, or near parallel, sides). The flakes consisted of 11 (2.2%) primary flakes, 57 (11.5%) secondary flakes, 173 (35%) tertiary flakes and 199 (40.3%) broken flakes. Of these, 6 were secondary blades, 70 were tertiary blades and 80 were broken blades. The size and shapes of the flakes and blades is reasonably restricted (Fig. 9.1) with the majority of the flakes being less than 50 mm long and 25 mm wide. The care taken in the production of the blades within the assemblage is demonstrated by the limited range of width seen in the blades. The blade widths ranged from 3 mm to 20 mm, although there was a marked concentration of blades within the 7 to 13 mm size ranges (Fig. 9.2). The latter group comprised 84% of the blades from the site. It would appear that the preferred blade width was approximately 10 mm with 20% of the blades from the site being of this width.

Only two cores and one core fragment were recovered within the assemblage. The cores were both irregular with a series of small flake removals from at least six different directions (Fig. 9.2, 14). The core fragment is a plunging flake from a blade core (Fig. 9.2, 14). A further 38 (7.7%) worked lumps were also recovered. These were small in size with an average weight of only 6 g. Apart from the tools the only other artefact to be recovered was a spall of flint. Thirteen (2.6%) tools were found, the majority of which were microliths of early Mesolithic types, although a side scraper and two retouched pieces

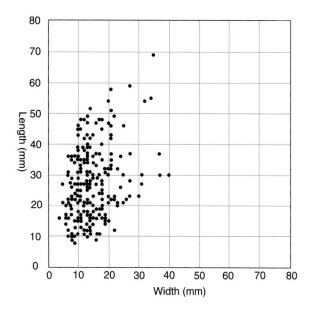

Figure 9.1 Hot Bath Spring: Scattergram showing distribution of flint flakes by size.

were also found (Fig. 9.2, 1). (For individual descriptions see report in site archive.)

The assemblage as a whole had a number of characteristics, which distinguished it from the assemblage from the Spa excavation. The majority of the assemblage, particularly the blade elements, are sharp and unrolled with only limited patination.

Raw materials

The range of raw materials used was also restricted. The same macroscopic raw material groups defined for the assemblage from the Spa site were used to analyse the flint assemblage from Hot Bath Spring. The range of raw materials used at the latter site was much smaller, with only 23 of the raw material groups being represented within the assemblage. Indeed 78% of the assemblage is from only five macroscopic raw material types, 8, 16, 18, 23 and 24. These tend to be the better quality flint from the local gravels. The range of raw materials used is unlike that within the gravels sampled during the Spa excavation, suggesting that deliberate selection of raw materials for this assemblage was taking place. (For more detail of raw materials see report in site archive.)

Heat treatment analysis

The deliberate heat treatment of siliceous materials has been demonstrated in a number of cross cultural ethnographic and archaeological studies (Olausson and Larsson 1982). The two main reasons for the use of heat on siliceous materials are the initial fracturing of intractable materials and the improvement of knapping quality of other materials.

The consistent nature of the blades from the material recovered from Hot Bath Spring and the occasional macroscopic sign of possible heating in

the form of glossy surfaces, suggested that deliberate heat treatment may have been used to produce at least some of the blades within the assemblage. Experimentation with flints from Brandon, Suffolk (Purdy and Brooks 1971) and at South Mimms, Hertfordshire (Griffiths *et al* 1987) has suggested that a temperature of around 250 C is optimal for thermal pre-treatment.

Ten samples were selected from the assemblage from the Hot Bath Spring for further analysis. The results showed that five of the samples would appear to have been heated to the temperature range suggested as optimal (250°–300°) for the thermal pre-treatment of flint with three samples being heated to higher temperature (350°–450°+) and two left unheated (>100°). Two of the "over heated" samples (Samples 3 and 10) had macroscopic signs of heat damage, although Sample 7 did not show any signs of heat damage. It is possible that these were slightly over heated in the attempt to improve the knapping quality, although other explanations may be equally valid. (For more details of analysis see report in site archive.)

The production of the blades from Hot Bath Spring would appear to have included deliberate heat treatment to improve the knapping quality in at least part of the assemblage. The consistency of the temperatures to which half of the samples examined were heated suggests that the results are not purely accidental. The temperatures represented are well above the temperature of the spring water in the Hot Bath Spring (48° C; Kellaway 1985, 7).

Illustrated flint

Fig. 9.2

1 **Obliquely blunted point** on a distal tertiary blade. The bulb of percussion has been snapped off. SF 1

2 **Lunate microlith** on a distal tertiary blade. The backing was produced by a series of direct removals along the right side. SF 2

3 **Obliquely blunted point** on a tertiary blade. The backing was produced by a series of direct removals along the right hand side. The bulb of percussion was removed by the removal of a transverse flake. SF 3

4 **Obliquely blunted point** on a distal tertiary blade. The tool was shaped with a series of crossed removals along the distal left section of the blade. SF 4

5 **Obliquely blunted point** on a tertiary blade. The blade is truncated by a series of direct removals along the distal right section of the blade. SF 6

6 **Obliquely blunted point** on a distal tertiary blade. The backing is formed by a series of direct removals along the distal left section of the blade. The bulbar end has been snapped off. SF 8

7 **Obliquely blunted point** on a distal tertiary blade. The tool was formed by a series of crossed removals along the distal left area of the blade. The proximal end has been snapped off. SF 9

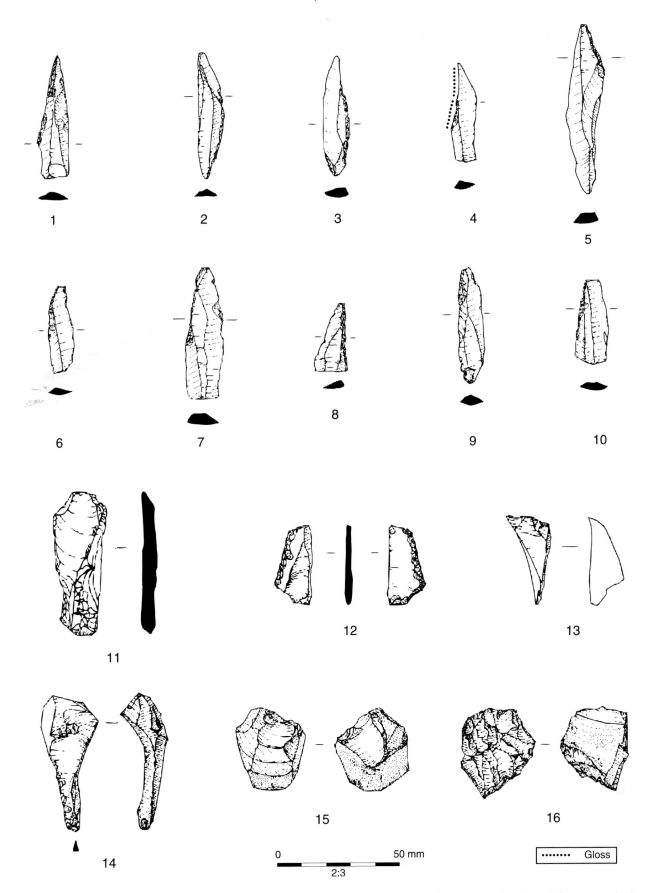

Figure 9.2   Hot Bath Spring: Flint tools: obliquely blunted points (1, 3–10), lunate microlith (2), side scraper (11), bifacially worked piece (12), retouched fragment (13), plunging flake from blade core (14), multi-platform cores (15–16).

8 **Distal end of obliquely blunted point** on a tertiary blade. The backing is formed of a series of crossed removals along the distal right sector of the blade. SF 10

9 **Obliquely blunted point** on a tertiary blade. The backing is formed of a series of direct removals along the distal left side of the tool. The distal end has been broken possibly by impact. SF 12

10 **Broken obliquely blunted point** on a tertiary blade. Both the proximal and distal ends have been broken. The backing was produced by a series of crossed removals along the distal left side. SF13

11 **Side scraper** on a secondary flake. The working edge was formed by a series of scaled, semiabrupt, short removals along the left side. The tool is slightly rolled and has a glossy appearance. SF 11

12 **Bifacially worked piece**. A fragment from a tertiary flake. The left hand side of the tool has been bifacially worked with a series of scaled, low angled, short removals. The bulb of percussion has been removed by a series of removals. The right and distal ends appear to have been snapped. SF 5

13 **Retouched fragment** on the fragment of a thick tertiary flake. The remaining section of the distal end of this broken flake has a series of sub-parallel, long, semi-abrupt removals. SF 7

14 **Plunging flake** from a blade core

15 **Multi-platform core.**

16 **Multi-platform core.**

Discussion

The assemblage recovered from the Hot Bath Spring is distinctive, both in its character and context. The assemblage would appear to be consistent and of a single period. The presence of large microliths suggests an early Mesolithic date. Three recognisable types of early Mesolithic assemblages have been defined based on their lithic components (Reynier 1998, 174). These groups are: "Star Carr" – dominated by broad, obliquely blunted points, with isosceles triangles and trapezoids the only other microlith types; "Deepcar" – with long, slender, partially backed points and "Horsham": with a diverse array of microliths. The assemblage from the Hot Bath Spring would clearly fit into the "Deepcar" grouping and Reynier (ibid., 175) has suggested that these assemblages date from after 9400 BP.

The assemblage would appear to be very restricted with only a limited range of artefacts being represented. The flakes and flake debris tend towards long flakes and blades. Only 28% of the assemblage had cortical surfaces and the bulk of these were the worked lumps with only 11 (2.2%) primary flakes. The range of tools was even more restricted with the majority of the artefacts being microliths. It also appears that deliberate heat treatment was routinely used for the production of the blades.

When the raw materials are examined the restricted nature of the assemblage is further emphasised. At a macroscopic level only five raw materials are identified suggesting a limited number of knapping episodes. This, however may be part of a larger pattern as Myers (1989, 133) has noted the exploitation of a few relatively high quality raw materials in the early Mesolithic.

The Hot Bath Spring assemblage is obviously distinct from the assemblage from the Spa excavations in date, content and context. It is also distinct from the flintwork recovered during the excavation of the King's Bath (Care 1985). Only 214 artefacts were found from the slope of the enclosure amongst the Roman piles and these were slightly mixed in nature, although there was a Mesolithic element to the assemblage. The differences between these two assemblages may be contextual as the King's Bath assemblage was found on the slopes around the spring whereas the Hot Bath Spring assemblage was from the spring pipe itself. The different character of the assemblages, however, and the potential extreme density of the Hot Bath Spring assemblage suggest that two distinct activities are represented.

The circumstances of the recovery of the Hot Bath Springs assemblage mean that it is difficult to judge the stratigraphic context of the assemblage. It is known that the material was from somewhere between 5 and 12 m below modern street level, but not whether it was in one horizon or spread throughout the borehole. Circumstantial evidence suggests there may have been considerable reworking of deposits by the spring water. However, the consistency of the assemblage suggests that it may have been from one context within the spring fill or at least was originally deposited as a single event. The density of flintwork is remarkable, if the density from the borehole is typical, with over 12,000 artefact/m^2. This can be compared to 500 artefact/m^2 at West Heath, Hampstead (Collins and Lorimer 1989, 16) and up to 900 artefacts/m^2 at Thatcham (Smith 1992, 124). Both of these were occupation sites where the density of flintwork would be expected to be high. Considerable care needs to be taken with such comparisons, as too little is known of the deposits within the spring. In volume the quantity of flint is approximately 1700 artefacts/cu m, but this figure is not readily comparable with other sites. Either set of figures is impressive and clearly sets the material from the Hot Bath spring apart from other sites.

The Hot Bath Spring is the hottest of the three springs rising in Bath (Kellaway, 1985, 7). If its structure is similar to King's Spring it will be a funnel shaped or tapering spring pipe. This may account for some of the density of flintwork in the deposits, with the artefacts being concentrated by the tapering of the spring pipe. The flintwork, however, would have to have been deliberately deposited in the area of the spring pipe to have moved down the pipe, thereby being concentrated by the shape of the pipe.

The function of the assemblage is difficult to define, its composition, density and context would all suggest that it is not part of the usual pattern of home base, field camps and kill, butchery or collecting sites (Smith 1992, 28). The context in particular may suggest a non-functional aspect to the site. Specially placed deposits, in wet contexts, are well known from the Neolithic to the Roman Period. From the jadeite axe and deposit of food in a pot besides the Sweet Track (Coles and Coles 1986, 59–60) to the deposits in the King's Spring in Bath (Cunliffe and Davenport 1985; Cunliffe 1988) the importance of watery context has been attested. As Cummins (2000, 32) has pointed out, the symbolic role of water has not been significantly discussed with reference to the Mesolithic, but may have been a metaphor for movement, journey or purification. The suggestion is strengthen by Bradley (2000, 32) suggesting that the relationship between shamanic sensations of swimming, when in an altered state, may provide an explanation for the importance of springs and other watery contexts as a transition to another domain. The effect of the Hot Bath Spring with the steam from the hot waters could only enhance such impressions. Whatever the detailed explanation for the deposition of this clearly special deposit, the recognition of what does appear to be ritual behaviour in the early Mesolithic period is of very significant interest and importance.

ROMAN PRESENCE

There is no evidence of continuous activity suggesting veneration throughout prehistory, though the association of the main spring at Bath with the Celtic deity Sulis indicates that the site was revered in some manner in the later prehistoric period. All the springs must surely have been seen as a unified phenomenon. It is possible that other items, such as libations or food offerings were the norm during prehistory, indeed Walker (1988) suggests that this could also have been the case during the Roman period, though there is no reason to think that the hazelnut shells noted above fall into this category. The presence of a single Durotrigian coin dating from the 1st centuries BC–AD may provide a firmer indication that pre-Roman votive deposits were being made. Coin deposition (Corney below) occurred throughout the Roman period, but was at its height during the early Roman period in the 1st and 2nd centuries AD, with the greatest intensity of deposition taking place between AD 69 and AD 161 (Vespasian to Antoninus Pius). There is then a dramatic drop in the quantity of coins, which Corney suggests must represent a marked break in the pattern of offerings into the Hot Spring. He concludes that in terms of the types represented, the patterns are broadly comparable to the large group recovered from the Sacred Spring (Walker 1988). The great divergence between the two sites occurs from *c* AD 161, after which date the Hot Bath Spring attracted very little coinage. Even allowing for the corrosive effects of the conditions of deposition (Corney below) and the methods of recovery, the evidence must indicate an profound change in the nature of

activity at the Hot Bath Spring at this period. The contrast with the Sacred Spring is stark. This might suggest that the spring itself was integrated into the redevelopment of the area, altering the status of and access to the spring in some way. An explanation may be that after redevelopment there was a change in the ways of veneration.

In addition to the artefacts that can be considered clearly votive in character, a variety of other material was found. Bone, glass vessel sherds, metal objects, fired clay, pottery and various building materials were identified. Some of the items such as a copper alloy button and some of the metal fragments appear to be post-medieval or later, probably relating to the construction work of John Wood, but others, such as the glass vessel sherds, are suggestive of earlier activity around the spring.

The building material appears to be Roman and is dominated by ceramic material, mostly small unidentifiable fragments of tile or brick, but a small number could be identified as *imbrex* fragments. There were also fragments of concrete, *opus signinum* and tufa and a single small, pale grey limestone tessera. This range of material either suggests that this spring was enclosed and roofed over, possibly in a similar manner to the King's Bath spring, or, just as likely, that roofed buildings were very close by. No box or voussoir tiles were apparent among the fragments, but it is possible that tufa was being used here as a light material for roof vaulting instead. A handful of potsherds was recovered, all Roman in date, but could not be more closely characterized than as black-burnished ware and an unsourced coarse reduced ware.

Clearly the material recovered from the very limited area of the borehole provides a tantalising glimpse of the early activity in and around this spring. The spring itself is often regarded as subsidiary to the King's Bath Spring as it is smaller and the flow less. However, the archaeological evidence suggests that the springs may have been treated in very similar ways in Roman times. It is clear that the fill of the spring pipe and the area immediately around the spring have a very high archaeological potential.

Roman Coins
by Mark Corney

Introduction

The assemblage from the Hot Bath Spring comprises approximately 330 coins (the number is approximate given the fragmentary nature of some pieces), all in copper alloy apart from the base silver Iron Age piece. Of this number, 219 are identifiable, 1 of Iron Age date and 218 Roman, representing 65.7% of the total. The overall condition of the group is very poor, the conditions of deposition having caused severe corrosion, masking significant detail and resulting in severe weight reduction. Walker (1988) also noted this factor in his highly detailed and informative analysis of the 12,595 Roman coins recovered from the Sacred Spring adjacent to the Temple of Sulis Minerva. In the case of the assemblage from The Hot Spring, the corrosive effects of the water have been particularly extreme, with many 1st and 2nd century *æs* being reduced to wafer thin fragments, totally devoid of detail. This may explain why so few later, smaller coins were represented in the assemblage; such coins could have been completely destroyed by corrosion. The circumstances of the assemblage discovery and recovery cannot be considered controlled and it can only be viewed as a random sample of the coins originally deposited in the Hot Spring. This factor may, in part, also contribute to the bias to earlier coins, the smaller issues of post *c* AD 260 being especially low. Despite this, the assemblage has produced a number of significant patterns that can be compared with the coins recovered from the Sacred Spring (Walker 1988).

A summary of the coins by emperor is given in Table 9.1. (The detailed catalogue of the individual coins is tabulated and can be found in the site archive).

Pre-Roman

The assemblage included one pre-Roman coin, a corroded and fragmentary issue of the Durotriges (catalogue no. 1). The Sacred Spring excavations produced eighteen Iron Age coins, including two of the Durotriges (Selwood 1988).

Roman

In discussing the assemblage from the Sacred Spring, Walker (1988), notes that the coinage of Roman Britain can be divided into two main periods

Table 9.1 Hot Spring: Summary of coins by emperor or period.

Pre Roman	1
TOTAL	1
Claudius	8
Nero	10
Vespasian/Titus	47
Domitian	35
Nerva	3
Trajan	45
Hadrian	27
Antoninus Pius	21
Marcus Aurelius	2
Faustina II	1
2nd century empress	2
Illegible 1st-2nd century	103
Early 3rd century empress	1
'Radiates'	2
House of Constantine	9
House of Valentinian	4
House of Theodosius	1
Illegible later 3rd-late 4th century	7
Total Roman	329

(ibid., 281). Prior to AD 260 supply of coin to Britain is irregular, although there are periods of significant input. Walker (ibid.) notes three phases within this period: the period of sporadic supply, AD 43–96; the period of regular supply, AD 96–197 and the period of minimal supply, AD 197–260. After AD 260, coin is supplied to the province in vast quantities and marks a change in the way coin circulates and is used. These divisions are employed in this report.

Period of sporadic supply AD 43–96

Claudian period issues c AD 43–6 – Eight coins attributable to Claudius were identified with certainty. Seven are definitely imitations, being products of irregular mints established in Britain and Gaul. All are *dupondii* or *asses*. The condition of the pieces does not allow attribution to specific production centres such as Colchester. One piece (no. 9) may be an official issue, but is in such poor condition that this cannot be confirmed. Where identifiable, the dominant reverse type is that of Minerva.

Neronian issues AD 64–67 – Ten coins attributable to Nero were identified: 2 *sestertii*, 2 *dupondii*, 3 *asses* and 3 *dupondius / as* module. The condition of the coins makes attribution of the mint, either Rome or *Lugdunum* (Lyons), difficult, only one (no.11) is clear enough to allow identification as a product of *Lugdunum*. However, the analysis by Walker (ibid., 285–6) and Macdowall (1967) would strongly suggest that the majority of the coins are products of *Lugdunum*, this mint supplying the majority of the Neronian *æs* found in Britain.

Issues of Vespasian and Titus AD 69–81 – Forty-seven coins attributable to Vespasian and Titus are present. For the latter emperor, three issues as Caesar struck during the reign of Vespasian were noted. The generally poor condition of the coins may mean that identification based on portrait alone may have led to issues of Titus being catalogued as Vespasian. This will not affect the overall analysis. Of the total identified, forty-six are *asses* and one a *dupondius*. No *sestertii* are present. Where attributable, the coins of this period conform to the two major periods of issue by the mint at *Lugdunum*, AD 71–3 and AD 77–8. The overall condition of the pieces is such that it was difficult to discern the globe at the base of the bust denoting the mint of *Lugdunum*. However, comparison with the assemblage from the Sacred Spring shows that of 149 coins attributable to the period AD 69–81, only six were issues from Rome, the remainder being products of *Lugdunum* (Walker 1988, 286). It is highly likely that the Hot Bath Spring group for this period will follow the patterns observed elsewhere in Bath and the province. The identifiable *as* reverse types are dominated by the *Aequitas* type, followed by the *Provident* altar series, *Fides* and the eagle on globe types. The high proportion of the *Aequitas* series contrasts with the Sacred Spring group, where the eagle on globe type dominates (31), followed by the *Provident* altar type (13) and then *Aequitas* (6) (ibid., 312).

Issues of Domitian AD 81–96 – Thirty-seven coins attributable to Domitian were identified. Of this total thirty-six are *asses* and one a *dupondius*. Fifteen of the coins can be identified with a reasonable degree of certainty, all being issues dateable to *c* AD 85–86. This dating once again conforms to the pattern observed at the Sacred Spring and the province overall and discussed at length by Walker (ibid., 286–8). Five reverse types are identifiable, a much lower total than the varieties recorded from the Sacred Spring (ibid., 313), however this figure must be offset against the high proportion (19) of the Domitianic issues where the reverse type cannot be identified.

Period of regular supply AD 96–AD 197

The 2nd century AD sees a more regular supply of coinage into the province and this is reflected in the Hot Bath Spring assemblage, with 101 issues that can be identified with certainty. The majority of these (97) fall into the period AD 96–161 and there is a more balanced spread of denominations: 8 *sestertii*, 15 definite or probable *dupondii* and 74 *asses*. A greater variety of reverse types is represented

Nerva and Trajan AD 96–117 – Forty-eight coins attributable to Nerva and Trajan were identified, three of the former and forty-five of Trajan. Of this total, three are *sestertii*, seven *dupondii*, eight *asses* or *dupondii* module and thirty *asses*. The Trajanic issues are especially badly corroded and only one reverse type, Arabia (no. 113) could be identified with certainty.

Hadrian AD 117–138 – Twenty-seven coins of Hadrian were identified, three *sestertii* and twenty-four *asses*. Six of the *asses* are of the 'Britannia' type issued in AD 119, a type that has an almost exclusively British distribution. In assessing the assemblage from the Sacred Spring Walker (ibid., 291–2) discusses issues of the 'casting mint', operating *c* AD 122–4 and copying issues from Nero to Hadrian. The condition of the coins from the Hot Bath Spring is so poor that no such issues can be recognised, although this does not preclude some of the Hadrianic and earlier *asses* being products of this mint.

Antoninus Pius and Marcus Aurelius AD 138–180 – Twenty-six coins of the period 138–180 were identified, two *sestertii* and twenty-four *asses*. The identifiable *asses* of Antoninus Pius are dominated by the 'Britannia' issues of AD 154–155, an output almost exclusive to Britain (ibid., 294). In addition, an *as* of Marcus Aurelius as Caesar, with a figure of Minerva on the reverse (no. 196) belongs to the same mint period as the Britannia issues. One issue of the Empress Faustina II and an *as* of Marcus Aurelius as Augustus plus two *asses* of unidentifiable Antonine empresses are the sum total for issues of the period 161–180.

The paucity of post AD161 coinage is striking and despite the circumstances of the assemblage recovery and condition, must represent a marked break in the pattern of offerings into the Hot Spring. No issues of Commodus or the early Severan dynasty were recognised, which contrasts markedly with the Sacred Spring (ibid., 319–20). Whether this implies reduced use or a change in the devotional pattern at the spring is impossible to discern from the numismatic evidence alone.

Period of minimal supply AD 197–260

This period more than lives up to its name in the assemblage with only one coin, an unidentifiable *as*, possibly of Julia Soaemias, AD 218–222.

Period c AD 260–402

This period, normally associated with vast quantities of coinage and widespread coin use in Roman Britain, is represented by only twenty-five coins, eighteen of which can be identified with any degree of certainty.

Only two 'radiates' of the period *c* AD 270–75 were noted and Constantinian issues, normally so common, show a marked bias towards the later period of *c* AD 350–61. Of note within this group is a cut-down AE2 of Magnentius, AD 350–353. This has been reduced in size to an AE4 module of 13 mm diameter. The original coin carried the reverse featuring a large Chi-Rho monogram. A very similar piece was noted by Walker from the Sacred Spring (ibid., plate XLVIII no. 13). The later 4th century is represented by only five coins, four of the House of Valentinian, AD 364–78 and one of the House of Theodosius, AD 399–402.

Discussion

The assemblage has, despite the conditions of deposition and recovery, provided valuable data on the numismatic votive depositional patterns at the Hot Bath Spring. The dominance of 1st- and 2nd-century coins down to *c* AD 161 would suggest a focus of deposition that ceases before the end of the 2nd century. In terms of the types represented, the patterns are broadly comparable to the large group recovered from the Sacred Spring (Walker 1988). The great divergence between the two sites occurs from *c* AD 161, with the Hot Bath Spring attracting very little coinage after that date. Even allowing for the corrosive effects of the conditions of deposition and the methods of recovery this period must indicate a profound change in the nature of activity at the Hot Bath Spring. The contrast with the Sacred Spring is stark. At the latter site over 4700 coins of this period were recovered, over one third of the total assemblage (ibid., 308–9). The patterns noted here must, however, because of the circumstances of recovery, be regarded as provisional.

GENERAL DISCUSSION

In the prehistoric period the hot springs must have attracted human interest but not necessarily habitation in the area. The interpretation of the flint deposits in the Hot Bath spring as evidence for early Mesolithic ceremonial or ritual suggests that these natural features inspired religious practices from a very early period. Although evidence for such practices has not been found for any other period until the late Iron Age (Cunliffe and Davenport 1985; Cunliffe 1988), it seems reasonable to think that the hot springs gave rise to such ideas and practices in the intervening period. Even if this interpretation is rejected, in the light of normal human reaction faced with such a phenomenon, the presence of mesolithic activity from early in the Holocene is of considerable interest. It is now clear from the material that has been found in the walled area of Bath and on the alluvial levels towards the river that the valley bottom was part of the resources of a Mesolithic population through the early to late Mesolithic periods. The potential for further study in the alluvium is considerable, as stratified flint spreads have been found there (Bell 1997) and work is about to begin (in Spring 2006) on large scale excavations which should expose sizeable areas.

Comparison with the King's Bath excavation has inevitably been made. However, at the latter site, no bore hole was made into the deep pipe deposits, and on the present site, no manual area excavation was possible. The contexts of the two samples are very different. Nonetheless the question must be asked, as it is raised for the Roman period, whether different activities, rituals or functions might have been specific to the various hot springs in the immediate vicinity. It would be obtuse to think they did not also change over the millennia.

Whatever the detail, probably largely irrecoverable, it is impossible not to imagine the Mesolithic populations, while exploiting the rich resources of the valley bottom, finding ways of dealing with the discovery of three steaming, bubbling, multi-coloured, probably weirdly-vegetated and certainly strange smelling springs in the heart of their territories. It is not likely to be confirmed that the springs ever were the sites of shamanistic ritual, nor that the deposition of flint was part of such ceremonies, but the suspicion that such rituals occurred is inescapable.

Nonetheless, we throw coins into water today with barely a nod to a belief system, let alone any noticeable ceremony, and we might think that the same could be true of the Roman deposition of coins in the springs and by extension backwards to Mesolithic activities. We are saved from any such minimalism by the indications provided by other objects, and in particular, the pewter inscriptions from the King's Bath, that there was a clear and powerful set of beliefs and rituals around the deposition of objects in the springs in Roman times.

The date ranges of the coin assemblage from the Hot Spring borehole seem to indicate that coin deposition started here as soon as Roman coins reached the area. The near cessation of deposition after 160, if taken at face value, is a strong reflection of the suggested date of construction of the main building on the Spa site. An obvious interpretation is that this mid-2nd century building development made the spring less accessible for the coin-depositing visitor and must have introduced a new kind of use or ritual into whatever observance now was undertaken. While it had no comparable effect on the deposition of coins in the King's Bath, the enclosure of the *Fons Sulis* in a vaulted chamber, probably before AD 200, perhaps reflects a related change in the way in which the springs were viewed (Cunliffe and Davenport 1985). The existence of coins right down to 402 indicates that the spring was still available, as a catchment at least, during their circulation. The fragments of other unfortunately undatable Roman objects hint at a period when such items were deposited as at the King's Bath. The absence of inscribed pewter plaques may be significant, for if there had been deposition of such objects in similar numbers to the finds in the King's Bath is unlikely that they would not have been found even by the bore pipe.

Chapter 10:   Bellott's Hospital: Salvage Excavation

By Marek Lewcun and Peter Davenport

OVERVIEW

Bellott's Hospital was founded by Thomas Bellott an important benefactor to Elizabethan and Stuart Bath. It was certainly in existence as a "new hospital for lame pilgrims" in 1608, but perhaps was not founded much before 1606 (Manco 1998, 76). Reforms to the Bath Charities in the early 19th century put Bellott's under the control of the Trustees of St John's Hospital, and in 1859 the original building was replaced with a rather clumsy design on two storeys with a full basement (ibid.). The latter were used for storage until plans were drawn up in 1996 to convert the block into a convalescent unit for inmates of the hospital which required the deepening of the cellars by 0.3 to 0.4 m and the insertion of below floor services of various kinds. Preliminary site investigations in the form of test pits had revealed structural remains and well-preserved deposits of Roman and medieval date below the cellar floors. A proposal for further investigation and/or mitigation was put to the Trustees but no conditions were placed on the planning permission and clearance work on the site went ahead in 1999 without any organised archaeological input.

During the development, however, access for monitoring was permitted to Bath Archaeological Trust and a small team, led by Marek Lewcun, was able to record much of what was revealed and removed. We are indebted to the contractors, Emery Brothers of Bath, for facilitating the work, even to the extent of delaying and rescheduling work to allow limited excavation and recording to take place. In the end, an overall plan of the deposits was achieved (Fig. 10.1), sample sections of the dark earth and some parts of the upper Roman deposits drawn, and detail sections of some deeper disturbances, such as a lift base, recorded (Fig. 10.2). In addition, it was possible to carefully excavate and sample the most important discovery on the site, a well-preserved, late Roman smithy.

The site is diagonally opposite the Spa site on the south side of Beau Street. At this point Beau Street, although a new street of 1830, closely followed the line of the medieval Bell Tree Lane and the hospital plot was at its junction with Bilbury Lane, which is thought to be of Saxon origin. As is commonly the case in Bath, the cellars had removed the medieval deposits, but in this case had left a dark earth over the Roman structural remains, sealed by the stone slabs of the 1859 cellar floor. It is possible that this area was an open space throughout the middle ages. When Bellott leased it for the new hospital, it was a garden and the intensive coverage of medieval pits supports the view that it was not built on for a large part of the middle ages. Although undated, the dark earth may therefore comprise the earliest garden soils that formed over the Roman remains. The almost level upper surface of the latter suggests long and aggressive cultivation. Careful observation at Aldridge's, Walcot Street (Beaton forthcoming) showed that the walls of the Roman buildings there had been robbed after cultivation was well established around them. Conditions were not conducive to such observations here.

In most of the site, a little less than one metre of Roman stratified deposits survived, over a buried soil macroscopically identical to the prehistoric levels at the Spa site. These layers were criss-crossed by substantial Roman wall-footings, gravel and rubble layers of a Roman street, and pits of probably medieval date (very few could be dug, but others were seen in section in modern trenches). The medieval pits, like those at the Spa site, were quarry holes or robber pits as well as rubbish pits, in as much as many clearly followed the lines of Roman walls.

Three phases of Roman building were identified, one apparently encroaching on the street line (something also seen at Hat and Feather Yard, Beaton in prep). In two rooms of Building 2, large quantities of smithing slag were found piled over the floors and one room contained *in situ* the stone block on which the anvil seems to have stood. Advice was sought from J. M. Mills on the appropriate sampling strategy and this was then implemented. Dr. Lyn Keys of English Heritage assessed the data and her assessment report is included in this section. It has not yet proved possible to carry out Dr. Keys' recommendations, but it is hoped to do this and publish a more detailed report on the smithy in another place.

This report is not based on a full stratigraphic analysis, as this has not yet been completed. Given the financial background to the project it is uncertain whether this will take place, except in so far as the iron-working phase is concerned. Instead, the results of the work are described in an interim fashion in order to make the information on this site available and enhance understanding of the adjacent Spa site.

PREHISTORIC ACTIVITY

A series of buried soils was noted at the base of the original test pit (264, 266, 267, Fig. 10.2, sections 2 and 3 and plan Fig. 10.1). The topmost was a dark grey-brown clay silt very like that at the Spa. It overlay a thin layer of brown sandy silt (266), itself sitting on the alluvial gravel (267). These contexts were not excavated further except that they were

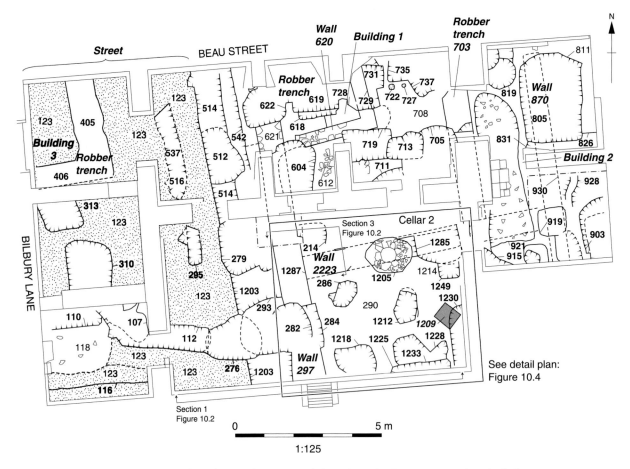

Figure 10.1   Bellott's Hospital: Plan of main features and deposits. The Roman street is stippled.

observed when the pit was extended eastwards by machine. While not very informative in itself, the observation does confirm that this pre-Roman soil extends across a large portion of the area south of Beau Street, while the Spa site and excavations at 31 Stall Street and the temple outer portico show that it extends north (Cunliffe 1969, 179–181; Davenport 1999, fig. I.59, layer 21).

ROMAN SEQUENCE

Street

A street, formed from a series of layers of gravel (Fig. 10.2, section 1, layers 269–273) with a cambered surface, was identified in the west end of the excavated area (Fig. 10.1). It was clearly visible after the first machine strip of the overlying dark earths. The road is collectively referred to as context 123. A foundation layer of stone rubble was seen in the south-west corner of the trench. Sequences of gravel deposits were seen in several places. Typically these comprised a layer of rubble acting as a foundation supporting at least five layers of gravel surfacing interleaved with grey silts. A typical sequence is listed below (from bottom to top):

2255	rubble foundation
550	gravel
549/1270	silt
275/535/533/548/1277	gravel
274/547	silt
273	gravel
272	silt
271	gravel
270	silt
269	gravel

The street was in general well-preserved but was cut by pits and gullies of later date. The minimum recorded width of the road was 5.8 m. The recorded depth of the street surfacing sequence was over 0.35 m from 269 down to the top of 273, implying that the whole sequence was over 0.50 m deep. It was not clear whether the gravels had been truncated, although this could not be ruled out as most of these layers were dug away by machine. The sequence of deposits below the rubble foundation was *not* investigated. The foundation layer of rubble does not necessarily represent the first phase of road construction. At the Hat and Feather Yard the main road had three 'foundation' layers spread through the sequence (Beaton in prep).

154

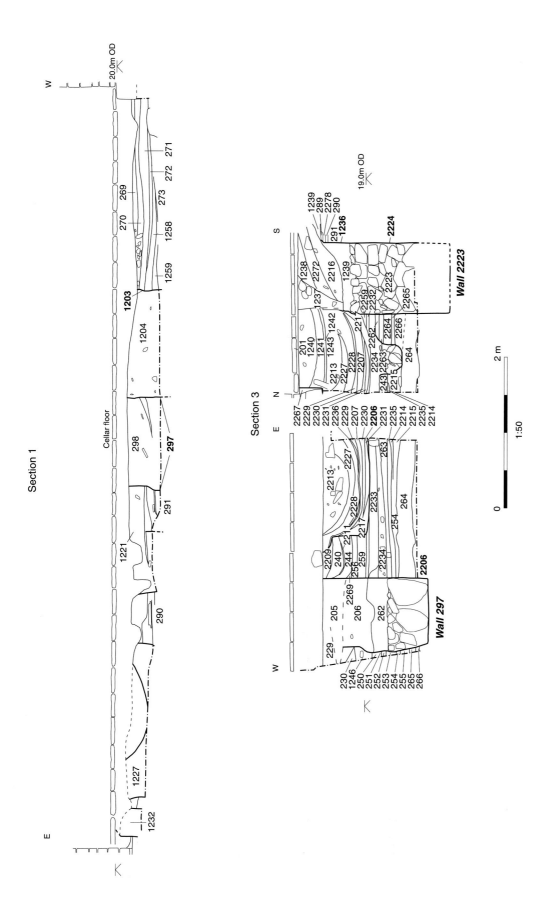

Figure 10.2 Bellott's Hospital: Section 1, east-west section located at south edge of trench; Sections 2 and 3, sections of Test pit. (See Fig. 10.1 for locations.)

Possible Timber building, Stone Building 1 and earlier deposits

The earliest recovered Romano-British stratigraphy has yet to be considered in detail, but seems to have consisted of a series of mortar layers, gravels, silts and loams forming floor and occupation deposits. These are in fact typical urban layers comprising mostly thin deposits that have built up over a long period. At the south end of cellar 2, east of the hatchway (marked by the steps on Fig. 10.1), two beam slots were recorded below the blacksmith's workshop floors, one running north-south, the other at right angles [2275, 2276]. Only short lengths were recorded in a hand-dug construction trench for new internal cellar walls. They presumably represent timber building. A gravel surface (2250) was recorded adjacent to beam slot 2275 and was either contemporary with or cut by it. Another cut feature, which may be related to the timber structures in the early phases of the occupation on this site, was recorded below pit 2206. The cut was only seen in section and was 0.40 m across, packed with stones 2234 (Fig. 10.2, section 3). It had small levelling stones at the top and may have been a foundation for a wooden sill beam. It might alternatively have been a stone packed post hole fortuitously sliced by the lift shaft cut. No comparable timber buildings of earlier Roman date have been recorded in central Bath, but examples were found and investigated in some detail at the Hat and Feather site and are indicated at Beehive Yard in the settlement along Walcot Street (Beaton in prep; Crutchley *et al.* forthcoming).

Another early feature was the south-east corner [620 = 729] of a stone-walled building (Building 1). The wall was largely robbed but mortared footings and a first course of squared rubble facing survived on the east-west run (620). Just north of 620 and probably contemporary with it was a gravel surface (660/642), which seems to have been an internal floor. Layers of burnt clay and gravel (661–664) under it suggest a previous phase of activity, but was not further investigated. Wall 620, was 0.42 m wide and was the narrowest of the walls discovered, was cut by the robber trenches of wall 621/209 and wall 617 (Building 2) and was on a slightly different alignment from the other walls. It is clear that this wall was earliest in the masonry sequence.

There is no stratigraphic evidence to establish the relationship between the possible timber structures under the smithy on one hand, and the earliest masonry structure and underlying burnt deposits on the other. Nor can the relationship between these structures and the street in the west part of the trench be established. Building 1 may have fronted onto the street [123] although not exactly on the same alignment. While it was clear that Buildings 2 and 3 (see below) were respectively contemporary with and later than the street surface, the relationship of Building 1 is less uncertain. It could have pre-dated the street, but it was not possible to check this point by excavation.

Building 3 (Figs 10.1 and 10.3)

This is represented by the south-eastern corner of a masonry building, much robbed and of broadly similar scale to Building 2 (see below). The foundations (417/418 and 420/424) were dug down to just over a metre from the surviving top edge of the robber trench [405/406] and were 0.67 m wide. Just over half the depth of footings survived robbing. Two other lengths of wall may have been associated with this building. To the south was wall 121, robbed by robber trench 110. The fill of the robber trench contained Pennant stone roof tiles, suggesting that this form of roof covering, common in Bath, was also used here. Less certainly associated was a rather irregular gully [537/516] filled with pitched stone footings and parallel to the east wall 424 = 405. Neither was directly connected with each other or with walls 418 and 424 and it is not certain that they were contemporary, although all were cut into the road surface.

Building 3 clearly encroached onto the road. The encroachment was on a considerable in scale, extending at a minimum over 2.5 metres into the known road, that is at least half way across it. This may indicate a simple narrowing of the street, with or without official sanction. Something similar was seen at Hat and Feather Yard where a new room was built out into the road from the arcaded or colonnaded passage on the front of one of the strip buildings. However, if 537/516 was really part of the building its presence implies the complete blocking of the road, or at best its transformation into a very narrow alleyway.

Building 2 (Figs 10.1 and 10.4)

Building 2 was a strongly built structure with mortared rubble wall footings over 0.8 m thick and 1.5–1.7 m deep from the street surface (curiously the internal cross wall was deeper set). Elements of three rooms were identified along the street frontage with a fourth, possibly an addition, at the rear to the east.

The front (west) wall [297] and the main east-west wall [2223] were the best preserved (Fig. 10.2, sections 2 and 3: 209, 297, 621; see also Fig. 10.3). The main east-west wall in the centre of the site still retained its massive, rubble footings (2223, Fig. 10.2, section 3), but had been extensively robbed. The east-west wall (617) to the north had been completely robbed away (robber trenches 621/209). The rear main wall was also completely robbed. Its robber trench (703) contained burnt tile, mortar and/or plaster (704). Parallel to 703 was a narrower wall (870 in foundation trench 871), which was heavily robbed but with coursing surviving in a small area at the north end. Its thinner dimensions suggest a single storey pentice or corridor along the rear of what was, to judge from the heavy footings, probably a two storied (or even higher) building. On the western street frontage ran a broad and in places shallow, robber trench [514/1203], and this

Figure 10.3 Bellott's Hospital: walls of Building 1 (620, in background) and Building 2 (wall 297 context 621, in foreground) in cellar 6.

might have been the location of a stone street-edge gutter, or of a continuous stone step along the front of the building. Whatever was removed from the robber trench was either cut into the street gravel or the gravel had built up against it (Fig. 10.2, section 1).

Within the building floors and destruction deposits were identified under the dark earth. Immediately beneath the dark earth was a layer of plaster and small limestone rubble and dust (1210) and beneath this spreads of Pennant roof tiles (1211) as distinct from stone floor slabs. These deposits are interpreted deriving from the collapse of the roof and the gradual weathering of the internal plaster and stone work. They sealed the latest floor levels.

In the south room (the 'smithy') at the front of the building the latest floors seem to have been of thin Pennant sandstone slabs laid either over make-up layers of gravel and clay or earlier gravel floors. The Pennant sandstone slabs were generally much broken and disarranged (eg. 612, 716, 813, 907, 909, 910, not on plan). They seem to have served as the floor of Building 2 when it was in use as a smithy and are much modified; they were sometimes placed in hollows. Overall they may be entirely an *ad hoc* arrangement of that period rather than a properly laid floor. The latter may have been represented by 291/2247, a concrete floor (described as crushed stone and mortar and gravel). This was seen, much worn away and punctuated by pits, over much of the southern room and was immediately under the layers of slags, Pennant sandstone and silts.

In the room to the north of the dividing wall 2223, the only floor was a gravel layer 708. To the east of the pentice or corridor wall 870 and therefore external to the building fragments of a surface or floor of light brown/yellow mortar (811) survived. Observation of pits and excavation for new footings showed stratified sequences of gravels and silts predating these floors.

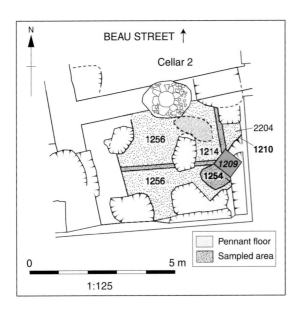

Figure 10.4   Bellott's Hospital: Plan of sampling of smithy.

Smithy and slag deposits

Within the south room of Building 2, large amounts of slag of various kinds (see Dr. Keys' assessment below) were spread around, and piled against the northern wall. (It is suspected that similar material lay to the south but was removed by machine before it could be fully recorded.) A small section (1256) was sampled here and suggested a thickness before machine

excavation of 0.35 m. On the east the build-up was sampled (2204) and reached a thickness of 0.48 m. This slag also formed the floor of the smithy, although probably more as a result of deposition through intensive working rather than being deliberately laid down (1214). The original floor may have been the Pennant stone spreads mentioned above, themselves acting as a repair to the concrete floor postulated there. Similar deposits of slag, but more dissected and damaged, were recorded to the north of wall 2223.

Sitting on the slag floor (1214) was a rectangular block of Bath stone 0.66 x 0.60 x 0.35 m [1209] (Figs 10.1 and 10.3). Its positioning post-dates the initial slag deposition but at least one phase of the Pennant paving butted it (indicating the *ad hoc* nature of this floor suggested above). Most of the later slag deposits post-dated the positioning of the stone. Clearly the block had been moved or replaced during the life of the smithy. The stone was interpreted as an anvil support block, and much smithing slag was indeed identified around it. Much ashy material was recorded, but no obvious hearth site. Dr. Keys points out that the hearth was probably raised, just as in traditional post-Roman ones, but that careful analysis of the materials on the floors may well allow its position to be fixed to some degree. Samples show that coal was at least one of the fuels used and this is, of course, locally plentiful, the nearest surface coal seams being only 2 miles away.

It is evident that at least two rooms were used as part of a blacksmith's workshop when the building was still standing and roofed. Little could be said

Figure 10.5   Bellott's Hospital: anvil stone (1209) in situ in cellar 2.

about the building before this use, but it seems extremely probable that it was not originally built as a smithy. The massive foundations suggest a substantial building for official use.

Dating

The material from the excavation has yet to be studied. However, the bulk of it seems to be of 2nd- to 4th-century date and is either from the upper Roman levels or residual from the robber trenches and medieval pits. The presence of 4th-century coins suggests activity in that period. Until the finds and stratigraphy are fully analysed, it seems reasonable to suggest that the smithing activity, at the end of the recognised sequence, utilised a run-down Roman building (itself not the earliest component of the stratigraphic sequence), quite probably in the 4th century.

Assessment of the iron slag
by Lynne Keys

Introduction and site methodology

The smithy was identified on-site in part because the Roman room it was in was much less disturbed by medieval pit digging than other areas of the site. The large square stone block on which it is believed the anvil once stood was still *in situ* towards one side. A trampled layer of iron slag was present, worn around the block but less so towards the wall. The larger slags such as smithing hearth bottoms remained piled against the walls of the room. The only feature absent from the smithy, as far as the archaeologists were concerned, was a hearth of any kind. Next to the smithy was another room which may have functioned as a shop or storeroom.

Sampling for hammerscale was carried out by means of subdivided strips across the floor and the anvil stone was recovered. A brief assessment of the slag was undertaken with a view to determining its significance and whether funding should be sought for full analysis and publication.

Archaeometallurgical methodology, explanation of terms and discussion

Almost 13.5kg of slag was examined for the assessment. This was only a small part of the recovered assemblage. In all, five contexts were selected for assessment. Contexts from the room adjacent to the smithy were not examined so the total quantity of slag present is not currently known.

The slag was examined by eye and with a magnet; samples were tipped out into a tray and similarly examined and tested. Smithing hearth bottoms were individually weighed and measured. Details of quantification are given in Table 10.1 below:

Some types of iron slags are diagnostic of smelting or smithing, while others are not. Slag may be said to be undiagnostic because it could have been produced by either process, or because it has broken up

during deposition, redeposition or excavation. Other types of debris sometimes encountered in slag assemblages may be the result of a variety of high temperature activities – including domestic fires – and cannot be taken on their own to indicate that ironworking was taking place. These include materials such as fired clay, vitrified hearth lining, cinder, and fuel ash slags. However if found in association with iron slag – particularly diagnostic iron slag – they can be considered as possible products of the process.

The diagnostic slags from Bellott's Hospital all point to smithing activity. This activity generates both bulk (larger) slags and micro-slags (invisible in the soil) which can supply information about the type of smithing which took place and how long it is likely to have taken place.

The smithing hearth bottom is the most characteristic bulk slag produced by smithing. Its plano-convex shape was formed as a result of high temperature reactions between the iron, iron-scale and silica from either a clay furnace lining or the silica flux used by the smith. The predominantly fayalitic (iron silicate) material produced by this reaction dripped down into the hearth base during smithing forming smithing slag which, if not cleared out, developed into the smithing hearth bottom. When removed from the hearth such bottoms were usually taken outside and deposited in the nearest pit or ditch, but the smith at Bellott's Hospital was either too lazy to do this or was prevented for some reason from depositing material outside. He piled the larger slags, including the undiagnostic pieces (which probably represent fragments of smithing hearth bottoms) against the inside walls of his workplace, where they remained.

Iron smithing also produces micro-slags (hammerscale) of two types: flake and spheroidal. Flake hammerscale resembles silvery fish scales and is the product of the ordinary hot working and hammering of a piece of iron where fragments of the oxide/ silicate skin flake off from the iron and fall to the ground. Spheroidal hammerscale consists of small solid droplets of liquid slag expelled from within the iron during the primary smithing of a bloom or the fire welding of two pieces of iron. Hammerscale is not visible to the naked eye when in the soil but is highly diagnostic of smithing activity, often remaining in the area around the anvil and near the hearth when macro-slags have been cleared out of the smithy and dumped elsewhere. Since it is generally highly magnetic, its detection with a magnet while excavating can allow the spatial relationship of the anvil to the hearth to be recorded and can pinpoint the smithing activity more precisely (Mills and McDonnell 1992). Significant amounts of hammer scale were present in the samples examined here and may allow the spatial layout of the smithy to be determined, as well as revealing the type of smithing carried out.

Virtually no material that could be identified as part of a hearth was seen in the assemblage.

Table 10.1   Quantification of the assessed iron slag by context (weights in grammes, dimensions in mm).

Con-text	Sample	Sub-division	Identification	Weight	Length	Width	Depth	Comment
290	32		hammerscale	23				lots flake, very occasional spheres
290	32		microslags	244				coarser sample: hammerscale flake, cinder, coal etc
290			smithing hearth bottom	380	110	80	50	
290			undiagnostic	320				
290			coal	32				laminated type
290			vitrified hearth lining	56				
290			undiagnostic	382				
290			smithing hearth bottom	114	55	55	40	good example of tiny; almost square
290			smithing hearth bottom	310	100	90	45	
290			smithing hearth bottom	350	90	85	50	
1214	6		sample	196				some flake hammerscale, iron shavings, coal fragments
1214	6		undiagnostic	78				two pieces
1214	6		fine sample	90				lots flake hammerscale and tiny spheres; iron shavings, coarse sand
1214	6		iron	4				
1214	9		fine sample	194				broken flake hammerscale, at least one tiny sphere; tiny fragments coal, fired clay, iron shavings
1214	9		coarse sample	418				smithy floor but a little less hammerscale flake than elsewhere and not so broken up, fragments coal etc.
1254	2		hammerscale	6				flake, large fragments
1254	2		microslags	0				irregular
1254	2		coal	14				
1254	11	2	hammerscale	92				flake and some tiny spheres
1254	14	5	fine sample	102				hammerscale flake and some spheres; very small fragments burnt coal
1254	17	8	fire/hearth debris	134				tiny fragments coal, ashy material and burnt ferruginous runs, hammerscale flake and occasional spheres
1254	23	14	fire/hearth debris	144				coarser sample: hammerscale flake (less broken), cinder, coal etc
1254	23	14	fine sample	490				includes flake hammerscale & v. occ spheres
1256	25	4	sample	316				hammerscale flake, not numerous but larger in size; tiny coal and slag fragments

Table 10.1   (Continued)

Con-text	Sample	Sub-division	Identification	Weight	Length	Width	Depth	Comment
1256	25	4	fine sample	150				flake hammerscale, possible occasional spheres
1256	28	7	hammerscale	76				flake, one tiny sphere and flakes of iron
1256	28	7	coal	6				
1256	28	7	microslags	4				
1256	28	7	fine sample	164				flake hammerscale, occasional spheres, coarse and
1256	98	11	fine sample	190				flake hammerscale, occasional spheres; charcoal and burnt coal
1256	98	11	undiagnostic	540				broken small fragments
1256	98	11	coal	24				
1256	98	11	coarse sample	368				occasional large hammerscale flakes, couple of spheres
1256	98	11	coal	13				
2204	33		fired clay	4				
2204	33		microslags	182				and coal, undiagnostic etc
2204	33		hammerscale	0				lots of flake, limited spheres
2204	33							
2204	33		fine sample	496				mostly broken flake hammerscale and very occasional spheres (16g+)
2204	34		undiagnostic	1850				probably smithing slag, hammerscale inclusions
2204	34		hammerscale	0				broken flake, charcoal and coal fragments
2204	41		undiagnostic	1442				
2204	41		undiagnostic	602				probably smithing slag
2204	41		smithing hearth bottom	726	125	125	65	
2204	41		stone (broken hone?)	0				removed for identification
2204	41		coal	0				as fuel
2204	41		hammerscale	0				broken flake
2204	34 & 95		smithing hearth bottom	2106	160	130	90	the two halves in different samples
			total weight	**13432 g**				

This may be because the firebed was on a raised base which was subsequently removed, perhaps for re-use of the material. Further support for this suggestion comes from the height of the anvil block, which was too great to have been used for ground level work and too low to have served on its own as an anvil; the smith would have been stooped over to such a degree that chronic back-ache would have ensued. An anvil probably stood on the stone – and, indeed, there is the trace of a wide wear mark on top where something heavy may have rested – allowing the smith to work comfortably standing up. If he was working in this way the implication is that the hearth may have been raised to a similar level. Analysis of the samples could answer this question as one would expect the hammerscale to be more frequent around the anvil and absent where a hearth had stood.

The question remains of why such a hearth might have been dismantled to re-use its materials while the large stone was ignored. A possible answer is that the stone has a crack towards one side (which may have originated at the time it was quarried), hence its use for something other than building and its abandonment when the smithy went out of use.

The fuel used for smithing was, in all instances, coal of a laminated type, probably from around the Bath area. Further analysis should be able to confirm this.

Significance of the assemblage

The assemblage represents smithing activity but because it has survived *in situ* in a Roman building where the layout of the activity can be ascertained, the slag and the site are of national importance.

MEDIEVAL AND LATER FEATURES

The removal of the Pennant slabs and make-up deposits for the basement floor of Bellott's Hospital revealed a layer of dark grey brown loam of varying thickness. This was only recorded in the edges of the excavated area. It was generally about 0.30 m thick and represented the last remnant of post-Roman and pre-1606 deposit. It covered the street surface and the demolition layers of the Roman buildings. It was presumably penetrated by the various pits and gulleys recorded cutting the Roman levels, but this could not be confirmed.

Apart from this material, post-Roman activity was represented by pits and scoops. All, as far as could be ascertained, were truncated by the construction of the 1859 basements. Between 20 and 25 of these features were recorded, in addition to the robber trenches, some of which were pit-like. The level from which they were dug remains unknown. Some idea of the ground level when the hospital was built in 1606 can be derived from trenches in the garden, and from the surviving fragments of that building in the east end of the present cellars. A pitched limestone surface was recorded in the south-west corner of the garden south of Bellott's Hospital and is probably part of the rear courtyard of the original hospital. Its top as recorded at 21.56 m OD, about 1.5 metres above the basement floors. The bases of what appear to be the ground floor fireplaces in the east wall are about 22 m OD, or about 2 m above the basement floor.

Many of the scoops and pits are clearly for quarrying, as demonstrated on the Spa excavation. Examples here are 1285, 622, 619 and 731. Features 112 and 276 are interesting as they may represent the removal of a transverse road drain such as was seen at a well-made side road at Hat and Feather Yard in 1989 (Beaton in prep) and could be part of the series of pits interpreted as a robbed drain alongside Building 2 (1203, 279, 514, 512). While some of the robbing was linear, most robber trenches were much wider and irregular at the top as if the exact line of the wall was not quite certain when digging commenced. By definition, these sorts of excavations are likely to be later than those more precisely targeted when the masonry remains were much more evident.

Other pits are likely to have been for rubbish disposal but it was not possible to excavate many of them in the appropriate manner to confirm this. Pit 2206 was not excavated, but its sections were recorded in the lift pit (Fig. 10.2, section 3). The pit was truncated by the cellar floor but was still almost a metre deep. It had been allowed to stand open for a short while after being dug, as the basal layer was a slow, steady filling of gritty, grey silt (2217), built up around the edges of the pit. Above this were two thin layers of brown and grey brown, gritty loam that were probably tips of material and a thicker, soft brown silt 2207. These were sealed by layer 2229, a thin lens of pure carbonised wood covering the whole pit, which suggests the dumping of the ashes of a wood fire. Above this were alternating tips of silts, thicker and thinner by turns (2228–1241). The upper silts were grey, and more mixed, as if they had accumulating quite quickly. Superficially, this pit appears to be a typical rubbish pit, but if so, it was not filled with anything highly organic, except possibly for layers 2207 and 2227 that were a soft brown silt which may represent decayed organic matter. Whether or not the fills were typical, pit 2206 certainly fell into the most common size range, of about a metre in diameter. There were, however, numbers of both larger and smaller pits.

GENERAL DISCUSSION

Much more analysis needs to be done on the data from this site, but it is already clear that the Roman remains are of considerable interest. A sequence with hints of a phase of timber buildings has not been found in central Bath before, and the topographical changes suggest significant alterations in the way the town was being organised. The complex history of the street and its changing relationship to the flanking buildings confirms the impression of fluidity of the town plan gained from other work.

The change in size and solidity of construction from Building 1 to Building 2 seems likely to reflect a noticeable change of use of the site, from a fairly average Roman masonry structure to a very substantial one. It is improbable that Building 2 had fewer than two storeys. It is also more likely than not that the building had some public, or at least non-domestic function, given the sheer massiveness of its footings. If the smith's hearth was in the ground floor of such a building, there must have been some arrangement for the smoke to get out, although this could have been as simple as pulling up a few floorboards in the floor above. Alternatively, if the thick walls mean that the lower floors were vaulted, then the fire resistant qualities of such a building may have attracted a smith. There is little evidence to support the idea of vaulting, however, and its presence is extremely unlikely if the interpretation of layer 1210 as roof collapse and dilapidation of the stone work is correct since any vaulting remains would have fallen before and been buried by the roof tiles, and none were seen. When the smithing data is properly analysed it will be possible to reconstruct much of the activity that went on in this phase.

It is likely that some evidence for the late and post Roman phases in Roman Bath survived until the

1999 work, but clearance of the site to the level at which archaeological recording began had removed most if not all of it. Further analysis may show some survival of data from this phase.

Analysis of the finds from the presumed medieval pits may allow some better understanding of this phase of activity, not least the dating. It can only be assumed at the moment that the pits are predominantly of 11th- to 13th-century date, as is usual in Bath. Dating of robbing activity is usually difficult but has been shown to be as late as the 13th century along parts of Walcot Street but evidence from the present site may be able to contribute to the argument. The excavation also showed that the rear garden of the present Bellott's Hospital is of very high archaeological potential.

Bibliography

Albarella, U and Davis, S, 1994 Mammal and bird bones from Launceston Castle: decline in status and the rise of agriculture, *Circaea* **12(1)**, 1–156

Allason-Jones, L and Miket, R, 1984 *The catalogue of small finds from South Shields Roman fort,* Society of Antiquaries of Newcastle upon Tyne

Ambrose, T and Henig, M, 1979 The small finds, in Greene 1979, 54–57

Anderson, F W, 1979 ** in P Rahtz, *The Saxon and Medieval Palace at Cheddar. Excavations 1960–62.* Brit Archaeol Rep (Brit Ser) **65**, Oxford, **.

Barrett, J H, 1997 Fish trade in Norse Orkney and Caithness: a zooarchaeological approach, *Antiquity* **71**, 616–38

Barrett, J H, Locker, A M and Roberts, C M, 2004a 'Dark Age Economics' revisited: the English fish bone evidence AD 600–1600, *Antiquity* **78**, 618–638

Barrett, J H, Locker, A M and Roberts, C M, 2004b The origins of intensive marine fishing in medieval Europe: the English evidence, *Proc Royal Soc, London, Series B* **271**, 2417–2421

Bath Archaeological Trust, 1997, 'The Hot Bath, Hot Bath Street, Bath; Archaeological Evaluation Report' (Unpub. Planning Report)

Beaton, M, forthcoming Excavations in Walcot Street, Bath

Bell, R D, 1997 Southgate Development. Archaeological Field Evaluation. Unpublished client report, B&NES SMR

Benhardt, D, 2003, The life and work of George Manners, architect, unpublished PhD thesis, Centre for Advanced Studies in Architecture, University of Bath

Betts, I M, 1985 A scientific investigation of the brick and tile industry of York to the mid-eighteenth century, unpub PhD thesis, University of Bradford

Betts, I M, 1991, Thin-section and Neutron Activation Analysis of brick and tile from York and surrounding sites, in A Middleton and I Freestone (eds) *Recent Developments in Ceramic Petrology,* British Museum Occasional Paper 81, 39–55

Betts, I M, 1995 Procuratorial tile stamps from London, *Britannia* **26**, 207–229

Betts, I M, 1999a Lower Common allotments, Upper Road, Bath. Assessment report on ceramic building materials (Unpublished archive report)

Betts, I M 1999b Oldfield Boys School, Bath. Assessment report on ceramic building materials, (Unpublished archive report)

Betts, I M, forthcoming The building material in Crutchley, Leverett and Riley forthcoming

Betts, I, Black, E W and Gower, J, 1994 *A corpus of relief-patterned tiles in Roman Britain,* J Roman Pottery Stud **7**

Biddle, M and Barclay, K, 1974 "Winchester Ware", in V I Evison, H Hodges and J G Hurst (eds), *Medieval pottery from excavations: Studies presented to Gerald Clough Dunning, with a bibliography of his works,* John Baker, London, 137–66

Bidwell, P T and Croom, A T, 1999 The Roman pottery, in Davenport 1999, 67–79

Bircher, J, 1999 The finds, in Davenport 1999, 89–105

Bircher forthcoming The Finds in Beaton forthcoming

Black, E W, 1995 *Cursus Publicus: the infrastructure of government in Roman Britain,* BAR British Series 241, Oxford

Black, E W, 1996 Box flue-tiles in Britannia: the spread of Roman bathing in the first and second centuries, *Archaeol J* **153**, 60–78

Blagg, T F C, 1999 Roman architectural and carved stonework, in Davenport 1999, 79–81

Blagg, T F C, 2002 *Roman architectural ornament in Britain,* Brit Archaeol Rep (Brit Ser) **329**, Oxford

Blázquez, J M and Remesal Rodríguez, J (eds), 1983 *Producción y comercio del aceite en la antigüedad,* Segundo Congreso Internacional, Madrid

Bradley, R, 2000 *An archaeology of natural places,* Routledge, London

British Geological Survey, 1965 Bath Sheet **265** Solid and Drift Edition, 1:63360

Brodribb, G, 1987 *Roman brick and tile,* Gloucester

Brooks, I P, 1989 The viability of micropalaeontology to the sourcing of flint, Unpublished Ph D. thesis, Univ of Sheffield

Brooks, I,1999 The flint artefacts, in Davenport 1999, 105–106

Brooks, I P, forthcoming Buxton Lismore Fields: flint thin sectioning, in D Garton, The excavation of a Mesolithic and Neolithic settlement area at Lismore Fields, Buxton, Derbyshire

Brown, A E, 1994 A Romano-British shell-gritted pottery and tile manufacturing site at Harrold, Beds., *Bedfordshire Archaeol J* **21**, 19–107

Brown, D, 1990 Weaving tools, in M Biddle, *Object and economy in medieval Winchester,* Winchester Studies 7.ii, Oxford, 225–232

Brown, L, 1984 Wiltshire-made pottery in B W Cunliffe, *Danebury: an Iron Age hillfort in Hampshire Volume 2: the finds,* Counc Brit Archaeol Res Rep **52**, fiche 8:C1–7

Brown, L, forthcoming The Roman pottery, in Crutchley *et al.* forthcoming

Brown, A G, Meadows, I, Truner, S D and Mattingly, D J, 2001 Roman vineyards in Britain; stratigraphic and palynological data from the Nene Valley, England, *Antiquity* **75**, 745–57

Browne, S, 1991 The animal bone [from Swallow Street], in Davenport (ed.) 1991, 89–96

Bull, G and Payne, S, 1991 Animal bones from Orange Grove and Upper Borough Walls: a synopsis, in Davenport (ed.) 1991, 31–2

Care, V, 1985 The flints from the spring, in Cunliffe and Davenport 1985, Fiche 3: A3–8

Clapham, A R, Tutin, T G and Moore, D M, 1989 *Flora of the British Isles* (3rd ed.), Cambridge Univ Press

Clarke, J, forthcoming Finds Report for Seven Dials, Bath, 1990

Coles, B and Coles, J, 1986 *Sweet Track to Glastonbury – the Somerset Levels Project,*Thames and Hudson, London

Collins, D and Lorimer, D, 1989 *Excavations at the Mesolithic site on West Heath, Hampstead 1976–1981. Investigations by members of the Hendon and District Archaeological Society*, Brit Archaeol Rep Brit Ser **217**, Oxford

Cool, H E M 2004 *The Roman Cemetery at Brougham, Cumbria. Excavations 1966–67*, Britannia Monograph **21**, London

Croom, A T, Bidwell, P T and McBride, R M, forthcoming The Roman pottery from Walcot, in Beaton forthcoming

Crummy, N, 1979 A chronology of Romano-British bone pins, *Britannia* **10**, 157–163

Crummy, N, 1983 *The Roman small finds from excavations in Colchester 1971–9*, Colchester Archaeol Rep **2**, Colchester

Crummy, P, 1992, *Excavations at Culver Street, the Gibberd School, and other sites in Colchester 1971–85*, Colchester Archaeol Rep **6**, Colchester

Crutchley, A, Leverett, M and Riley, G, forthcoming Excavations at The Tramsheds, Beehive Yard, Bath 1999–2001

Cummins, V, 2000 Myth, memory and metaphor: the significance of place, space and the landscape in Mesolithic Pembroke, in R Young (ed.), *Mesolithic lifeways: current research from Britain and Ireland*, Leicester Archaeol Mono **7**, Univ of Leicester, 87–96

Cunliffe, B, 1969 *Roman Bath*, Rep Res Comm Soc Antiqs London No. **33**, London

Cunliffe, B, 1971 *Excavations at Fishbourne 1961–1969, Volume II: The finds*, Rep Res Comm Soc Antiqs London No. **27**, London

Cunliffe, B (ed.), 1979 *Excavations in Bath, 1950–1975*, Comm Rescue Archaeol in Avon, Gloucestershire and Somerset Excavation Rep No. **1**

Cunliffe, B, 1986, *The City of Bath*, Sutton, Stroud

Cunliffe, B W (ed.), 1988 *The Temple of Sulis Minerva at Bath. Volume 2 the finds from the sacred spring*, Oxford Univ Comm Archaeol Mono No **16**, Oxford

Cunliffe, B and Davenport, P, 1985 *The temple of Sulis Minerva at Bath. Volume 1(I) the site*, Oxford Univ Comm Archaeol Mono No **7**, Oxford

Dannell, G, Dickinson, B and Vernhet, A, 1998 Ovolos on Dragendorff form 30 from the collections of Frédéric Hermet and Dieudonné Rey, in J Bird (ed.), *Form and Fabric: Studies in Rome's material past in honour of B. R. Hartley*, Oxbow Monograph **80**, Oxford, 69–109

Darling, M J, 1977 Pottery from early military sites in western Britain, in J Dore and K Greene (eds), *Roman pottery studies in Britain and beyond*, Brit Archaeol Rep (Suppl Ser) **30**, Oxford, 57–100

Davenport, P, 1991 *Archaeology in Bath 1976–1985*, Oxford Univ Comm Archaeol Mono **28**, Oxford

Davenport, P, 1999 *Archaeology in Bath: Excavations 1984–1989*, Brit Archaeol Rep (Brit Ser) **284**, Oxford

Davenport, P, 2002 *Medieval Bath uncovered*, Tempus, Stroud

Davenport 2004 An archaeological evaluation on the site of Old St Andrew's Church, Julian Road, and Victoria Park, Bath, (Unpublished Planning Report, N & NES SMR)

Davenport, P, forthcoming An Iron Age and Roman site at Bathampton Meadows, Somerset

Davies, B, Richardson, B and Tomber, R, 1994 *A dated corpus of early Roman pottery from the City of London*, Counc Brit Archaeol Res Rep **98**, London

Davis, S, 1991 *Faunal remains from the late Saxon-medieval farmstead at Eckweek in Avon: 1988–1989 excavations*, Ancient Monuments Laboratory Report No. **35/91**

Davis, S J M, 1992 *A rapid method for recording information about mammal bones from archaeological sites*, Ancient Monuments Laboratory Report No. **19/92**

Dickson, C and Dickson, J, 2000 *Plants and people in ancient Scotland*, Tempus, Stroud

Dickinson, B and Dannell, G D, 1991 The samian ware, in N Holbrook and P T Bidwell, *Roman finds from Exeter*, Exeter Archaeol Rep: Volume **4**, Exeter City Council and Exeter University

Dimbleby 1969 A Sample of silt from the floor of the Temple Precinct, in Cunliffe 1969....

Dobney, K, Jacques, D and Irving, B, 1996 *Of butchery and breeds: report on the vertebrate remains from various sites in the City of Lincoln*, Lincoln Archaeol Stud **5**, Lincoln

Dowden W A, 1957 Little Solsbury Hill Camp, *Proc Univ Bristol Spel Soc* **9(3)**, 177–182

Fox, G E, and St John Hope, W H, 1894 Excavations on the site of the Roman city at Silchester, Hants, in 1893, *Archaeologia* **54** (1), 199–238

Fulford, M G, 1975 *New Forest Roman pottery*, Brit Archaeol Rep (Brit Ser) **17**, Oxford

Gale, R and Cutler, D, 2000 *Plants in archaeology*, Westbury and Royal Botanic Gardens, Kew

Gerrard, C M, Gutierrez, A, Hurst, J G and Vince, A G, 1995 A guide to Spanish medieval ceramics, in C M Gerrard and A G Vince (eds), *Spanish medieval ceramics in Spain and the British Isles*, Brit Archaeol Rep (Int Ser) **610**, Oxford, 281–295

Grant, A, 1979 The animal bone, in Greene 1979, 60–70

Grant, A, 1987 Some observations on butchery in England from the Iron Age to the medieval period, *Anthropozoologica*, Premier Numéro Spécial, 53–58

Grant, A, 1988 The animal resources, in G Astill and A Grant (eds), *The countryside of medieval England*. Blackwell, Oxford, 149–187

Grant, A, 1989 Animals in Roman Britain, in M. Todd (ed.), *Research on Roman Britain: 1960–98*, Britannia Monograph Series **11**, 135–146

Green, F, 1991 Landscape archaeology in Hampshire: the Saxon plant remains, in J Renfrew (ed) *New light on early farming*, Edinburgh Univ Press, 363–77

Green, S and Young, C, 1985 The Roman Pottery, in Cunliffe and Davenport 1985, 143–160

Greene, J P, 1979 Citizen House, 1970, in Cunliffe (ed.) 1979, 40–70

Greig, J, 1982 The interpretation of pollen spectra from urban archaeological deposits, in Hall and Kenward 1982

Griffiths, D R, Bergman, C A, Clayton, C J, Ohnuma, K, Robins, G V and Seeley, N J, 1987 Experimental investigation of the heat treatment of flint, in G de G Sieveking and M H Newcomber (eds), *The human use of flint and chert. Proceedings of the Fourth International Flint Symposium held at Brighton Polytechnic 10–15 April 1983*, 43–52

Grimes, W F, 1965 *Excavations of defence sites 1939–45*, HMSO, London

Hall, A R and Kenward, H K (eds) 1982 *Environmental archaeology in the urban context*, Counc Brit Archaeol Res Rep **43**

Hall, A R and Kenward, H K, 1990 *Environmental evidence from the Colonia: General Accident and Rougier Street*, The Archaeology of York. Volume 14, fasc. 6, CBA, London

Hartley, B R, 1972 The samian ware, in S S Frere, *Verulamium Excavations, Vol. I*, Rep Res Comm Soc of Antiqs of London **28**, Oxford, 216–262

Hartley, B R, 1985 The samian ware, in L F Pitts and J K St. Joseph, *Inchtuthil, The Roman legionary fortress*, Britannia Mono **6**, 314–322

Hartley, K F, 1998 The incidence of stamped mortaria in the Roman Empire with special reference to imports to Britain, in J Bird (ed.), *Form and fabric: Studies in Rome's material past in honour of B. R. Hartley*, Oxbow Mono **80**, Oxford, 199–217

Henig, M A new star shining over Bath, *Oxford Journal of Archaeology* **18.4,**

Hermet, F, 1934 *La Graufesenque (Condatomago)*, Paris

Higbee, L, n.d.1 The faunal remains from St Swithin's yard and Hat and Feather Yard, Walcot Street, Bath, unpublished report for Bath Archaeological Trust

Higbee, L, n.d.2 The faunal remains from Tramsheds, Beehive Yard, Walcot St, Bath, unpublished report for Bath Archaeological Trust

Higbee, L, n.d.3 The animal bone from Union Street, Bristol, unpublished report for Bristol and Region Archaeol Services

Higbee, L, n.d.4 The animal bones from Abingdon Court Farm, Cricklade, Wiltshire, unpublished report for Bristol and Region Archaeological Services

Hill, D, 1969 The Burghal Hidage:the establishment of a text, *Medieval Archaeology* **13**, 84–92

Holbrook, N and Bidwell, P T, 1991 *Roman finds from Exeter*, Exeter Archaeol Rep No **4**, Exeter

Jones, A K G, 1982 Intestinal parasites: prospects for a quantitative approach. in A R Hall and H K Kenward (eds), *Environmental archaeology in the urban context*, Counc Brit Archaeol Res Rep **43**, **

Jones, A K G, 1984a The fish bones, in A Rogerson and C Dallas, *Excavations in Thetford 1948–59 and 1973–80*, East Anglian Archaeol **22**, 192–4

Jones, A K G, 1984b Some effects of the mammalian digestive system on fish bones, in N Desse-Berset (ed.), *2nd Fish Osteoarchaeology Meeting, 1983*. Notes et Monographies Techniques **16**, C.N.R.S. Centre de Recherches Archéologiques, 61–5

Jones, A K G, 1986 Fish bone survival in the digestive systems of the pig, dog and man: some experiments, in D C Brinkhuizen and A T Clason (eds) *Fish and archaeology*, Brit Archaeol Rep (Int Ser) **294**, Oxford, 53–61

Jones, A K G, 1990 Experiments with fish bones and otoliths: Implications for the reconstruction of past diet and economy, in D Robinson (ed.), *Experimentation and reconstruction in environmental archaeology*, Symposia of the Association for Environmental Archaeology (Roskilde, Denmark) **9**, 143–6

Jones, A K G, 1991 The fish remains from excavations at Freswick Links, Caithness, Unpublished D. Phil. Thesis, University of York

Jones, A K G, 1995 The fish material, in C D Morris, C E Batey and D J Rackham, *Freswick Links, Caithness: Excavations and survey of a Norse settlement*, Historic Scotland, Edinburgh, 154–191

Jones, J, 1999 Macroscopic plant remains, in Davenport 1999, 114–121

Kellaway, G, 1985 The geomorphology of the Bath region, in Cunliffe and Davenport 1985, 4–8

Kellaway, G, 1991 *The Hot springs of Bath. Investigations of the thermal waters of the Avon valley*, Bath

King, A, 1978 A comparative survey of bone assemblages from Roman sites in Britain, *Institute of Archaeol Bull* **15**, 207–232

King, A., 1984 Animal bones and the dietary identity of military and civilian groups in Roman Britain, Germany and Gaul, in T F C Blagg and A King (eds), *Military and civilian in Roman Britain: cultural relationships in a frontier province*, Brit Archaeol Rep Brit Ser **136**, 187–218

King, A, 1999 Diet in the Roman world: a regional inter-site comparison of the mammal bones, *J Roman Archaeol* **12**, 168–202

Knorr, R, 1919 *Töpfer und Fabriken verzierter Terra-Sigillata des ersten Jahrhunderts*, Stuttgart

Knorr, F, 1952 *Terra-Sigillata-Gefässe des ersten Jahrhunderts mit Töpfernamen*, Stuttgart

Lambrick, G H and Robinson, M A, 1979 *Iron Age and Roman riverside settlements at Farmoor, Oxfordshire*, Counc Brit Archaeol Res Rep **32**, London

Lauwerier, R C G M, 1988 Animals in Roman times in the Dutch Eastern River Area, *ROB Nederlandse Oudheden* **12**

Leach, P, 1982 *Ilchester volume 1; excavations 1974–5*, Western Archaeol Trust Mono **3**

Levitan, B, 1982 The faunal remains, in Leach 1982, 269–283

Lovett, J, n.d. The animal bones from Nelson Place 1989, unpublished report for Bath Archaeological Trust

MacDowall, D W, 1967 Group of early Imperial Aes from Augers-en-Brie, *Numismatic Chronicle* **7**, 43–5

Maltby, J M, 1979 *Faunal remains from urban sites: the animal bones from Exeter 1971–1975*, Exeter Archaeol Rep **2**, Sheffield Univ: Dept of Archaeol and Prehist

Maltby, M, 1985 Assessing variations in Iron Age and Roman butchery practices: the need for quantification, in N J R Fieller, D D Gilbertson and N G A Ralph, *Palaeolbiological investigations: research design, methods and data analysis*, Brit Archaeol Rep (Int Ser) **266**, 19–32

Maltby, M, 1994 The meat supply in Roman Dorchester and Winchester, in A R Hall and H K Kenward (eds), *Urban-rural connections: perspectives from environmental archaeology*, Symposia of the Association for Environmental Archaeology No. 2, Oxbow Monograph **47**, 85–102

Manco, J, 1998 *The spirit of care. The eight hundred year story of St. John's Hospital, Bath*

Manco, J, 1999 The history of Binbury: medieval to modern, in Davenport 1999, 122–5

Mann, J, 1982 *Early Medieval Finds from Flaxengate 1: Objects of antler, bone, stone, horn, ivory, amber and jet*, Lincolnshire Archaeol Trust

Manning, W H, 1993 *Report on the Excavations at Usk 1965–1976: the Roman Pottery*, Cardiff

Marsh, G D, 1978, Early second century fine wares in the London area, in P R Arthur and G D Marsh (eds), *Early fine wares in Roman Britain*, Brit Archaeol Rep (Brit Ser) **57**, Oxford, 119–223

Mees, A W, 1995 *Modelsignierte Dekorationen auf südgallischer Terra Sigillata*, Forschungen und Berichte zur Vor- und Frühgeschichte in Baden-Württemburg, Band **54**, Stuttgart

Mills, A and McDonnell, J G, 1992 The identification and analysis of the hammerscale from Burton Dassett, Warwickshire, Ancient Monuments Lab Rep 47/92

Moore, P D, Webb, J A and Collinson, M E, 1991 *Pollen Analysis* (2nd ed), Blackwell Scientific Publications

Morris, E, forthcoming The prehistoric pottery, in Davenport forthcoming

Murless, B J, 1991 *Somerset brick and tile makers: a brief history and gazetteer*, Supplement Somerset Industrial Archaeol Soc Bulletin **58**

Murphy, P, 1984 Carbonised fruits from building 5; and the charred cereals from Building 45, Room 6, in P Crummy, *Excavations at Lion Walk, Balkerne Lane, and Middlesborough, Colchester, Essex*, Colchester Archaeol Rep **3**, 40 and 108

Myers, A M, 1989 Lithics, risk and change in the Mesolithic, in Brooks and Phillips (eds) *Breaking the Stony Silence* Brit Archaeol Rep (Brit Ser) **213**, 131–60

O'Connor, T P, 1988 *Bones from the General Accident Site, Tanner Row*, The Archaeology of **York 15/2**, Counc Brit Archaeol, London

Olausson, D S and Larson, L, 1982 Testing for the presence of thermal pretreatment of flint in the Mesolithic and Neolithic of Sweden, *J Archaeol Science* **9**, 275–285

Oswald, F, 1936–37 *Index of figure types on terra sigillata*, Univ of Liverpool Annals of Archaeol and Anthropology, Supplement

Peacock, D P S and Williams, D F, 1986 *Amphorae and the Roman economy*, Longman, London

Pritchard, F, 1984 Late Saxon textiles from the City of London, *Medieval Archaeol* **28**, 46–76

Pringle, S, forthcoming The building material, in C Cowan, L Wheeler and A Westman, *Roman Southwark: origins, development and economy*, MoLAS Mono Ser

Pugsley, P, 2001 Of Timotei and boxwood combs, *Roman Finds Group Newsletter* **21**, 3–6

Purdy, B A and Brooks, H K, 1971 Thermal alteration of silica minerals: an archaeological approach, *Science* **173**, 322–325

Radford, C A R, 1972 Excavations at Cricklade, *Wiltshire Archaeol Magazine*, **67**, 61–111

Reynier, M J, 1998 Early Mesolithic settlement in England and Wales: some preliminary observations, in N Ashton, F Healy and P Pettitt (eds), *Stone age archaeology. Essays in honour of John Wymer*, Oxbow Mono **102**, Lithic Studies Soc Occ Paper **6**, 174–184

Rigby, V, 1982 The coarse pottery, in J S Wacher and A D McWhirr, *Cirencester excavations I: early Roman occupation at Cirencester*, Cirencester, 153–200

Robinson, M, 2000 A preliminary investigation of waterlogged sediments from the early fort ditches at Alchester for environmental evidence, in E W Sauer, Alchester, a Claudian 'vexillation fortress' near the western boundary of the Catuvellauni: new light on the Roman invasion of Britain, *Archaeol J* **157**, 64–5

Rogers, G B, 1974 *Poteries Sigillées de la Gaule Centrale I, les motifs non figurés*, Gallia Supplement **28**

Rogers, G B, 1999 *Poteries Sigillées de la Gaule Centrale II, Les Potiers*, premier Cahier du Centre Archéologique de Lezoux,

St John Hope, W H, and Fox, G E, 1896 Excavations on the site of the Roman city at Silchester, Hants, in 1895, *Archaeologia*, **55**, 215–56

St John Hope, W H and Fox, G E, 1899 Excavations on the site of the Roman city at Silchester, Hants, in 1898, *Archaeologia*, **56**, 229–50

Saunders, P and Saunders, E (eds), 1991 *Salisbury Museum Medieval Catalogue Part 1 Harness pendants, seals, rings, spurs, tiles, coins, mortars, etc.*, Salisbury

Scarth, H M, 1864 *Aquae Solis*, London

Sellwood, L, 1988 The Celtic coins, in B Cunliffe (ed.), *The temple of Sulis Minerva at Bath Volume 2 The finds from the sacred spring*, Oxford Univ Comm Archaeol Mono **16**, Oxford, 279–80

Silver I A, 1969 The ageing of domestic animals, in D Brothwell and E S Higgs (eds), *Science in archaeology*, 2nd ed., Thames and Hudson, London, 283–301

Sims-Williams 1975 Continental influence at Bath Monastery in the seventh century, *Anglo-Saxon England*, **4**, 1–110

Smith, C, 1992 *Late Stone Age hunters of the British Isles*, Routledge, London

Stanfield, J A and Simpson, G, 1958 *Central Gaulish potters*, Durham

Swan, V G, 1975 Oare reconsidered and the origins of Savernake ware in Wiltshire, *Britannia* **6**, 36–61

Sykes, N, 2001 The Norman Conquest: a zooarchaeological perspective, PhD thesis, University of Southampton

Sykes, N, 2002 The animal bones from the 1998–9 and 2002 excavations at Malmesbury, Wiltshire, unpublished report for Bristol and Region Archaeol Services

Symonds, R P, 1990 The problems of roughcast beakers, and related colour-coated wares, *J Roman Pottery Stud* **3**, 1–17

Timby, J, 1998 *Excavations at Kingscote and Wycomb, Gloucestershire*, Cotswold Archaeological Trust, Cirencester

Tomber, R and Dore, J, 1998 *The National Roman Fabric Reference Collection; a handbook*, Mus of London Archaeol Services Mono **2**, London

Tyers, P, 1996 *Roman Pottery in Britain*, Routledge, London

Van der Veen, M, 1989 Carbonised grain from a Roman granary at South Shields, North East England, in H Küster (ed.), *Der prähistorische Mensch und seine Umwelt (Festschrift U. Körber-Grohne)*, Forschungen und Berichte zur Vor- und Frühgeschichte in Baden-Württemberg **31**, 353–365

Vince, A G, 1979 The Medieval Pottery: Fabric Types, in Cunliffe (ed.) 1979, 27–38

Vince, A G, 1985a Part 2: the ceramic finds. in R Shoesmith (ed.), Hereford City Excavations: Volume 3. The Finds, Counc Brit Archaeol Res Rep **56**, London, 34–82

Vince, A G, 1985b The Saxon and medieval pottery of London: a review, *Medieval Archaeol* **29**, 25–93

Vince, A, 1991 The medieval and post-medieval pottery [from Swallow Street], in Davenport (ed.) 1991, 70–81

Vince, A, 1999 The Saxon and medieval pottery, in Davenport 1999, 81–3

Wainwright, G J, 1967 The excavation of an Iron Age hill fort on Bathampton Down, Somerset, *Trans Bristol Gloucestershire Archaeol Soc* **86**, 42–59

Walker, D, 1988 The Roman coins, in B Cunliffe (ed.), *The temple of Sulis Minerva at Bath Volume 2 The finds from the sacred spring*, Oxford

Univ Comm Archaeol Mono **16**, Oxford, 281–358

Webster, G, 1983 The function of the Chedworth Roman 'villa', *Trans Bristol and Gloucestershire Archaeol Soc* **101**, 5–20.

Webster, P V, 1993 The post-fortress coarse wares, in Manning 1993, 227–360

Webster, P, 1996 *Roman samian pottery in Britain*, Counc Brit Archaeol Practical Handbook in Archaeology **13**

Wedlake, W J, 1979 St. John's Hospital, 1954, in Cunliffe (ed.) 1979, 84–85

Wedlake, W J, 1982 *The excavation of the shrine of Apollo at Nettleton, Wiltshire, 1956–1971*, Rep Res Comm Soc Antiqs London **40**, London

Wheeler, A, 1969 *The fishes of the British Isles and north west Europe*, Macmillan, London

Wheeler, A and Jones, A K G, 1989 *Cambridge manuals in archaeology: fishes*, Cambridge Univ Press, Cambridge

Wheeler, R E M, and Wheeler, T V, 1932 *Report on the excavations of the Prehistoric, Roman and post Roman site in Lydney Park, Gloucestershire*, Rep Res Comm Soc Antiqs London No **9**

Whitaker, R, 2000 *The archaeology of Combe Down and Bathwick, Bath*, Unpublished MA thesis, University of Bristol

Williams, D F, and Peacock, D P S, 1983 The importation of olive oil into Roman Britain, in J M Blazquez and J Remesal Rodriguez (eds), *Produccion y Comercio del Aceite en la Antiqedad. II Congresso*, Madrid, 263–80.

Willcox, G H, 1977 Exotic plants from Roman waterlogged sites in London, *J Archaeol Science* **4**, 269–282

Wilkinson, M, 1979 The fish remains, in Maltby 1979, 74–81

Young, C J, 1977 *The Roman pottery industry of the Oxford region*, Brit Archaeol Rep (Brit Ser) **43**, Oxford

Abbreviations

RIB: Roman Inscriptions in Britain
RIC: The Roman Imperial Coinage
HK: P V Hill and J P C Kent. *Late Roman Bronze Coinage Part I. The Bronze Coinage of the House of Constantine AD324–346*
CK: R A G Carson and J P C Kent. *Late Roman Bronze Coinage Part II. The Bronze Roman Imperial Coinage of the Later Empire AD346–498*

Index